An American Icon

Brother Jonathan Suited Exactly.

Star Dealer "ALLOW ME TO RECOMMEND THIS VEST, SIR; IT WILL SUIT YOUR FIGURE EXACTLY."
Jonathan. "WALL, I GUESS I'LL TRY IT ON, FOR THE PRESENT, BUT TOTHER'S THE GARMENT, I CALC'LATE, WOULD FIT ME BEST OF ALL!"

Brother Jonathan Suited Exactly. *The Lantern* 2 (1852): 172. (*Courtesy of the University of Wisconsin Library Rare Book Collection.*)

An American Icon

Brother Jonathan and American Identity

Winifred Morgan

DELAWARE

NEWARK: University of Delaware Press
LONDON AND TORONTO: Associated University Presses

Associated University Presses
440 Forsgate Drive
Cranbury, NJ 08512

Associated University Presses
25 Sicilian Avenue
London WC1A 2QH, England

Associated University Presses
2133 Royal Windsor Drive
Unit 1
Mississauga, Ontario
Canada L5J 1K5

The paper used in this publication meets the requirements
of the American National Standard for Permanence of Paper
for Printed Library Materials Z39.48-1984.

Library of Congress Cataloging-in-Publication Data

Morgan, Winifred, 1938–
  An American icon.

  Bibliography: p.
  Includes index.
  1. American literature—1783–1850—History and
criticism. 2. Brother Jonathan (Nickname) in
literature. 3. National characteristics, American,
in literature. 4. American literature—Revolutionary
period, 1775–1783—History and criticism. 5. Brother
Jonathan (Nickname) 6. United States—Popular culture.
7. Popular literature—United States—History and
criticism. 8. American wit and humor—History and
criticism. I. Title.
PS217.B75M67   1988   810′.9′351   86-40597
ISBN 0-87413-307-6 (alk. paper)

Printed in the United States of America

Contents

Acknowledgments

I WISH TO THANK PROFESSORS HARRY OSTER, ALBERT STONE, MARGARET McDowell, David Schaal, and Bruce Gronbeck from the University of Iowa, and Professors Esther Heffernan, Michael Lybarger, and William Duddleston from Edgewood College, who all read and criticized parts and earlier versions of this manuscript. I particularly thank E. McClung Fleming, Winterthur Research Associate, who read this manuscript for the University of Delaware Press. In addition, I thank my family and my community, the Sinsinawa Dominicans, for their support. Finally, I thank all of the librarians I have encountered at the University of Iowa, Edgewood College, the University of Wisconsin, The Historical Society of Wisconsin, the University of Chicago, Northwestern University, the Chicago Art Institute, the Newberry Library, Indiana University (Bloomington), the University of Illinois (Champaign), and Northern Illinois University.

Illustrations

LIST OF ILLUSTRATIONS

Preface

DURING THE FIRST SIXTY-FIVE YEARS OF THE EXISTENCE OF THE UNITED States, de Tocqueville and other visitors like him often remarked upon the fiercely independent individualism of American citizen. Some visitors even disparaged Americans as "Brother Jonathans." In so characterizing Americans, however, visitors and other commentators on the American scene attempted to make sense of their cultural encounter by equating the people they met with a stereotype from popular culture. At the same time, they missed the humor and complex social tension the stereotype embodied.[1]

To the question "What is an American?" came the popular answer "Brother Jonathan." While the United States produced relatively few memorable creative works before the literary flowering of the 1850s, preparatory to producing a distinct national literature, the country needed to domesticate its own myths. Brother Jonathan belonged to the effort at understanding what sort of "new man" traded with his neighbors, joked at their expense, and—especially—voted for elected leaders. Republican government could succeed only if ordinary citizens accepted their responsibilities. Jonathan represented those valued but worrisome citizens.[2]

While his popularity did not rival that of the Western hero who later gripped the American imagination, Brother Jonathan was a significant cultural icon in antebellum America. He provided a commonly accepted definition of what to expect from an ordinary American. Europeans and Americans alike accepted the definition. His popularity spanned four generations, all parts of the country, the entire popular culture, and every social class. In addition, his limitations as a character and as a symbol actually suggest elitist reservations about the early national consensus regarding the role of the ordinary citizen. The humor involving Brother Jonathan, in fact, offers the opportunity to trace some fault lines of social, sectional, and international tension.

A media construct, Jonathan reflected social reality during this early period in the United States' history. Particularly before 1840, the white rural males symbolized by Jonathan seemed to be the bedrock of American civilization. Other nations gloried in the heroism of the Cid or Henry V.

And, actually, after 1800 Pastor Weems's biographies, responding to an established sense of reverence for the nation's first president, encouraged a similar cult of George Washington in the United States.[3] Nonetheless, during the early and middle national periods of United States' history, the idea that each American citizen had the potential to "take charge" sparked the most overwhelmingly popular understanding of America's greatness. Eventually, the Jonathan character of popular media also developed into someone who excelled at taking charge. But before the character became universally recognized as a typical—and admirable—American, he underwent several permutations. These changes delineated one tributary of American self-discovery.

As far as is known, Brother Jonathan appeared first in a political cartoon published in 1776. Then in 1787 he first appeared in a popular American stage comedy. Over the next three decades, the figure of Jonathan reappeared on stage in a dozen popular comedies. The character's name also became attached to the fumbling adventures of a country boy who appeared in occasional verse during the same three decades. In the 1830s and 1840s, almost a third of all published comic almanacs featured anecdotes about Jonathan, as did occasional political broadside cartoons and the benefit-night performances of most American stage Yankees. But the character appeared with less frequency during the 1850s and gradually he disappeared from American popular media after the Civil War.

As a popular media construct, the Brother Jonathan figure supposedly represented the ordinary American. But since Jonathan was constructed by people who did not consider themselves "ordinary," the figure may tell us more about the producers of and myths about the ordinary American than about the ordinary American himself. In political cartoons, for example, the character was intended to express "everyman's" observations on the political scene. But in cartoons as well as jokes and stage comedies, the Jonathan character was often the object of condescension.

In addition to eliciting affectionate condescension, however, the Jonathan character also became associated with particular patriotic causes and, specifically, with Yankee patriots. As a patriot, Jonathan could not be only derided. This led to an intriguing characteristic of Jonathan jokes: i.e., in popular media, the Jonathan figure was usually set up as a comic fool; yet the joke frequently twisted around so that someone else was made to look even more foolish. As Rourke, Blair, and others have remarked, this has served as a characteristic situation in American humor.

Moreover, the presentation of Brother Jonathan varied significantly according to the medium. Stage comedies, for example, naturally developed the character far more amply than did the brief anecdotes found in jest books and almanacs. Each medium, in turn, experienced periods of greater and lesser importance in early republican culture. Only with the rise in popularity of the stage Yankees during the 1820s did the Jonathan figure become a staple of the American stage. And cheaper production methods made possible by commercial lithography encouraged the popularity of cartoons during the 1830s and 1840s. Comic almanacs, as well, exploded in popularity only after 1830. All of these popular forms, however, offered images of Brother Jonathan during the politically, economically, and socially stormy period of the Jacksonian Era—roughly from 1828 to 1848. During these twenty years, both political unrest and new developments in all the popular modes of entertainment encouraged the wide dissemination of the figure of Brother Jonathan.

The widespread popularity of the Jonathan character during the first several decades of the nineteenth century, its almost exclusive limitation to the popular media, and its consequent rapid decline as a vibrant cultural icon naturally raise questions about the causes of these changes. Searching for relationships between this symbol and the culture it served, this book explores several shapes and meanings of Jonathan as a characteristic antebellum image of the American. It argues, as well, for the likelihood of a relationship between the decline of Jonathan and an altered consensus about the role of the common man in American society. Finally I suggest that the humor surrounding the Jonathan figure and the way it was framed probably indicated that established groups often experienced tension in their relations with the mass of ordinary citizens who had little interest in accepting roles as passive supporters of elite leaders, but who instead viewed themselves as economically and politically important contributers to the republic.[4]

Because Jonathan developed his own visual, verbal, and action tags as well as characteristic patterns of action, the formulaic structure of the comedies, for instance, suggests a key to attitudes and opinions held by both genteel and ordinary Americans. In addition, humor worked as a prism so that incidental anecdotes also gave a refracted—bent but related—image of genteel attitudes toward the common folk. The Jonathan figure and the situations he appears in present—to use John Cawelti's phrase for popular literary formulae—a comfortable "moral fantasy."[5] The Brother Jonathan of these pieces, for example, is consistently inept in his dealings with women. Furthermore, his inability to function socially with any *savoir faire* could comfort the genteel observers to whom Jonathan was a potential economic and social threat. The social assumptions expressed by the humorous surroundings of the Jonathan character are hardly unexpected, but the action involving Jonathan does seem to illustrate social, economic, and sometimes geographic tensions that we might expect to encounter in a young country trying to define itself.

Although today's students of American culture recognize the name of Brother Jonathan, most people know the figure through either Constance

Rourke's fine but short exposition of the Yankee's contribution to early American humor[6] or through Royall Tyler's *The Contrast*. Actually, even before the publication of Rourke's book on American humor, Jennette Tandy had already started to trace the role of the Jonathan figure as one of several nineteenth-century satiric creatures who both sprang from and railed against the ordinary people.[7]

Scholarly attention to what Kenneth Lynn has called "the great age of American humor"[8]—the pre–Civil War era—became active in the 1930s. Six years after the publication in 1931 of Constance Rourke's *American Humor*, Walter Blair returned to the subject in his *Native American Humor*.[9] Emphasizing somewhat different materials than Rourke, he examined the Yankee countryman of whom Jonathan was the prime exemplar and described thereby the "beginnings" of American humor. More recent writers, such as Jesse Bier, whose *Rise and Fall of American Humor* came out in 1968,[10] barely found time or space to mention the Jonathan character. Walter Blair's more recent book on American humor, co-authored by Hamlin Hill, mentions Brother Jonathan only in passing.[11] David E. E. Sloane's (1983) *The Literary Humor of the Urban Northeast, 1830–1890* provides a fuller treatment.[12] Yet, none of these writers— neither the original students of the thirties nor later scholars of the sixties, seventies, and eighties—were interested enough to pinpoint in detail the various sources out of which the Jonathan figure developed. Nor have any commentators made any attempt to examine the patterned structure of the Jonathan character's appearances in different media. This study tries to do both.

An American Icon

1

Jonathan's Territory

FROM THE START OF THE AMERICAN REVOLUTION, BOTH AMERICANS AND
Europeans wanted an answer to Crevecoeur's question: Who was this "new
man" who dared to question British and even his own leaders' preroga-
tives? Jonathan embodied one popular answer. But the way his definition
varied in different places and actually changed over time also illustrated
how difficult it was to maintain a consensus about what set Americans apart
and what was laudable in their difference.

The figure of Jonathan became a loose metaphor for a group on whom
the turmoil following the revolution focused new attention. An individual
most commonly controls a metaphor's significance, as Sallie TeSelle explains:

> In the modern literate era, a poet, playwright or fiction writer often cre-
> ates a metaphoric representation that literally dramatizes what a concept
> means. In fact, the more complicated the concept, the less satisfactory
> any one representation will be. So in hopes that one attempt will clarify
> another, the writer may return again and again to amplify the concept
> through further metaphoric representation.[1]

The Jonathan figure stood for this sort of effort complicated by the fact
that many people were involved in the popular and communal effort of
delineating what the figure signified. And even when Jonathan was most
successful at signifying America's "new man," other popular metaphors
vied for recognition or acceptance.

Not only did the representation of Jonathan alter from time to time, the
figure itself developed from an earlier notion of America embodied in the
figure of Yankee Doodle. In turn, Brother Jonathan gave way to Uncle
Sam. Jonathan's reign as an American icon lasted only for the period between the American Revolutionary and Civil Wars. Before the revolution,
Yankee Doodle seemed to serve the population's cultural needs; after the
Civil War, Uncle Sam apparently answered to them. Because, however, of
the period's political and social ferment as well as the many media used to

depict Jonathan, his representation evolved far beyond either of the relatively static figures of Yankee Doodle and Uncle Sam. During the eighty-five years of his active life, Brother Jonathan offered the world insight into the power and weakness of the American everyman. As a representative American, Jonathan acquired both a pseudo-scholarly origin and a richly imagined life of adventure and discovery. Both cut through to popular early nineteenth-century perceptions of an American difference.

Origin

In 1901 Albert Matthews effectively demolished the popular nineteenth-century fakelore regarding the origin of Brother Jonathan. The popular tradition had held that George Washington used to say of his friend and counselor, Governor Trumbull of Connecticut, "Let us consult Brother Jonathan." In time then, by the process of extension, the country itself came to be called Brother Jonathan. Repeated in many newspaper fillers, the story took on the presumption of fact. And it had the ring of truth about it, until Matthews' examination pointed out that neither Washington nor Trumbull ever referred in writing to the story; nor did their contemporaries seem to know it.

> [it was] a story unheard of until forty-seven years after the death of Washington, sixty-one years after the death of Trumbull, and seventy-one years after Washington took command of the American forces; [it was] a story the author of which [had] never been discovered, but which [came] from an unknown octogenarian, who, as he was upwards of eighty years of age in 1846, was therefore upwards of *nine* years of age in 1775, and whose services as "an active participator in the scenes of the Revolution" could scarcely have been of an arduous nature; [it was] a story unsupported by one iota of corroborating evidence,—to such a story obviously no credence [could] be given. It [was], in short, a newspaper story pure and simple, and as such should have been received with caution from the beginning.[2]

REVOLUTIONARY DERIVATION

Then in 1935 Matthews attempted to establish a more legitimate etymology for the figure of Brother Jonathan. At that time Matthews concluded that while between 1776 and 1783 loyalists and British soldiers applied the term in mild derision to those who espoused the American cause,[3] no definitive proof existed to show that the term had wide currency before the American Revolution. In addition, until after that war was over, Americans reacted sensitively to being called either Jonathan or Yankee.[4] Without discovering a single or exact source for Jonathan, Matthews did nonetheless explore several suggestive lines of investigation. He showed, for example, that Jonathan was a popular first name in seventeenth- and eighteenth-century New England; he noted as well that many ships carried the name.[5] Finally, Matthews found English accounts written during the nineteenth century by usually reliable travellers who recalled having heard the name used as early as 1765 to refer to Americans. Unfortunately, when published, their recollections were already as much as fifty years old.[6] So although the name Jonathan may have been used much earlier in the eighteenth century to indicate someone's essentially boorish provincialism, Jonathan's existence as a widely recognized icon may have come to life only with the Revolution.

JONATHAN'S COLONIAL PREDECESSOR

Not the only American icon before the revolution, Yankee Doodle was a major representative of America in the popular arts and Jonathan's immediate predecessor. Like Jonathan, he was a representative American bumpkin. Other essential identifying traits also connected Jonathan with Yankee Doodle. Thus for example Jonathan—like the Yankee Doodle of song and stage references—was a country boy who often appeared foolish but beneath whose seemingly bland and slow surface lay a threat of comeuppance. Jonathan was even named as one of the Yankee crowd in the ballad's earliest known broadside edition, the "Lexington March."[7] Unlike Jonathan, however, Yankee Doodle had a far less sketchy background. Actually, a good deal of evidence exists to show that Yankee Doodle's roots spread widely throughout colonial culture.

General Burgoyne's farce *The Blockade of Boston* (early 1776) already implied widespread recognition of the meaning of Yankee. In Burgoyne's satire, an orderly-sergeant in country dress accompanied Washington, who appeared as an uncouth figure wearing a large wig and carrying a long rusty sword.[8] The countryman presumably represented an American national type. National stereotypes, after all, provided a staple of stage humor during the eighteenth century. One account of the performance—no copy of the play itself has been found—also related that another, real sergeant burst upon the stage crying "The Yankees are attacking our works on Bunker Hill!" and produced chaos among the officers attending the performance.[9]

Yet Burgoyne's was not even the first stage reference to "Yankee Doodle." In 1767, under the pen name of Andrew Barton, an American, Thomas Forrest, had published a comic opera *The Disappointment; or, The Force of Credulity*. The play was advertised that year as well, but it was withdrawn before it could be performed. In addition to burlesquing local personalities,[10] *The Disappointment* contained a song with instructions that it be set to "Yankee Doodle."[11] So a song antedated these stage references to Yankee Doodle.

While the song "Yankee Doodle" was not published until a broadside entitled the "Lexington March" appeared—probably between 1782 and 1794[12]—the melody presumably dated from early seventeenth-century England.[13] Thus, though he questioned their authenticity, Oscar Sonneck noted a variety of imputed sources for the song, including its possible roots in an air called "The Roundheads and the Cavaliers" that was sung in ridicule of Cromwell.[14] Even acknowledging that another early broadside containing a prerevolutionary version of "Yankee Doodle" and entitled "Yankee Song" might have been printed from an earlier broadside or manuscript, J. A. Lemay more recently concluded that this imprint did not occur until the 1810.[15] The evidence consequently points to a widespread oral knowledge of "Yankee Doodle," predating by at least decades the actual printing of the song.

The relatively late printing of this well-known song may have encouraged the often-accepted tradition that one version of the lyrics was written by Edward Bangs only shortly before the revolution.[16] In interesting contrast with the then-prevailing belief that "Yankee Doodle" originated as a song written by an English officer and sung by English soldiers in ridicule of the colonial American militia, during the American bicentennial year LeMay cogently argued that the ballad was, in fact, "an American folk song, reflecting American humorous traditions and American self-characterization," probably dating from the late 1740s.[17]

LeMay's argument rested heavily on "Yankee Doodle's" being an ironic song, an American joke at English credulity. Hence, when in spite of evidence to the contrary, the English insisted on believing Americans cowardly yokels, Americans could—by exaggerating the stereotype to absurdity—laugh at English gullibility. Later on, Jonathan certainly continued in that characteristically American vein. As F. O. Matthiessen quoting Max Eastman noted, American "'demigods were born in laughter; they are consciously preposterous; they are cockalorum demigods. That is the natively American thing—not that her primitive humor is exaggerative, but that her primitive exaggerations were humorous.'"[18] Humor belonged to Jonathan's essence. And if LeMay correctly established "Yankee Doodle" as ironic, Jonathan's humor probably derived from the same sources. The sly humor of both Yankee Doodle and Jonathan provides a key to what Americans of the periods before and after the revolution acknowledged about themselves.[19]

Yankee Doodle, the irreverently humorous joker gradually developed in ballads and plays, then set the stage for the more overtly nationalistic figure of Brother Jonathan. As part of the process involved in what Walter Blair has referred to as "a slow accretion of details until at last native figures came to be generally perceived,"[20] the Yankee Doodle of colonial songs and comedies—while never entirely fading as a separate entity—also became assimilated into the figure of Jonathan who took on a fuller existence after the revolution. On the one hand, Yankee Doodle contained early rumblings of dissatisfaction with English dominance and the growing sense of an American difference; on the other hand, Brother Jonathan came to make additional political, social, and sectional statements about America. Of the transition from Yankee Doodle to Brother Jonathan, Alton Ketchum has suggested that the former "didn't quite fit" the "expansive and industrious time" of which Americans believed they were part, following independence. Yankee Doodle "was too simple and ingenuous to exemplify the new spirit of the continent-tamers."[21]

Identity

In most segments of the popular media, Brother Jonathan represented the ordinary American; and since the rhetoric first of the British, and then of Americans as well, insisted that the ordinary American best represented what one could expect to encounter in most Americans, Jonathan came to be the American. Until the Civil War, Jonathan held his own as a representative American. He did this despite competition from other representative Americans, such as those of the Indian Maiden and Liberty in cartoons, plus Columbia in cartoons and songs,[22] and from the Yankee Doodle of song, the Jack Downing of political satire, and the Uncle Sam of later political cartoons.[23]

A COUNTRY BOY FROM NEW ENGLAND

Because Jonathan appeared in most popular media, he was capable of greater development than other images of the United States that were tied to one or another media. Yet three elements remained constant in his makeup, however his nonessentials varied. First of all, he came from rural New England. Even when he appeared as a sailor or a peddler, he continued to be a Yankee and a country boy, though making his living at sea or on the road. He combined the humor of Yankee Doodle and that of the traditional stage yokel.

Brother Jonathan was a projection of what many wanted to think was American. As such, Jonathan belonged to the kind of small community where neighbors, greeting one another in the morning on their way to work in their fields or small shops, acknowledged their kindship with the honorific "Brother" attached to one another's name. The title suited a cohesive circle of people who shared the same life style, ideals, and limitations. The men of the community knew that they were brothers in all but blood;

sometimes they were blood kin. The "simple" American projected by the image of Jonathan was, of course, no more naive than Benjamin Franklin, who affected Quaker dress during his stay at Versailles.[24] Ironically, the title echoed the speech pattern of a religious sect, but while the Jonathan figure originated in the folk characteristics of Puritan New England, he clearly represented a secular viewpoint. The Masonic practice of calling fellow members "brother" may actually have had more influence on Jonathan's title than any Puritan practice.

Jonathon's first characteristic, fresh from the farm, led to his second, his apparent but deceptive simplicity.

MASKED IN FOOLISHNESS

Jonathan invariably wore a mask.[25] His naïveté was both real and assumed, yet no one could penetrate which was which. Just as the Yankee Doodle of the "Lexington March" exaggerated his own naïveté—pretending that he could buy a military commission (when they were not for sale in America) for the price of a cow or that he feared French cannibalism—the Jonathan of *The Contrast* (1778) pretended utter ignorance of urban life. Both these and later Yankees assumed a bland simplicity at which onlookers loved to laugh. Yet while the joke usually started at Jonathan's expense, it normally boomeranged. Jonathan early mastered the technique of the "last laugh."

The anecdotes found in almanacs, jest books, and magazines probably provide the quickest illustration. The Jonathan of one anecdote, baulked by a punctilious Canadian customs inspector, tricked the poor man into investigating too closely the sawdust-filled false bottom of his wagon. Overset and unable to extricate himself, the inspector then received a free ride over a corduroy road.[26] The same sort of humorous behavior characterized the stage Jonathan, who, for example, sent a supercilious London cabbie in futile search for a nonexistent fare after the man had cast aspersions on Jonathan's provincial ignorance of the city.[27]

Although Jonathan seldom actually broke into overt violence, the character gave the impression, in some cartoons at least, that rash action suited him far better than rational discourse.[28] Jonathan's humor and rebelliousness went hand in hand. As Neil Schmitz reaffirmed in his recent study of American literary humor, "Humor . . . is skeptical of any discourse based on authority—[thus humor] mispeaks it, miswrites it, misrepresents it."[29] Jonathan frequently resorted to all three. And his humor especially functioned as "an aggressive argument, an imperative statement about knowledge as power."[30]

Quick-witted and inventive as it was, Jonathan's humor was still one-dimensional. He seldom relaxed enough to enjoy life's ironies and his own role in contributing toward those ironies. Nor was this humor a means of understanding or accommodating to the difficult or painful experiences everyone has to face. It lacked "the freedom to let go of small or narrow viewpoints and see things from a playful distance, to appreciate rather than fear contrast and irony, to enrich . . . dialogue with freshness."[31] Part of his defensive posture toward the world—the world being almost any place or anyone from beyond his village's boundaries—his humor responded only to real or imagined slights. Not surprisingly then, by the 1840s and 1850s, Jonathan's mask began to limit the character's representative role. Like a turtle or crab unable to grow beyond the confines set by his cara-pace, Jonathan was garbed in an armor that eventually cut him off from new experiences. From behind his mask of foolishness, however, during his active career he manipulated most situations so that his humor func-tioned as a weapon and as protective coloring.

CANTANKEROUSLY INDIVIDUALISTIC

Jonathan needed protective coloring because he always constituted a threat to someone. "Americans" or "Yankees" might include upper-crust capitalists like John Hancock or wealthy landowners like George Washing-ton, but Brother Jonathan came from a humbler background. He repre-sented a volatile element in American society forever insisting that while not everyone was his peer, he was the equal of anyone. The attitude was self-contradictory but it is hardly uncommon even now. Jonathan's un-abashed individualism would appeal to the contemporary *posse comitatus*.

Throughout his career, Jonathan opposed—or to use Royall Tyler's word, stood in contrast with—anyone with pretensions. Consequently, Jonathan first came to life in contrast to British affectation. In time, how-ever, he stood just as solidly in opposition to American governmental, social, sectional, or economic leaders. Accordingly, a song published in the 3 September 1795 *City Gazette & Advertiser* fully expected "Jonathan" to mount intense opposition John Jay's unsatisfactory treaty with England.[32] And on the stage Jonathan invariably deflated someone's social preten-sions while in jest book and almanac anecdotes, Jonathan loved to rattle the poise of city slickers, local wits, and pompous Englishmen.

In her book on American humor, Constance Rourke traced a relation-ship between Yankee humor—of which Jonathan offered a prime example —and emotional repression.[33] Jonathan's early and frequent resort to aggressive humor in defense of what he perceived to be his embattled status suggests a dissatisfaction on the part of people who might be called petite bourgeois: owners of small farms, skilled workmen, peddlers, and shop owners eager to make a profit from the sale of their limited stocks of goods. These men seem to have resented the continuing hegemony exercised

by revolutionary leaders when the rhetoric of the American Revolution
had promised a more democratic society. As Kathleen Smith Kutolski
pointed out in a 1982 issue of the *American Quarterly*, scholarly investigation now supports the argument that even during the Jacksonian Era,
"Concentration, not distribution of power, and oligarchy, not democracy,
characterized governing elites and politics in many types of commu-
nities."[34]

In any case, by the 1850s the character had changed. In the increasingly genteel humorous productions emanating from Northern presses,
Jonathan lost his wicked edginess; in the South, he kept his aggressive edge
but lost his humor. In fact when he appeared in political cartoons and
illustrations with a Southern bias, he became the visual Simon Legree—or

OUR VISITORS.
JONATHAN. "Ah! Mister, and, pray, what can I do for you?"
JAPANESE VISITOR. "If you please, I would like to borrow a little of your light."

Our Visitors. *Harper's Weekly* **4** (1860): 352. (*Courtesy of the State Historical Society
of Wisconsin Rare Book Collection.*)

after the Civil War—a carpetbagger. Until the loss of his humorous acuteness in the fifties, however, Jonathan allowed his creators to indict what they considered creeping inequities in society and a loss of revolutionary fervor.

Although Jonathan did sometimes seem a carping small-minded dissenter, as the representative common man with none of the traditional entrées to status such as aristocractic lineage, great learning, or social cachet, Jonathan primarily recalled everyone to the reality behind revolutionary rhetoric. The "every man" referred to in the Declaration of Independence and the Constitution had to include him. As a reminder of human dignity, he embodied an admirable ideal. But when the popular media attempted to reflect this inclusive vision of Jonathan, he became a vague and generalized abstraction—worthy of the idealized multitude but only vaguely human.

As long as he remained a laughable and contentious hick, Jonathan said something about a major portion of American society. But too many forces worked against his retaining that identity: the limitations of his one-dimensional humor, the prickly quality he stood for, and the homogenizing force of Victorian gentility all encouraged him to change. By the 1860s when Uncle Sam had absorbed the paternal qualities of "Father" Abraham Lincoln, Brother Jonathan had smoothed out enough to contribute his distinctive costume. After all, by then only his dress set him apart.

Stages in Development

1776–1800

Jonathan's early period from 1776 to 1800 coincided with the revolutionary and federalist eras in the United States. During this time, the character appeared in political cartoons, on the stage, in occasional verse, and in almanac anecdotes as the common man—sometimes admirable but more frequently a clod capable of substituting self-interest for the common well-being. Hence, the Jonathans of the first known political cartoon to feature the character, as well as the Jonathan of the "Lexington March," seem more worried about the cold of winter and the heat of battle than the fortunes of their new nation.

1800–1840

Jonathan's fullest development occurred roughly between the Republican victory that Thomas Jefferson referred to as the Revolution of 1800 and Martin Van Buren's presidential defeat in 1840. At no time since in peacetime history, except perhaps the 1930s, have the popular media in the

United States so exalted the essential strength, courage, and wisdom of the common man. For these forty years Jonathan was the preeminent representative of the American everyman. As the political myths of the day stressed the worth of the ordinary citizen, the character retained his original definition—rural, slier than his outward appearance might lead one to expect, and fiercely independent—but these same qualities were now envisioned as admirable sources of strength.

This shift in emphasis can be seen in an original tale by J. K. Paulding published in an 1831 issue of *The New York Mirror* and entitled "Jonathan's Visit to the Celestial Empire." Recounting the absurdly exaggerated adventures of young Jonathan, the tale detailed how in 1783 he "fitted out his sloop, a tarnal clever vessel of about eighty tons, and taking a crazy old compass for his guide, his two cousins, one a lad about sixteen, and a great Newfoundland dog for his crew, and a couple of rusty revolutionary swords for an armament, . . . [he] boldly set forth on a voyage to the celestial empire."[35] Naturally, he overcame all difficulties and limitations and made half-a-million dollars as the first person to sell ginseng to the Chinese. He achieved success by first convincing the Chinese that he was a poor, slow-witted country boy of whom they were taking advantage. In the process, of course, Jonathan made the Chinese authorities look especially foolish.

That is the only tale I know of approaching the length of a short story. Besides this appearance, Jonathan achieved much fuller development in cartoons from the 1810s onward, on the stage from the 1820s onward, and in almanac humor after 1830. In addition, on ongoing barrage of incidental verse and political writing kept the figure active in opposition to one person or another's source of annoyance.

1840–1865

During the decade before the American Civil War, Jonathan continued to appear frequently in the popular media, but his essence changed. He remained a man from the country; however after 1840 he lost much of his sly contentious humor. Actors playing stage Yankees were busier with delineating the sartorial and verbal quirks of the Yankees they had encountered than with thinking through Jonathan as a national or even a regional type. Some actors, in fact, like James Hackett, were branching out beyond the constraints of Yankee humor to other comic roles. Almanac and jest book humor never had much room for developing character. In any case the writers and publishers of anecdotes were primarily interested in entertaining as a means of selling. They had considerably less interest in social or political humor. (At its most vibrant, the Jonathan figure had invariably been a means of humorous commentary.) From the 1830s onward cartoons tended to concentrate on individual political characters. (Provincial at heart, political caricature of the period hardly seemed aware of anything happening beyond the nation's borders.) Jonathan was also present in these cartoons, yet increasingly, his jaunty self-confidence outstripped his humor. Jonathan's political sympathies lay with the Loco Focos. Established as *the* ordinary American, Jonathan easily became the focus of xenophobic feeling directed against Catholic immigrants, Jews, and blacks, who by nativist definition lacked Jonathan's inherent individualism, love of freedom, and independence of spirit. Jonathan's virtues were thus made to contrast with the sins of the "servile races" inundating the American consensus.

By 1850 the costume today recognized as Uncle Sam's was almost set. But from the 1850s all too often Jonathan functioned as the mouthpiece of narrow-minded bias. Thus Jonathan no longer spoke for the underdog of the revolutionary period but for the Know-Nothings in American (1855)[36] and British (1862)[37] political cartoons entitled "More Free Than Welcome." Issued as a broadside, the earlier American cartoon was anti-Catholic and implicitly opposed to Irish immigration. The later British cartoon from *Punch* was antiblack. Present even in early plays,[38] by the 1850s prejudice predominated in the character of Jonathan. During the 1860s Jonathan aged rapidly. Though many writers had tried a literary development of the character that might have kept him alive as a cultural symbol, they had met with limited success.

After the Civil War Jonathan gradually disappeared from American popular culture. In Europe, however, particularly in England, the cartoon figure lived an extended existence lasting to the end of the nineteenth century. As late as 1898, *Punch*[39] and *Judy*[40] represented the United States as Jonathan in cartoons critical of American actions during the Spanish-American War. Nonetheless, by this date the cartoon figure was little more than a fossil remain.

Analogs and Direct Competition

Between the Revolutionary and Civil Wars in America, Jonathan maintained a unique place in popular culture as an exemplar of the common man. Concurrently, elite culture encouraged other symbols of America. Elite and popular media fed off one another, developing in the process, a few of the more lasting American symbols.

COLUMBIA

In the eighteenth century, America's few political cartoonists still copied almost without variation the symbols and sometimes the very sketches of

British artists. But eighteenth- and nineteenth-century British caricaturists liked to contrast the stately, restrained figure of Britannia with an uncouth American Indian figure. Naturally, Americans did not maintain the same enthusiasm for the British depiction of the United States as a savage. They preferred instead an equally formal and classical figure such as Liberty or Columbia to parallel England's Britannia.

So, from the earliest national period, American artists drew the latter images. As McClung Fleming has shown, the heyday of the Indian princess image of America passed with colonial and revolutionary times. The classical figure of a Greek goddess, variously called Liberty of Columbia, superseded the Indian princess and predominated until after the War of 1812. The image of Liberty, of course, had been closely linked with the imagery of the republic particularly up to and during the French Revolution. But popular recoil from the violent excesses of the terror may have limited popular enthusiasm for the radical republicanism for which it stood. The consequences, after all, of the French and American Revolutions appalled English and American Whigs despite their initial support for these revolutions.[41] Actually, serious and caricaturized versions of this figure have never entirely lost their popularity. The paramount serious exemplar resides on Staten Island in New York City's harbor. From atop state houses across the country, other equally sober goddesses bless legislative and executive proceedings.

Any figure can be caricaturized, but in comparison with most national symbols, Columbia has seldom suffered that ignominy. Columbia speaks of the ideal of liberty. With a touch of the sacred, she represents an ideal that neither Americans nor others have cared to mock. During the federalist period, numerous patriotic songs acclaimed Columbia; and after George Washington's death in December of 1799, still more songs strengthened the association of a god-like Washington with a goddess of liberty.[42] In addition, the image of Columbia never belonged to the marketplace in the same way as Jonathan or Uncle Sam. Far more than these the product of an elitist self-image, she belonged to the impulse that encouraged Horatio Greenough to sculpt a statue of Washington in the costume of an ancient Greek. Columbia's image associated the American republic with Athens and early Rome.

Columbia thus symbolized an ideal America, the home of liberty. As such she appeared in cartoons with both Jonathan and Uncle Sam but spoke of a different quality in American life. In a *Vanity Fair* cartoon, for example, of 8 December 1860, Nurse Columbia dressed as a prim middle-class housewife but wearing her god-like crown of stars, objected to Doctor Disunion's prediction of amputation for Brother Jonathan. According to her, "Good nursing [an infusion of patriotic idealism?] will do anything—everything—if you will only give him the opportunity."[43]

BROTHER JONATHAN LAME.

Doctor Disunion.—POOR FELLOW! HIS CONSTITUTION IS SO RUN DOWN THAT I FEAR HE CANNOT SURVIVE WITHOUT AN AMPUTATION.
Nurse Columbia.—O! *don't* GIVE IT UP, DOCTOR. GOOD NURSING WILL DO ANYTHING—EVERYTHING—IF YOU WILL ONLY GIVE HIM THE OPPORTUNITY.

Brother Jonathan Lame. *Vanity Fair 2 (1860): 285. (Courtesy of the University of Iowa Rare Book Collection.)*

WASHINGTON

Some real men of the period between the Revolution and the Civil War, raised while still alive to the level of legendary heroes, also functioned as American icons—human embodiments of all that was admirably American. George Washington served that purpose, as did Benjamin Franklin, and later—in different ways—so did Daniel Boone, Davy Crockett, and Abraham Lincoln. Each man incarnated what was considered one type of American greatness. The most significant cult attached to and started with the figure of Washington.

Even Washington's contemporaries, David Humphreys and Jonathan Mitchell Sewell, favored the epithet "god-like" in referring to Washington.[44] Seymour Martin Lipset points, in fact, to Washington's charisma and subsequent lionizing as an important source of legitimization for the authority of the early American republic.[45] Well-known and respected even before the revolution, Washington was raised after his death to supreme cultic status.[46] Especially influential among the mountains of tributes to Washington were the "fictionalized biographies"[47] written and peddled by Mason Locke Weems, an itinerate preacher, fiddler, and book-seller. Known to have tested out on his listening audiences his tales about Washington before incorporating them into literary editions,[48] Weems's "Sunday school hero"[49] versions of Washington's life saw eighty-four printings by 1829.

If Columbia signified America's adherence to the ideal of liberty, the Washington of song, biography, verse, public oratory, and statuary represented an ideal of preternatural public virtue. As high culture symbols, both Columbia and Washington found their way onto coins and greenbacks as well as onto more obviously transient popular artifacts. Idealized versions of American virtues, neither symbol offered the potential for controversy inherent in popular cultural symbols of the early nineteenth century. The major imaginative symbols of the United States and of the American people between the wars—the Yankee, Jack Downing, Jonathan, and Uncle Sam—actually represented real and thus fallible people; these figures, therefore, also provided ready targets for caricaturists. Toward the end of the century, because the American eagle represented a real, militaristic manifestation of American pride, European artists also caricaturized the eagle.

THE YANKEE

To this day, Yankee,[50] shortened from Yankee Doodle, means both a New Englander and an American; the term had the same double significance before the Civil War. Thus much as a contemporary Southerner might speak, in 1861 an acquaintance of Mary Boykin Chesnut objected to her British friend that Southerners were not Yankees.[51] And, of course, during the Civil War combatants and noncombatants alike distinguished between Yankees and Southerners, though even then Yankee need not mean exclusively New Englander.[52] The efforts of New England writers like Whittier, Longfellow, and Beecher to mold the "American" into a "New England" image and later to link the antislavery and free soil movements with the American ideal, may have served only to foster the identification of the Yankee with New England alone. Their efforts for these causes certainly help to explain Southern resistance to being identified as Yankees.

While foreigners have always been more likely than Americans to refer to all citizens of the United States as Yankees, even during the early part of the nineteenth century—as reflected in popular songs of the period— Americans already called themselves Yankees.[53] But since Yankee could mean American or New Englander or Northerner, the character in the songs did not signify a distinct persona such as Jonathan had developed.

The Yankee did have a greater presence on the stage than in most other popular arts. On the stage, actors developed a roster of Yankee types. While Jonathan was one of the most eccentric and memorable of these Yankee types, other Yankee characters also served as *sui generis* Americans.[54] Not every Yankee character was necessarily a Jonathan, but like him for the most part a Yankee character could be expected to prove shrewd and canny. With contemporary actors continuing to exploit Yankee stereotypes, variations in the character remain familiar even today. Some actors like Percy Kilbride's Pa Kettle of a generation ago and, more recently, Tom Poston's unhandyman George on the Bob Newhart show emphasize the comic potential inherent in the Yankee's hesitant verbal delivery. Others, like James Stewart, have made a career of playing variations of the Yankee as the quintessential American. So the tradition continues to thrive.

But it started during the nineteenth century when comedy stars first produced a range of Yankee characters such as James Hackett's Deuteronomy Dutiful in *The Vermont Wool Dealer* (1839), Joshua Silsby's Solon Shingle in *The People's Lawyer* (1839), and the various renditions of Rip Van Winkle culminating after the 1860s onward in Joseph Jefferson's version. Up to mid-century, Yankee roles emphasized comedy, but about mid-century more writers began to mold together the comic aspect of the Yankee type with the more laudable qualities of the genteel heroes of early nineteenth-century comedy. For example, the more sedate hero of *Our American Cousin* (1858), the play Lincoln was watching the night he was shot, retained some Yankee humor but had aged as well and was acted with far more decorum than any Jonathan character. In Tom Taylor's melodrama turned farce, the "quaintly comic"[55] hero, Asa Trenchard, combined the altruism of *The Contrast's* Colonel Manly with the sharp wit and country ways of Jonathan.

JACK DOWNING

Among early republican fictional Yankees, only Jack Downing rivaled the popularity of Jonathan. Like Jonathan, Jack Downing appeared in more than one medium and represented a countryboy turned entrepreneur. The character originated in mock letters written between 1830 and 1833 by Seba Smith for his newspaper, *The Portland Courier*. In 1833 Smith published this series as *The Life and Writings of Major Jack Downing*. Through the persona of Jack Downing, whose character, according to Smith's recent biographer, combined innate innocence with a spirit of foolish ambition and proud ignorance,[56] Smith provided a conservative critique of mass democracy during Jackson's presidency. From Smith's jaundiced point of view, the sad lessons to be derived from Jack Downing's experiences as a would-be congressman showed that even the least qualified man could achieve public office, that election resulted from party solidarity rather than merit, that issues were better avoided because their clarification lost votes, and that the votes of society's riffraff could assure party control.[57]

Jack Downing's rural background and his potential for upsetting the established order resembled Jonathan's background and similar propensity. In contrast, however, Downing was invariably political. Except in political cartoons, Jonathan's role did not need to be political. During the 1830s Jack Downing commonly appeared in political cartoons, and a chronology of Seba Smith's career notes that several spurious, imitative Downing letters appeared as newspaper series during the 1830s and 1840s.[58] Nonetheless, Downing did not have Brother Jonathan's coverage in every media. Regardless of his imitators, Jack Downing remained primarily the creation of Seba Smith. Jack Downing also differed from Brother Jonathan in that Downing's character was often "uncomprehending."[59] More often than not, Jonathan only pretended incomprehension. Jack Downing's opinions and actions satirized the ignorant. Jonathan's satirized both the ignorant and the knowledgeable.

Smith literally resurrected Jack Downing during the 1840s in order to satirize Polk's incumbency. Between the summer of 1847 and January of 1856, Downing's letters to his people back in Maine regularly appeared in the Washington, D.C., *National Intelligencer* to let them know of his new adventures as President Polk's friend and advisor. Pushed into action by a rival series of "Downing" letters, Smith had his favorites from this series published in 1859 as *My Thirty Years Out of the Senate* (a satirical play on

Uncle Sam Sick with La Grippe (1836). (*Courtesy of the Prints and Photographs Division, Library of Congress.*)

the title of Thomas Hart Benton's autobiography). By then the heyday of both Jack Downing and Brother Jonathan was over.

UNCLE SAM

Although Uncle Sam in time acquired some traits and the clothing of Jonathan and Jack Downing, he always had an essentially different meaning. As Albert Matthews pointed out in 1908, Uncle Sam differed from any other national nickname in that he always referred primarily to the government of the United States rather than the nation as a whole.[60] Still, from his first appearances during the War of 1812, the character gained steady acceptance as an important symbol of America. Thus an American cartoon from Van Buren's presidency, "Uncle Sam Sick with La Grippe" (1836 or 1838) put Uncle Sam in the picture's foreground with Jonathan outside playing the puckish commentator on the government's malady.

Uncle Sam was unequivocally American in origin, and Europeans took their time about accepting him as a symbol of America.[61] The English, for example, preferred Jonathan, since they could think of him as John Bull's oafish offspring, by nature subordinate. While American political cartoons of the 1830s, 1840s, and 1850s featured Brother Jonathan and Jack Downing as frequently as Uncle Sam, during the Civil War Uncle Sam gradually became the more common American symbol. During and after the Civil War, as Uncle Sam took over Jonathan's more easily recognized garb and Abraham Lincoln's beard, Uncle Sam gained absolute ascendancy. During the Civil War, British and American cartoons had caricatured Lincoln, presenting him in the stars and stripes earlier reserved for Jonathan.[62] The identification of Uncle Sam and Lincoln may also have been assisted by the latter's widespread recognition as a Yankee original. Even Mary Chesnut and her Confederate friends referred to Lincoln as "the cleverest Yankee type." She recalled as well that Stephen Douglas had told her husband that Lincoln was "the hardest fellow to handle" he had ever encountered.[63] Chestnut's—and perhaps Douglas's—choice of words echoed a common way in popular literature of describing a "cute" Yankee.

Conclusion

Jonathan clearly inhabited a slightly different symbolic space than any other American icon of his time. A development of the colonial figure of Yankee Doodle, Jonathan emerged in response to the patriotic call for a national image; but since the people Jonathan stood for were all too "common," the figure increasingly represented dissenters: political, economic, or social outsiders cut off from effective power. Among twentieth-century cartoon characters, Bill Mauldin's Willie and Joe probably most closely approach Jonathan's irreverent spirit.[64] Langston Hughes' Jesse Simple offers another kindred spirit.

In his role as the representative of the ordinary man, Jonathan differed from other popular, elite, and folk presentations of the American. When in fact literary men used the word "Jonathanism," they meant some sort of verbal barbarism.[65] Anecdotes by and about the figure of Jonathan tended to demonstrate the tension during the early years of United States history between what Lipset refers to as our basically conflicting values, egalitarianism and achievement.[66] Since Jonathan embodied both the egalitarian spirit and American pride in achievement, the figure sometimes presented a Janus-like appearance. One moment he insisted on his independence and equality; the next moment he was bragging about his special talents and unique achievements.

Not only did the figure of Jonathan suffer from this innate division, he also suffered from a structural confusion. On the one hand, Jonathan flourished as a popular visual and verbal embodiment of romantic individualism in the United States. On the other hand, since that individualism was expressed in dialect and frequently in a boorish sense of humor, Jonathan's popular expressions ran counter to the overwhelming genteel

JONATHAN'S ADVICE TO LOUIS NAPOLEON.

"DON'T YOU THINK YOU'D BETTER TAKE YOUR DOG HOME?"

Jonathan's Advice to Louis Napoleon. *Vanity Fair* 5 (1862): 311. (*Courtesy of the State Historical Society of Wisconsin.*)

trend toward eliminating "the taint of vulgarity and of humor"[67] in American colloquial styles. Unfortunately for his survival, these elements belonged to Jonathan's essence. Nonetheless, as long as he retained his bumptious humor, he remained a weather vane for tensions in American culture. Once he lost his edge, he faded into the figure of Uncle Sam.

While this may prove only partially demonstrable, it seems that Jonathan's shift in status from a lout to a hero[68] and back again to a lout paralleled a similar shift in self-definition within American culture. During the first several decades of the nineteenth century, American political trends and social organizations had favored Jonathan's establishment as a primary American icon. If Alan I. Marcus, for example, is correct in his analysis, until the 1840s citizens considered themselves free agents, only needing or interested in government services in extreme circumstances.[69] The individual presumably could deal with anything short of a catastrophe. Jonathan's attitude reflected this highly individualistic approach. By the 1840s, with the development of questions about how unbridled capitalism might affect workers and particularly when the Civil War demanded the submersion of individual preferences to national necessity, Jonathan became archaic.

2

Brother Jonathan on the Stage

THE JONATHAN CHARACTER WHO APPEARED IN ROYALL TYLER'S *THE CONTRAST* (1787) shocked and delighted American audiences with an enjoyable sense of recognition. For the first time they saw a distinctly American type on stage. A contemporary critic, for example, signing his name "Candour" in *The Daily Advertiser* on the day after the opening performance, commented that Jonathan was "very well drawn."[1] Although Candour was making a specific judgment about Jonathan's account of his inadvertent attendance at "the devil's drawing room,"[2] a theatrical performance, the reviewer was, in effect, also describing the character himself.

This chapter explores what Candour and the rest of the audience accepted as an especially "well drawn" American. In addition, it shows that in actual fact the depiction of the Jonathan character in *The Contrast* and in the comedies by other playwrights that followed Tyler's lead during the next several generations did not present only the ordinary American whom Brother Jonathan was supposed to represent. More than a picture of the ordinary American, the Jonathan character offered a view of how writers, actors, and theater audiences believed or wanted to believe the ordinary American acted. Thus the portrait not only reflected reality, but also attempted to influence it.

In addition to *The Contrast*, the main comedies featuring an American character explicitly referred to as Jonathan included Joseph Atkinson's *Match for a Widow* (1786), J. Robinson's *The Yorker's Stratagem* (1792), John Minshull's *Rural Felicity* (1801), Lazarus Beach's *Jonathan Postfree* (1807), A. B. Lindsley's *Love and Friendship* (1808), J. K. Paulding's *The Bucktails* (c. 1815), Charles Mathews's *Trip to America* (1824), R. B. Peake's *Americans Abroad* (1824), Charles Mathews's "Jonathan W. Doubikins" and "A Trip to Natchidoches" (1820s), Samuel Woodworth's *The Forest Rose* (1825), George Colman's *New Hay at the Old Market* reprinted as *Sylvester Daggerwood* (1827), James Hackett's *Jonathan in England* (1828), Thomas Dibdin's *Banks of the Hudson* (1829), William

Dunlap's *A Trip to Niagara* (1930), George Stevens's *The Patriot* (1834), and William Moncrieff's *Tarnation Strange* (1838). (Notes on these texts and their stage production appear in Appendix B.)

Moral Fantasies

As formulaic stories, *The Contrast* and later Jonathan comedies belong to the category of what John Cawelti calls "moral fantasies" whose actions exclude "the disorder, the ambiguity, the uncertainty, and the limitations"[3] of real life in the early United States. These moral fantasies allowed the genteel element in the audience to "confirm their own already held idealized self-image,"[4] which contrasted with the Jonathan character's lower-class limitations. But the delight that Tyler's audience experienced arose from the fact that his Jonathan introduced what Cawelti could call "a new element into the formula." Tyler and his followers brought a "personal vision" to the depiction of what had been the role of a rural buffoon who like Sheridan's Tony Lumpkin occasionally showed flashes of native ingenuity or wit. The Jonathan character, like the Harlequin of the *commedia dell' arte*, started as a cloddish buffoon resembling his European ancestors; but Jonathan developed into a wily force to be reckoned with.

Throughout the character's career, his country origins clung to his person like grains of hayseed. The Jonathan formula did not materialize out of nowhere. It was primarily a new twist braided into several established traditions. The next chapter will outline the force these influences (from dramatic history, stage practice, the national need for an American icon, and the way that humor sometimes functioned as a weapon) had in helping to mold the Jonathan character as it appeared on American and European stages before the Civil War.

Sly Simplicity

In her book on American humor, Constance Rourke demonstrated that the Yankee's mask of naive ignorance was also the first identifiably American type of humor.[5] Jonathan in *The Contrast* was the original version of these not-so-innocent innocents. In one of the most widely known scenes from *The Contrast*, for example, Jonathan ingenuously recounted his misadventures in the city, including an unknowing visit to a playhouse. The audience of *The Contrast* could not be sure: Did Jonathan realize that he was really watching Sheridan's *The School for Scandal*? Was he fooling himself or his audience as he recounted the experience? Surely a magic show with its overtones of devil worship should have been even more severely interdicted than playgoing. According to Jonathan's account, however, that was what he had intended to attend; yet somehow the raising of the curtain allowed him to listen to and watch the Teazles and Surfaces. Jonathan appeared to take the whole scene quite seriously and to get properly incensed over the perfidy of Charles and the lightweight moral sense of Mrs. Teazle.

The deadpan delivery of an exaggerated piece of absurdity salted with occasional touches of realistic detail is, as Mark Twain later reminded his contemporaries, quintessentially American. As Twain put it:

> To string incongruities and absurdities together in a wandering and sometimes purposeless way, and seem innocently unaware that they are absurdities, is the basis of the American art. . . . Another feature is the slurring of the point. A third is the dropping of a studied remark apparently without knowing it, as if one were thinking aloud. The fourth and last is the pause.[6]

Tyler's Jonathan already knew these tricks.

Thus when Jessamy, the servant of the foreign villain and Jonathan's foil, and the audience first met Jonathan in Act II, scene 2, Jonathan appeared rude and untutored. Jonathan was nevertheless quick to learn. Recounting an earlier encounter with a "deacon's daughter," he was apparently still unaware of her questionable virtue. In any case he would have visited her apartment in New York's "Holy Ground" except that a brawling crowd of sailors chased him off.

Malapropism

Tyler was clearly indebted to the playwright Sheridan. The characters, structure, and comedic form, for example, of *The Contrast* all bore notable resemblances to *The School for Scandal*.[7] The humor revolving around the best known of *The Contrast's* characters, Jonathan, was also influenced by the most memorable character from Sheridan's *The Rivals*. Mrs. Malaprop certainly earned the right to have her named affixed to the verbal blunder we call a malapropism. It is difficult to envision even an adequate peer to her misplaced bragging. And though not her peer, Tyler's Jonathan also can be identified, along with other tags, by his recourse to malapropism.

Like Mrs. Malaprop, Tyler's Jonathan indulged in unexpected turns of speech such as "a pungency of tribulation" (p. 45) for a poignancy of tribulation—one of his better malapropisms. The phrase implied a comic interplay between the elegant locution that tribulation was poignant and the implied colloquial statement, that trouble stank. Tyler's Jonathan regularly substituted inappropriate words for others with a similar pronunciation. But as Mark Auburn noted in *Sheridan's Comedies*,[8] Mrs. Malaprop misused language in a couple of ways. Not only did she substitute a like-sounding antonym for the word she meant, e.g., "malevolence" for "benevolence"; she also and more commonly substituted words whose misapplication conveyed inadvertently amusing sense despite her patent nonsense. Jonathan indulged in something similar. Nonetheless, unlike Sheridan's Mrs. Malaprop, Jonathan did not misuse pretentious words in order to impress others.

Instead, Tyler's dialect vocabulary for Jonathan provided him with a sufficient stock of words with which to utter double-edged malapropisms. Despite Jonathan's apparently naive misapprehension, the joke's barb usually stung someone else. On his tongue insurgents became "sturgeons" (p. 36) making a sort of edible fish out of would-be heroes. He expected and got a kind of hocus-pocus (p. 53) when he visited the theater. Jonathan inadvertently but accurately referred to a "dissolvable knot" (p. 63) of marriage in his pursuit of Jenny. He had no intention, after all, of getting tied with an indissolvable knot. In *The Contrast's* last scene, angry at Dimple, Jonathan demanded, "Don't you see you have frightened the young woman into hystrikes?" (p. 100). Perhaps Jonathan thought that Charlotte feared a rape attack from Dimple (he strikes). In its way, the notion was as logical as the etymology of "hysterics," a female emotional disturbance related to the womb. Earlier in a still better malapropism, Jonathan neatly reinterpreted Jessamy's explanation of the ritual of gallantry as the practice of "girl-huntry" (pp. 37–38).

On Jonathan's tongue malapropism became a two-edged sword. Tyler's Jonathan was only apparently guileless. Like many of his countrymen during the first half-century of United States history, the Jonathan character knew he did not know about sophisticated women, about cities, about much of the larger world; so sometimes life cast him in a foolish position and sometimes he only acted the fool. The doltish role provided a convenient mask for him to wear while he attempted to find his way in unfamiliar surroundings. Malapropisms and various other forms of twisted language allowed him to control would-be predators. The use of malapropisms provided the Jonathan character with an opportunity to preserve what Flannery O'Connor called the ominous silence[9] until he could figure out how to turn the situation to his own advantage. One wonders if the Jonathan character's subsequent identification with a guileful innocence did not grow in part out of Tyler's early insistence upon the perverse logic of Jonathan's malapropisms in *The Contrast*.

Related to his use of malapropisms, Jonathan often managed a guileful reworking of Jessamy's phraseology. Jessamy's ironic recollection, for example, of "the blooming cherub of consequence smiling in its angelic mother's arms" ten months after his master's all too successful "gallantry" metamorphosed into Jonathan's query whether he might also expect "such little cherubim consequences" (p. 44) if he were to follow Jessamy's advice about practicing gallantry. Later when Jessamy tried to explain Jonathan's lack of success with Jenny as resulting from his lack of social grace,

Jonathan complained, "Grace! Why does the young woman expect I must be converted before I court her?" (p. 89).

This early Jonathan—like many later Yankee characters—had a disingenuous trick of taking another character's words at face value, and by insisting on their literal meaning, turning aside the other's attempt to dominate or assert superiority. Jessamy, for example, was made even more foolish in his insistence that the "rules" for acceptable levels of amusement be acknowledged while listening to a joke (pp. 88–93) because Jonathan took seriously each part of the joke. Jonathan also got literal when Jenny railed against his lack of feeling for the "delicacy" of her sex. Since she had just slapped his face, he objected, "Feeling! Gor, I—I feel the delicacy of your sex smartly" (p. 62).

The Jonathans of later comedies were not all equally adept at turning the cutting edge of a malapropism against their tormentors, but many of them used the mask of simplicity to great effect. In a comic misunderstanding, somewhat like a typical malapropism, the author of *Love and Friendship* (1809), for example, had Jonathan assuming that the young gentleman Mr. Seldeer, is Mr. Sell-dear.[10] Jonathan believed in buying cheap and selling dear; thus he assumed that Sell-dear was an apt name for any right-thinking person. Or perhaps his "mistake" was a slyly ironic comment on the disinterested motives of "gentlemen" merchants. In *The Bucktails* (c. 1815), as well, Jonathan crossed verbal swords with the king of the gypsies, who informed Jonathan that he was a king by virtue of descent from a courtier who had gotten in the habit of begging and a maid who kept her virtue so well that no one knew she had any. With a straight face, Jonathan queried, "O—ay—I guess that's being what they call a legitimate king?"[11] And in Hackett's adaptation of Colman's *Who Wants a Guinea*? renamed *Jonathan in England* (1828), Solomon Swap—the Jonathan of the piece—responding to the incensed householder Torrent's demand that he leave the room, retorted, "Don't s'pose I'm going to take it with me, do ye?"[12]

In addition, Jonathan Ploughboy, in the extremely popular *Forest Rose* (1825), piqued by what he considered a man's superior attitude, twisted a traveller around with simplicity and indirection. When Blanding, the traveller, asked how far he was from the Eagle Tavern, Jonathan wondered aloud, "You don't belong to these parts, I calculate?" And when Blanding tried to insist on an answer, Jonathan continued, "Maybe you are from New York? How does buckwheat sell?" Blanding's attempt to return to the subject by mentioning the innkeeper's name merely encouraged more pointed questions from Jonathan. "You a'n't acquainted with the major, are you? He trades at my shop. If I may be so bold, sir, what may I call your name?" Irascibly, Blanding blurted, "Stupid!—Pshaw! I will keep my temper," thus giving Jonathan another opening to ponder, "Stupid Shaw. S'pose you a'n't any ways related to 'Squire Shaw of Taunton, are you?—he that married the widow Lovett, mother of Ichabod Lovett, who was tried for horse-stealing?"[13]

When Captain Horner from *Love and Friendship* (1808), grew choleric, Jonathan protested, "Capun, don't swear so, I beg on't; for the land sake and masies alive, what would our parson say? you're a darned sight wos'n a methodist preacher."[14] The author, Lindsley, could not, it seems, resist a jibe at the itinerant ministers proliferating through every area during this period of religious enthusiasm.

Following the well-defined tradition for stage clowns, Jonathan Seabright of *The Patriot* (1834) also favored traditional malapropisms and puns. Speaking to a young woman, for example, he gushed, "Any man may speak *pottery*, when he speaks *truth*—smite me! may he not, my cherry-lipped tender-leaved-blossom of thy soul-consuming race?"[15] Stevens perhaps had Jonathan reminding the audience that rather than expressing lofty and inspired thought, much alleged poetry was flimsy earthenware. And toward the end of the comedy, sailor Seabright promised "Never will be *smitten*, do you see, so long as all the members of our noble Frigate, the United States' Constitution, live in union one with the other."[16]

Thus, while malapropism was not the only or even the most prominent characteristic of Jonathan's language and humor, it played a central role in turning a joke's edge against his tormentor. And while not all of the foregoing illustrations are malapropisms, they are all related to the use of malapropism—a traditional clown's tool—readjusted to make others as well as Jonathan look foolish. Tyler's appropriation of the characters, dramatic form, and style of R. B. Sheridan and other eighteenth-century playwrights led him to emphasize malpropism in the speech of Jonathan; but in his reordering of malapropisms for Jonathan, Tyler hit upon the happy accident of altering the joke's usual form and thus helped to set a pattern for what came to be a characteristic type of American humor.

At the same time that they characterized the ordinary American as novel and admirable, Tyler and those who followed his lead retained a healthy distrust of that group of possible usurpers, also ordinary Americans, whom they typified in the character called Jonathan. So on the one hand, Jonathan's speech and humor showed him as a potentially strong and worthy opponent capable of slipping out of an inferior position; but on the other hand, Jonathan retained his role as bumpkin. At any moment he might say or do something stupid. His audience never knew when he would give them the opportunity to feel superior any more than they knew when he would slyly gain the upper hand.

Although malapropisms provided a key to the depiction of the ordinary American as portrayed in the Jonathan character, the stage personality was quickly identified through verbal, physical, and action tags. The majority of these undoubtedly originated in fact. Real people spoke, dressed, or acted in this fashion. A symbolic character, the Jonathan figure, attracted these tags from a variety of individuals. Some tags hung on the figure as awkwardly as iron filings on a magnet; others seem molded into the character.

Tags

PHYSICAL

Jonathan's physical tags were first associated with his clownish lower-class country origins. His costume developed from peculiarities of country dress noted and copied by actors playing this role. The character was at first indistinguishable from the British northcountryman Hodge; but in the relatively standardized garb eventually adopted by Yankee actors of the 1820s, 30s, and 40s, Jonathan wore a long Yankee coat, striped trousers and vest, a wig of long lank hair, and a top hat. This of course is the same basic costume that later came to identify Uncle Sam.

On the antebellum stage, however, props as well as costume became recognizable visual tags for Jonathan. The character often carried either a whip or a jews harp; and consonant with the occasional confusion between Yankee and frontier stereotypes, he sometimes became identified with prowess as a rifleman.

VERBAL

Besides the physical tags of costume and props, the stage Jonathan quickly identified himself through verbal and action tags. His action tags primarily involved characteristic modes of behavior, such as prying. Because of Jonathan's obvious identification with Yankee dialect, however, his verbal tags were perhaps more pervasive and more easily isolated than his action tags. In almost every comedy, Jonathan either sang "Yankee Doodle," referred to himself as Yankee Doodle, or was called Yankee Doodle. That name was an almost universal verbal tag. In individual plays particular dialect words or phrases also became tags. So Jonathan repeated *ad nauseam* "I vow" in *Match for a Widow*, "how the witch" in *Jonathan Postfree*, "it beats all nature" in *Love and Friendship*, "I reckon" in *The Bucktails* and *Tarnation Strange*, "I calculate" and "I wouldn't serve a negro so" in *The Forest Rose*, "I calculate" in *Americans Abroad, The Yankey in England*, and *Tarnation Strange*, "I reckon," "I expect," "I guess" in *Jonathan in England*, "I guess" in *A Trip to Niagara*, "smite me" in *The Patriot*, and "tarnation strange, but very true for all that, besides it was in the papers—oh, yes!" in *Tarnation Strange*.

In addition to tags made from particular dialect words and phrases,

Jonathan's localized speech pattern itself became a verbal tag. His speech reflected his New England background. His stage dialect was concrete and homey and usually a source of amusement. But it also made the character who he was.

Jonathan's sly simplicity was most apparent in his speech. It came to the forefront with his offhand references to the courting custom of couples' "bundling" up in a quilt through the long New England evenings. The word alone must have gotten a reaction from audiences who vividly envisioned the unseen and unelaborated scene. In addition, "cute" in context came to mean "acute, quick, aggressive perhaps to the point of dishonesty in trading."[17] At the end of *Americans Abroad* (1824), for example, Jonathan voiced admiration for his Uncle Ben's "cute" trick in spreading the rumor that an American commercial house had gone bankrupt because Ben had thus managed to buy stock cheaply. And in *Jonathan in England* (1828), when Torrent objected to how slow his messenger was in arriving, Amy disagreed, saying, "Slow! There's not a cuter young man in the village than Solomon Swap."[18]

Also "cute," the Jonathan Ploughboy of *The Forest Rose* (1825), preferred to avoid blatant dishonesty; yet he managed to obtain a "generous reward" and "no questions ax'd"[19] for returning Lydia's locket despite having kept it for some time. Jonathan had to return the locket but he preferred to return it in his own good time and at a profit. The Jonathan character typically acted in this manner even though at times he also played the fool.

From comedy to comedy Jonathan's clownish simplicity, aided by his innate wiles, generally got him out of trouble. The characteristics surfaced in Hackett's adaptation of Colman's play. Thus when Torrent became incensed with Solomon-Jonathan, for letting a glass lamp break, Jonathan assured Torrent that nothing was out of order since he had escaped injury. A little later Solomon appeared to have been outmanuevered by Andrew Bangs, who had traded five guineas and a nonexistent watch for Solomon's watch, but then it turned out that Solomon's watch was only a shell. In any case Solomon got even that shell back later on.

Jonathan's clumsy clownishness often covered sly intentions. Even in Atkinson's *Match for a Widow* (1786), Jonathan's recurrent bouts of "forgetfulness" when he referred to Captain Belmor as "Madame" helped to convince Lady Bloomingdale, who had forsworn the company of men, that her visitor was not a man but a woman dressed as a man. From the opening scene in *The Yorker's Stratagem* (1792), as well, Amant as Jonathan Norrad played the bumpkin, referring to madeira as a French wine, and leading Acid, whom he intended to lull into overconfidence, to comment in an aside, "What an ass you are."[20] Jonathan could stand a good deal of insult for the sake of gulling his victim. When Fopling in

Jonathan Postfree (1807) tried to hire Jonathan for "secret" nefariousness, they proceeded with this absurd dialogue:

> Fopling: You see that house, next to the three story brick?
> Postfree: Yes, I do; and is that to be kept a secret?
> Fop: Mind me—in that house is a young lady—
> Post: Well, I won't tell of that.
> Fop: Behind the house is a garden—
> Post: I didn't know that before—that's a secret sure enough.[21]

Jonathan Postfree acted the buffoon, tripping over carpets and complaining that they were at fault, carrying the mail in his hat, prattling about inconsequentials; yet he was also clearly able to act with dispatch whenever he pleased.

While Tyler's Jonathan was not as sly and shrewd as many later Jonathans, his double-edged use of language indicated that he too was shrewd enough. Later Jonathan plays, working off the folk tradition about wily, eccentric Yankees, capitalized on the popular presumption of Jonathan's shrewdness and often exaggerated the character's guile—as when he became a conniving trickster peddler[22] or when they compounded the role playing and the Jonathan character was actually a New Yorker or an Englishman pretending to be a Yankee.[23]

Finally, almost every Jonathan was a storyteller. Part of the difficulty in ascertaining what these performances were like is that the actors who enlivened these plays with their characterizations of Jonathan were adept at ad lib storytelling but jealous of their material; so the original tales were seldom written down. Fortunately, almanac anecdotes suggest the content of Jonathan's shorter tales. So also the tales told by the popular Yankee actors of the 1840s and 50s and reprinted in book form indicate the tenor of the longer ramblings. These tales were humorous but they also contained a barb. Occasionally the humor was self-deprecating. More commonly, the humor stung a foreigner, city person, or a wit from another part of the country who tried to challenge Jonathan.

ACTION

Action tags were sometimes difficult to separate from verbal tags. Many of Jonathan's lines, for example, were designed to accentuate his ignorant singlemindedness. Thus, in *Americans Abroad*, Jonathan complained to the waiter at a local hotel, "Du you call this a land of liberty, where I cannot larrup my own nigger without being ordered out of the house? du explain to me the principles of the British constitution!"[24] Other lines, such as these from *Jonathan in England*, seem designed to illustrate his delicious incongruity with the British caste system. Asked why he came into the room, he told the master of the house,

> I was sent on an errand, to tell you that there's a chap out yonder in the hall—(Voice without.) Now, if there ain't that squalling sarpent of a cook. (Calls off.) What's the matter with you now, rot ye? Why, that cook is as shallow as a clam-shell. Why she never blushed when she told me she never heard about Indian dumplings and pork and molasses. I guess she's about as fit to be a cook as a hog is to wear a side-saddle. I say, squire, do you remember when you went cachunk into that horse-pound?[25]

Jonathan was as a rule so consistently lacking in finesse in his dealings with women that this became an action tag. In *Jonathan Postfree* the title character was the leading champion of virtuous maidens, but most of the Jonathan characters appeared simply ignorant of how even to speak to a woman. In the time-honored practice of closing comedies with paired-off couples, several of the plays ended with Jonathan finding a mate; but the plays left little doubt that he could hardly have won her through verbal blandishments. In a duet sung by Jonathan Ploughboy and Harriet, one of the village girls in *The Forest Rose*, Jonathan opined:

> I cannot tell the reason but I really want a wife, And everybody tells me 'tis the sweetest thing in life;
> But as for cheeks like roses, with pouting lips, and such, I know no more about them, than Ponto knows of Dutch.

When Harriet's reply, a mocking imitation of his stanza, wondered if he worshiped the ground she walked on, he continued,

> I'll tell you that sincerely, nor think it any harm,
> I love the ground you walk on, for 'tis your father's farm.
> Could that be mine without you, I'd be a happy man,
> But since you go together, I will love you if I can.

Nonetheless, after Harriet mused aloud about moving to town and flirting with numerous beaux, Jonathan reacted:

> If that's your calculation, we never can agree
> For such a mode of living will never do for me—
> And as for beaux and lovers, though you may like the fun,
> I guess the deacon's Sally, will be content with one.[26]

Jonathan had a knack for deflating romance.

Women might find Jonathan a failure at romance, but he was a dependable patriot and a thoroughly independent soul. Unfortunately, he could also be at once inquisitive and secretive, tight with his money, and appallingly intolerant. In these comedies Jonathan's xenophobia and anti-Semitism vied with his baiting black characters. Part realistic treatment and part wishful thinking, this view of the ordinary American emerged from the symbolic Jonathan character's stage tags.

The physical, verbal, and action tags attached to the stage character were identifications that audiences quickly accepted as "real" because in some cases they had met specific people who dressed or talked or acted in a similar manner. In other cases, however, some tags—such as the deceptive quality of the Jonathan character's simplicity, the Jonathan character's unbridled instinct for financial gain, or the character's utter inability to rise above his class and rural social limitations—suggest unconscious uneasiness among established elites that the Jonathan character and the hordes he symbolized would not, indeed, "keep their place."

Formulaic Pattern

While the tags provided quick identifications for the Jonathan character and implied social and economic tensions within the country, the formulaic presentation of the character in American comedies provided a dramatic framework that indicated further conflict.

In the American comedies, the authors usually set up a triangle of opposition. The Jonathan character and the genteel American hero together represented American virtue repulsing the dangers of European moral decay embodied in the villian. The two American characters in turn represented realistic and idealistic American portraits. Since the real American, Jonathan, could be dramatized through the use of physical, verbal, and action tags drawn from folk sources and already familiar through popular sources, the Jonathan character was naturally far more active and interesting than the vaguely conceptualized gentleman. And even though the playwrights assumed that the genteel character was the hero, in practice the comic actors who took the role of Jonathan became the stars.

FOREIGN VILLAIN

The hero, the villain, and Jonathan were thus defined in contrast with one another. In 1837 Emerson defined the American scholar by what he was not. Above all, he was not European. In the Jonathan plays, Americans were already defined by what they were not. Americans were not overly refined, corrupt men who imperiled what Americans valued: the heroine, her wealth, and her virtue. The pattern in these plays became almost allegorical.

Sentimental dramas of the period already included a villainous lecher; this group of plays also made the villain unAmerican. Sometimes the villain was explicitly identified as a foreign national. The would-be kidnapper in *The Forest Rose*, for example, was a traveller from England who promised to "remember" the rest of the cast when he published his "Three

Months in America."[27] (Woodworth thus neatly painted the villainous character of people who returned to Europe and published derogatory accounts of American life and manners after having been guests in America; he also managed to suggest the whole cloth out of which their accounts had been manufactured.) Dimple in *The Contrast* was English. An impoverished Irishman, the wastrel Lord Noland in *The Bucktails*, intended to recoup his fortunes by forcing Jane Warfield, the American heiress, to marry him. Another impecunious Irish lord was the villain in *Jonathan in England*. In other comedies the villain, though American-born, was tainted by contact with Europe. Dick Dashaway in *Love and Friendship* was thus an American infected by a European education; Fopling in *Jonathan Postfree* was similarly marred.

AMERICANS: ACTIVE JONATHAN AND PASSIVE GENTEEL HERO

Consistent with Humphreys's distinctions among Yankee types,[28] these comedies presented a genteel hero who belonged to the class of idealized gentlemen that both British and American audiences liked to believe existed. The comedies also presented a Jonathan character who, with only an elementary formal education, constantly compensated for this limited education through acute social observations. Less inhibited by genteel forms and traditions than his upper-class counterpart, Jonathan was the more active character; and while the genteel Yankee's innate talents and capabilities were assumed (since he was, after all, a gentleman), Jonathan demonstrated his capabilities in the course of the play's action. The Jonathan character was a mover. Things happened because he made them happen. Even in the very British version of *American Abroad*, where Jonathan W. Doubikins was crass, abrasive, and arrogant in contrast to the genteelly innocuous American, Delapierre, Doubikins vibrated with life and energy.

Although Jonathan was no hero and often did not win any girl, much less the comedy's heroine, he—rather than the play's titular hero—was responsible for the girl's rescue from the inevitable melodramatic toil. Consequently, in the last scene of *The Contrast*, Jonathan rather than the staid hero offered to fight Dimple. Particularly in plays with a melodramatic complications, Jonathan brought about the villains' downfall.

Indeed, the Jonathan character was almost always the most lively one in any comedy, but a particularly active one appeared in *Jonathan Postfree*. This character was prying, independent, intractably "common," a comical buffoon who dropped the mail he carried in his hat, pried into everyone else's business, and took more prat falls than Chevy Chase. But Jonathan's refusal to help Fopling abduct Maria, followed by his keeping track of the villain just in case Fopling should hire someone else to do the dirty work, and finally Jonathan's physical defense of Maria saved her from Fopling's intrigues. In contrast, the ostensible hero, Jemmy Seamore-Herdy, came on stage just long enough to receive directions, reestablish good relations with—and thus the hope of an inheritance from—his wealthy father, and get his suit with Maria approved by her parents.

A similar pattern emerged in *The Forest Rose*. Here, however, Jonathan Ploughboy lacked Jonathan Postfree's disdain for shady deals; he was tempted by the villain's pay, and not just for the sake of buying cookies to give to the local children, as Jonathan Postfree indicated he would do. And yet, Jonathan Ploughboy was probably a funnier character. He wanted to avoid helping the kidnapper but at the same time to find a way of keeping his pay for helping the kidnapper. In addition, like Jonathan Postfree, Jonathan Ploughboy was the butt of physical jokes. Irked by his lack of romantic finesse, his girl Sally tricked him into caressing a fat tabby cat instead of her; and later, when his eyes were closed, she tricked him into kissing the black serving girl, Rose. Not unexpectedly, Sally rather than Jonathan thought of substituting the willing Rose in order to foil Bellamy's attempt to abduct the genteel heroine, Lydia. Jonathan Ploughboy followed Sally's directions; nevertheless, he—not the hero, Blandford—saved the heroine.

Again, in *The Bucktails*, Henry the hero offered to walk in the garden with the heroine and thus showed his disdain for petty social rules. But Jonathan Peabody sounded out Lord Noland's servant, figured out the wicked plot, and was in the forefront among Jane's would-be rescuers.

The Jonathan character that appeared in Tyler's *The Contrast* and those later Jonathan characters that followed were "well drawn." But they were well drawn in the sense that any good nonphotographic portrait is "true." The plays captured in tags and formulaic actions some specific characteristics common to many ordinary working Americans; at the same time the artists—particularly the actors and playwrights—projected on the Jonathan character their fears and hopes about the masses whom he symbolized.

After all, actors like John Bernard and Charles Mathews considered themselves socially akin to the "gentleman" Shakespeare rather than to the rowdy patrons of American theaters such as appeared in the Auguste Herve illustrations for Mrs. Trollope's *Domestic Manners* (1832). In his memoirs John Bernard carefully distinguished among social classes in the United States, and Mathews openly resented the egalitarian manners of American workers. The playwright David Humphreys also distanced himself from the sort of man symbolized by Brother Jonathan.

Jonathan's role was ambiguous. The character never became entirely admirable. His feet of clay remained all too visible. Yet as a symbolic projection of American patriotism, the Jonathan character offered many admirable qualities. From his start in Tyler's *The Contrast*, the Jonathan character's use of malapropisms merely foreshadowed the character's role in subsequent plays as a wise fool and an oddly admirable shyster.

The Jonathan character almost had to be an ambiguous presentation. Influenced by nationalist fervor, American actors and playwrights were proud of what they perceived as the American difference that showed up in even the most ordinary people. At the same time they may have feared the energy, the singleminded acquisitiveness, and the intransigent toughness of ordinary Americans. This social tension, as well as others, was part of the stage presentation of the Jonathan character and will be discussed in the next chapter.

3

Sources of the Stage Jonathan

THE TAGS AND FORMULAE THAT IDENTIFIED THE STAGE JONATHAN RE-sulted from a combination of influences including an American cultural milieu that was almost frantically casting about in search of usable national icons, a theatrical tradition that had grown to expect national figures embodied in typical characters, and an uneasy mélange of British and American writers and actors perhaps unconsciously attempting to enforce through laughter the hegemony of society's "better sort" over rude parvenus whose origins matched those of the Jonathan character.

A National Icon

Although the Brother Jonathan character was admittedly not in every way unique, he did answer the popular call for a national icon. The public wanted such a formulaic identification of national characteristics. The success of the Jonathan character on the stage may well have been related to the way the character embodied in himself and in his relations with other characters recurring tensions in the early American republic. His humor, his language, and his formulaic parts in the plot enabled the character to embody and dramatize geographic, social, and economic strains. Incarnating both the American and a regional or social "other," Jonathan allowed the audience to experience and perhaps in part to resolve the social tensions the character embodied.

EMBODYING GEOGRAPHIC TENSIONS

To begin with, the Jonathan character allowed the actors and the audiences who saw them to explore regional tensions between the city and the country, the North and the South, and between the United States and Europe. Belonging to the long line of comic simpletons, the Jonathan character was generally a countryboy. His foil, by contrast, usually belonged to the villain tradition, so he was both bumpkin and sly fox. Garbed in the identifying verbal, visual, and action tags of New England Yankees, Jonathan could be expected to be parochial and localized in meaning. But during his early years he was not. The Jonathan character at once embodied the quirky Yankee, complete with local prejudices and limitations, and the American everyman.

The singing of "Yankee Doodle" by Tyler's Jonathan illustrated both his provincialism and patriotism. As a New England Puritan, he should know only hymns; but the proud patriot also admitted to knowing "Yankee Doodle." Jonathan disparaged this latter facility, however, with characteristic drollery, since he knew "but a hundred and ninety verses."[1] Patriotism—and thus an identification with the entire nation—typified the Jonathan character from the start of his career. He associated personal independence with political independence. So his very touchy New England sensitivity became part of a national pride. The national and patriotic flavor of Jonathan appeared in an incipient form in *The Contrast*, but it became part of a clear pattern in later Jonathan plays. Just as today people often use "Yankee" and "American" interchangeably, the terms were evidently interchangeable in the late eighteenth and early nineteenth centuries as well. Appropriately enough, though the Jonathan character wore all the trappings of a New England Yankee, in none of the plays was he set at odds with Southerners or Westerners—as he was at odds with all foreigners.[2]

EMBODYING SOCIAL AND ECONOMIC STRAINS

Besides his role as a regional figure, Jonathan also incarnated the tension between radical social democracy and the genteel aspirations of many in America's growing middle class. Tyler's Jonathan was vehement about his personal independence. But the Jonathan character and his fellows perhaps already recognized that status in America would be as often tied to money as to rank or accomplishments. The altruism personified by Colonel Manly was undoubtedly meant to glorify the more noble republican virtues, but all sections of the audience must have realized that Jonathan did not believe he could afford Manly's refined moral code. In contrast with Manly, Jonathan based his singleminded determination to get ahead on a clear perception of social reality. Unnervingly so to genteel observers, Jonathan was pushy. Even when they intended to present Jonathan as a sympathetic—because patriotic—character, playwrights had reasons to feel uncomfortable with his aggressiveness.

Both native and British playwrights generally belonged to a precariously genteel class whose families had once had the means to educate them, even though, in fact, the playwrights were not making much money from their writing. These authors could hardly be expected to glorify the character who embodied economic and social competition from would-be capitalists. Tyler, for example, despite his eventual position as chief justice of Vermont's Supreme Court, was rejected early in life as an unacceptable suitor for John Adams' daughter Nabby. Later, as an old man, he came to depend on his children's generosity for financial support. Tyler's precarious position was not uncommon among the playwrights who wrote the Jonathan plays.[3]

Theatrical Traditions

To achieve Jonathan's estimable status, writers and actors remodeled a type character and altered somewhat the familiar form in which he appeared. Audiences already knew both the character and the form quite well. Jonathan was descended from a long line of naive countryboys in dramatic literature. The English northcountry bumkin, Hodge, Jonathan's immediate predecessor and a staple role for eighteenth-century comic actors, represented a sort of thick-headed good humor. In fact, Thomas Wignell, the comic actor who first played Jonathan, wore the wig and costume of Hodge, the Northumbrian simpleton, when he introduced the role at New York's John Street Theatre.[4] In addition, comic national types— Irishmen, Frenchmen, Germans—also commonly graced eighteenth-century comedies.

A national type, the Jonathan character belonged to the much larger genre of stage Yankees. The practice of populating the stage—particularly the comic lines of acting—with national types was quite common in the eighteenth century and can be traced back through most of Western European stage comedy. Much of what can be said about the Jonathan character appearing in these comedies could be extended further to other Yankee characters. Other Yankee plays, however, are beyond the scope of this study. Because the comedies with a character clearly identified as Jonathan were more limited in number and maintained a consistent formulaic presentation of that character, they offer a more circumscribed assemblage than the larger group of Yankee plays for examining the cultural significance of Brother Jonathan during the early republican period in the United States.

Jonathan represented, after all, only one current in the turgid stream of American humor during the early part of the nineteenth century. As Tandy, Rourke, and Blair demonstrate, typically American humor emerged as a recognizable national trait during this period. Blair's definition of "native" humor posits the dual need for characters who reflected the customs and thinking of the people and for a technique with which to effectively develop that subject matter.[5] Working with the figure of Jonathan provided humorists with a clearly American type and an established comic pattern. Both the character and the pattern had their limits, yet they suggested ways to exploit the comic possibilities of the American scene and the American character.

In a sense all humor, but particularly American humor, tends toward the theatrical. The humorist has in mind the "play" involved in recounting a laughable experience.[6] And American humorists have often been performers. The tie between humor and the stage was preeminent in America from the 1820s through the Civil War. During that period the best-known comics and comic traditions of the period all appeared on the popular stage. Stage comics were the first American actors to achieve star status. Ever eager to widen and prolong their popularity, they showcased Yankee and frontier humor, Shakespearean and literary humor.

The Contrast, for example, was an extension of the established pattern of sentimental comedy.[7] The characterization of Jonathan, however, came closest to transcending the form's limitations. However ancient his type and regardless of what costumes the actors wore, Jonathan was clearly American. The character was so distinctly American, in fact, that the early critic, Candour, resented Wignell's inability to mimic exactly the Yankee twang that Jonathan ought to have spoken. Jonathan's humor and his language, after all, felt unequivocally American.[8] His humor and language as well as his conscious difference from Europeans made Jonathan a welcome novelty for theatergoers.

The title of *The Contrast* highlighted the comedy's conscious comparison of American and European characters and values; but later Jonathan plays also contrasted the United States with Europe. The naive simplicity and loyal worth of Jonathan in *The Contrast* opposed the sophistication of Jessamy, the villain's servant, while the self-effacing Colonel Manly, the ludicrously high-minded republican hero to whom Jonathan attached himself, stood in bold opposition to the self-serving Dimple, Jessamy's master. From now on, these American comedies were not only to have a villain, but a foreign villain.

Even though American audiences perceived his Yankee quirks as indications of Jonathan's independence, the character still belonged to the ranks of comic national types. As a comic type, the Jonathan role would as a matter of course fall to an acting company's comic actor. Acting troupes were in the practice of assigning each player a particular type of acting, called a "line of acting"—regardless of the dramatic vehicle; and the British actors who dominated the comic stage until the late 1820s imprinted a British stamp on the presentation of the stage Jonathan. Even as more plays came to be written by Americans, these English actors were bound, even if only as part of their cultural thought patterns, to retain their national and social assumptions about the ordinary American they presented in Jonathan.

Following an English tradition dating from Shakespeare's time, travelling companies of actors and actresses led by a manager (often himself one of the actors) performed a repertory of plays for as long as an area supplied adequate audiences. This practice prevailed both in England and in America until the star system took over. These troupes treated America as the inconveniently distant province that it was until the revolution. Thus in the 1790s, even a leading troupe, the American Company, toured four or five cities a year. Lesser companies, like the one led by the Ryans in the early 1790s, tried to maintain headquarters in one place but were forced by financial pressures to do even more travelling. As the trans-Appalachian "West" opened up, a series of travelling troupes formed to serve the new population centers by steamboat, cart, or on foot and horseback. These troupes performed for a night or two and then moved on.

By the practice of limiting themselves to "lines" of acting, performers cut down the strain of memorizing for only intermittent performances dozens, even hundreds, of plays. One actor, for example, would play the comic role—whatever the comedy and whatever its other requirements. In this way he could reuse much of the same physical stage movements, business, mannerisms, and speech patterns, even costumes, that had already worked effectively in that type of role. Similarly the same actor and actress regularly took the romantic leads. Someone else always played the elderly roles. Each performer stuck closely to the assigned line of acting. In fact, the practice of holding on to a line of acting regardless of changing circumstances sometimes led to decidedly odd stage groupings, such as the youthful Lewis Hallam's playing Romeo to his widowed mother's Juliet.

YANKEES PORTRAYED BY BRITISH ACTORS

British actors, familiar with this system, were naturally used to playing national character types—the stage Irishman, the stage Frenchman or Dutchman, or the bumptious English countryman Hodge. These actors clearly envisioned the Jonathan character in *The Contrast* and in other early comedies written by Americans as an extension of the northcountry yokel they were used to playing in comedies generally written by British playwrights.[9] This assumption about the Jonathan character showed up in the costume of Thomas Wignell, the actor who first made a name for himself playing Jonathan in *The Contrast*. As Francis Hodge comments, "Wignell was first an Englishman, then an actor, and he could not be expected to tell an audience much about genuine native Americans."[10]

British actors playing Yankee roles persisted in thinking of the Jonathan character as a country clod, a Yorkshireman transplanted to the colonies. John Bernard, an English actor active on the American stage between 1797 and 1811, explained in his memoirs to his mainly British readers the decidedly lower-class role that a Yankee could be expected to take:

> The Yankee is a man of the lower orders, sometime a farmer, more
> often a mechanic (the very spirit of mechanism embodied), and yet more
> usually a travelling trader. The Yankee is the Yorkshireman of America;
> the same cunning, calculating, persevering personage, with an infusion
> of Scotch hardiness and love of wandering. Like him, he goes upon the
> principle that all men are rogues, and like him he is instanced by his
> customers as the best illustration of the doctrine. He has the same talent
> for expedients; the same keen eye to character and to expedite a sale;
> the same want of nicety in regards to means, so long as they are not
> legally offensive (going to jail he considers not so much a disgrace as a
> waste of time).[11]

Bernard's ancedotes illustrating these imputed Yankee peculiarities continued for another ten pages, pigeonholing the Yankee (and by extension
all Jonathan roles) as "Yorkshire" and "Hodge" roles. Though he probably brought to London the manuscript copy of Humphreys's *Yankey in
England*[12] and was as sympathetic and knowlegeable as any Englishman
about Americans, Bernard was also, as Hodge says of Wignell, "an Englishman first" and culturally unable to recognize the complex of strengths
and weaknesses Americans found in other Americans.

In British comedies about Jonathan, the character seldom exhibited the
admirable qualities that he showed in American plays where, though often
ludirous, he was dependable. Similarly, it is likely that British actors demonstrated the Jonathan character's potential for ridicule without suggesting his strengths to their audiences; they probably were not even aware
that the character could be more than a butt of humor. Where the British
writers and actors saw only truculence, Americans recognized the Yankee's sly humor.

The English monopoly on starring roles in American plays on the American stage was eventually broken, in part through the example of the eminent British comic star Charles Mathews. After gathering material about
American eccentricities during his starring tour of the United States in
1822 and 1823, Mathews developed first a sketch called *Trip to American—*
which included a Jonathan character surnamed Doubikins. Later he had
Richard Peake help him put together a comedic vehicle entitled *American
Abroad* (titled at that time *Jonathan in England*). Mathews's success as a
stage Yankee led a host of American comics to emulate him. As natives
they were after all closer to their material and quicker to pick up nuances
than even the most gifted of foreign mimics.

YANKEES PORTRAYED BY AMERICAN ACTORS

Main credit for the spread and popularization of the Jonathan figure belonged to the Yankee actors, Americans who made Jonathan their chief stock in trade. These actors standardized Jonathan's costume and the props that became his physical tags. The Yankee actors also became, as Richard Dorson calls them, a "living bridge" between stage comedy and oral humor.[13] The link was most apparent in Jonathan's language and tale-telling. Exaggeration, for example, such as that heard by Captain Marryat in the 1830s ("I wish I had all hell boiled down to a point just to pour down your throat")[14] found an echo in the language of almost every stage Yankee.

The first of the Americans to try to take over the comic lead via roles as a stage Yankee was James Hackett, who appeared as a guest star in London during the spring of 1827. Using much of the same material with which Mathews had already become identified, Hackett was not a success at Covent Garden. Audiences thought he was imitating Mathews when, in fact, both humorists were probably retailing the parlor entertainments of John Wesley Jarvis.[15] In any case, British audiences simply were not attuned to the relaxed pace of Hackett's genuine American folk humor. The rambling Yankee tales told by Hackett were in all probability closer than Mathews's to the sort that might have been heard in the American hinterland, but London audiences could not know that. As the auditioning Sylvester Daggerwood, for example, Hackett portrayed Jonathan meandering through tales that had more twists and turns than the Mississippi. Although not a success in London, Hackett continued to develop Yankee material for the American stage. Within the next five years, he did achieve star billing.

During this period one of the vehicles he used to showcase himself as a comedy star was his own version of George Colman's *Who Want a Guinea?*, which Hackett retitled *John Bull at Home*, or *Jonathan in England*. The comedy is now catalogued under the latter title. By late 1828 Hackett was starring in this adaptation. The character who had appeared as a cloddish boor when played by Mathews in England became an egalitarian hero when played by Hackett in America.[16] Jerome Sommers maintains that by fixing the focus of attention on Swap, Hackett tightened and strengthened the earlier play.[17] Hackett certainly shortened Colman's comedy. From 1828 on, Hackett appeared in a series of Yankee roles and eventually branched out to Shakespearean comedy as well, often playing Falstaff and a diverse range of dialect comedy roles.

Once Hackett had achieved star status, a number of other American actors, beginning with George H. Hill, began to assume Yankee roles. One of the best known actors to play Jonathan and all of the Yankee roles of his time, Hill recalled in his memoirs, "from boyhood I noticed the dialect of farm boys and the peculiarities of character since identified with stage Yankees."[18] In Hill's portrayal, these tricks of speech, dress, and action became the character.[19] Those who saw Hill enthusiastically supported his contention that he portrayed exactly the idiosyncrasies of real people he had been in contact with since childhood:

> Mr. Hill's Yankee was the real critter. It was not, as are almost all the representations of other actors I have seen, a mixture of Western, Southern and Eastern peculiarities of manner and dialect, but the unalloyed, unadulterated down-easter. Mr. Hill did not merely imitate their tone, dialect and manner, but felt and thought like them. It was this faculty, to use a hackneyed phrase, of throwing himself, body and spirit into a part, which gave to his Yankee a richness and truthfulness not approached by any other actor before or since his time. He did not merely put on a flaxen wig, a long-tailed coat, a short vest, a bell-crowned hat, and straps to his pantaloons long enough for suspenders, nor thus attired did he content himself by imitating the peculiar drawl and queer expressions of the Yankee, for the veriest bungler on earth can do all this, but the spirit of Yankeedom pervaded every action of his boy, peeped from his expressive eyes with such sly meaning.[20]

As is here pointed out, almost any impersonator depended on tags to delineate the Yankee. Hill, however, must also have had the means to convince his audience that they were encountering the "original" Jonathan.[21] The character always remained a type, although reified in a series of individual Jonathans. As Joseph Arpad correctly notes, Brother Jonathan "accumulated all the idiosyncrasies that had ever been attributed to the Yankee character and mentality, as well as some borrowed from regional types and some that were sheer fabrications purportedly in the Yankee vein."[22] These accumulated idiosyncrasies repeated on stage made a success of Hill's portrayal.

Yankee roles provided the route to stardom for Danforth Marble, Joshua Silsbee, and a host of lesser actors in the 1830s and 1840s. The playbills from regional theaters throughout the antebellum United States show these stars following one another around the country, each appearing in his own preferred round of Yankee roles. Among these roles, nevertheless, *Jonathan in England* and *The Forest Rose* were almost unanimous choices, even when the stars played in the South.

In the course of the American actors' appropriation of Yankee roles, the characterization altered. While Jonathan's origins remained visible as an American countryboy and as the clownish servant from the sentimental tradition, in the actors' eagerness to fill our their characterizations, Jonathan moved beyond those stereotypes. He became a local embodiment of national spunk, and he also came to act out some of the social strains in the young republic.

Aggressive Laughter

In addition to stage influences, developments in dramatic history, and the culture's evident need for national icons, the comic element of these plays also formed an essential part of their function in early nineteenth-century culture. Two points are relevant here. First of all, "the rich, the able, and the well-born" did use humor as a means of trying to contain social and political changes. Humor does not function, after all, only as a means of amusement.[23] Secondly, with the advent of Jonathan, humor on the stage assumed a characteristically American cast. As a British critic writing in the 1830s explained in a review of books on American humor, "Humor is national when it is impregnated with the convictions, customs, and associations of a nation."[24] Jonathan's appearance on the stage instituted such a national humor. As the same English writer noted, humor is "impregnated with character."[25] And the character who vivified these comedies was Brother Jonathan.

All of the Jonathan roles were essentially comic; and the Jonathan plays were more aptly termed comedies or farces than anything else. The fact that Jonathan was often the butt of the humor, even when he controlled the action, complicated the picture. As a host of modern theorists like to point out, humor often serves as a means of aggression or at least as a means of cutting a rival down to size.[26] Robert Sklar, in fact, theorizes that early nineteenth-century American humor developed as it did because conservative writers tried to "deflate the pretensions and expose the follies of democracy in American,"[27] by making the over-reaching democrats look foolish. Sklar also assumes that these authors, to whom he refers as Brahmins and members of the Southern plantation gentry, "did not quarrel fundamentally with the broad democratic developments in American society."[28] However, the pejorative humor employed to depict Jonathan, who represented the hoi polloi particularly, although he also stood for Americans as a group, strongly suggests that these writers felt at least unconsciously extreme discomfort with the general leveling effects of popular democracy in America. And as Bruce Ingham Granger points out, the tradition of satire's serving "the cause of virtue by ridiculing irrationality and error," already held a secure place in American humor even as Jonathan prepared to take the stage.[29]

Stow Persons contends that during the postrevolutionary period, tensions existed between the personally confident and able social, professional, and political elites who preferred liberty (they excelled after all in competition), and the masses who, resenting the deference paid to these elites, espoused equality as the premier value for their society.[30] This social tension between the aspirations of ordinary people and the privileges of elites surfaced in the ambiguous handling of the Jonathan character who was at once laughable and a sort of "salt of the earth" bedrock on whom all of society relied. Whig writers and publishers embodied in the person of Jonathan their sense of unease with the social and economic revolutions that were accompanying and even outstripping the goals of the political revolution Whigs earlier had initiated and supported.

All of the Jonathan characters were laughable. They were often the only enjoyable elements in otherwise predictable and forgettable comedies. Yet the pattern of action suggests that the people Jonathan portrayed were objects of affectionate but often uneasy condescension. The audience could condescend toward and laugh at the foolish Yankee bumpkin; but since Jonathan also represented the innate wisdom and wiles of an American everyman, the audience knew they had to respect and sometimes be leary of Jonathan. The ordinary American represented by the Jonathan figure was essential to American society. His originators recognized his importance as the ordinary citizen, but their personal ambivalence toward the ordinary American also showed in the comedies. Their ambivalence underlined what Jesse Bier finds to be the "paradox of pluralistic American life . . . that our special history has furnished our humor simultaneously with both its targets and weaponry."[31]

LITERARY VS. POPULAR HUMOR

The pre–Civil War period when these comedies were most frequently produced saw, additionally, a major development in more than one distinctly American expression of humor.[32] Often American humor during the period before the Civil War is subdivided into literary humor—appraised according to English or European norms—and popular humor—judged according to its acceptance by the populace. Cash receipts demonstrated popularity. Down-East (Yankee) humor and the humor of the old Southwest (the pre–Civil War frontier that now constitutes the Deep South) furnished the two main currents of popular humor. In addition, humorists identified significant minorities such as blacks—lampooned in song and jest by the period's minstrel shows—and Irish immigrants whose boisterous exhuberance bubbled in the "b'hoy" Mose. Both minstrel shows and Irish comics flourished during the 1840s. Like Jonathan and most frontier characters, they were apt to express themselves in what Blair and Hamlin label subversive humor.[33]

YANKEE HUMOR

Jonathan's humor, like that of most Down-East comic figures, depended on a reversal of expectations. The Yankee humor of Down-East best represented the characteristic humor of New England, while the violent exaggerations of the old Southwest best illustrated the burgeoning excitement of the frontier. At first, neither of these typically American expressions of humor bore much resemblance to the literary humor popular with members of genteel elite culture. Gradually, however, the comic stage appropriated both the Yankee and the frontiersman as well as their humor. Dramatized on stage, each character increased his hold on the popular imagination. In turn, Jonathan and other Yankee characters helped keep Down-East humor alive on the stage through most of the nineteenth century.

Even while the Jonathan character came out of the Yankee tradition, some elements of the popular Southwestern humor that developed in the South during the thirty years before the Civil War also showed up in Jonathan plays. In Moncrieff's *Tarnation Strange*, in fact, Jonathan Jonah Goliah Bang is—despite his name—a Kentuckian and an almost incessant storyteller. He relates incredible anecdotes to illustrate every conceivable conversational gamut. Jonathan Bang, however, does not appear to wear the Jonathan character's usual mask of wise stupidity. Rather, Bang seems to be fooling himself instead of his audience. But, since Moncrieff was a British playwright, he would not necessarily realize how important Jonathan's mask was to the authentic American interpretation.

What primarily set almost all Jonathan plays off from the humor of the old Southwest was not, however, the dialect humor, the comic invention, the delightful comic exaggerations and absurd common folk, or the ludicrous incidents. The Jonathan plays shared these elements of American humor with the tales of the old Southwest. What did set them apart was first, the fact that the Jonathan plays did not deal with frontier situations. Rather, the action in these plays belonged in settled territory. The formula assumed an established social order—even if it was one under siege. Secondly, the Jonathan character belonged to Aristotle's category of *eirons*, self-deprecating comic heroes, rather than the *alazons*, the imposters—or as Walter Blair calls them, the comic braggarts—of frontier humor. People from places or classes opposing Jonathan preferred to depict him as a buffoon.[34] Nonetheless, he used even this role to mask his intelligence and strength. Finally, Jonathan retained something of the buffoon—Susanne Langer's "personified *elan vital*."[35]

The Jonathan figure appearing on the American stage was thus an amalgam forged in great part from a variety of influences found in the popular culture. The shift from English to American comic stars made it possible for actors to alter the emphases given to Jonathan roles. The comedies themselves fit into the sentimental tradition. An expression of the vogue for comic action, the Jonathan plays also served a deeper need to express unease with changing social, economic, and eventually political patterns. In addition, these formulas offered an opportunity for writers, actors, and audiences to explore some of the tensions engendered by these changes.

Although clearly a product of popular and folk culture, the Jonathan figure had fewer and more tenuous ties with high culture. While references to Brother Jonathan were relatively common even in literary works before the Civil War, the figure clearly fed from the oral folk culture of early America; and for a period of about a generation, the figure literally dramatized many of the young republic's most potent tensions.

Even in the skewed vision of Jonathan fomented in British-influenced comedies, the character was the center of action. More than a catalyst, he initiated and directed action. In a triumvirate of major characters with the hero and villain of the melodramas, Jonathan defined himself as the effective force in contrast to these others. As a stage figure, Jonathan could be quickly identified through tags developed earlier in oral yarn-spinning. Given the basic simplicity of action in these comedies, the limited role of the Jonathan character, and his stock identification through the use of tags, the innate paradoxes of the Jonathan figure gained imporatnce. These probably helped him win wide acceptance in the 1830s and 1840s when the figure was most popular; they also provide a continuing source of interest and puzzlement. The stage Jonathan was both a local and national figure; he was wise and foolish; a radically independent democrat and a perfectly trustworthy citizen of the republic. Much of the character's tension and ambiguity can, however, be traced to the differing purposes he served—as a national symbol, for example, and as a comic type.[36]

4

The Cartoon Character: Beginnings and Heyday

WHILE THE WRITERS AND ACTORS WHO DEVELOPED THE JONATHAN CHARACTER on stage were limited by the traditions of sentimental comedy and its stereotypes, they at least had the advantage of working in a literally dramatic form. As a result, in their hands the character could grow and develop a personality. In contrast, the artists who drew the nineteenth-century lithographs featuring Jonathan literally flattened the character into two dimensions. In addition visual artists were straightened by the form and tradition in which they worked as well as by the marketing practices and politics of their time.

As an emblem of America in political cartoons, the Brother Jonathan image belonged especially to the forty or fifty years following the War of 1812. Such examples, as well as those from the comic stage, appeared before this period, and Jonathan-like Uncle Sams cropped up throughout the nineteenth century. But the character's widest currency belonged to the two generations between the War of 1812 and the Civil War. During this period technological improvements in printing and political unrest both encouraged the spread of political cartoons.

Lithographs

The development of commercial lithography in the United States during the late 1820s and early 1830s made for relative ease in producing prints. Earlier illustrations in books, newspapers, and magazines—as well as in the broadside cartoons where political caricatures were more often found —had been engraved, etched, or cut on steel, wood, or copper plates. In comparison with these time-consuming techniques, the lithographic process—invented in 1796, patented by a German in 1801, and then introduced into the United States during the late teens—was cheap and much less tedious.

Lithography involves drawing with crayons on smooth limestones, which are then soaked and inked. The oily ink adheres to the design but not to the water-soaked stone. The design can then be transferred to paper using a special lithographic press. Unlike engraved plates, these stones can be run almost indefinitely, or they can be cleaned, polished, and used again. In addition to taking longer and costing more, engraving on steel and copper requires more specialized training than lithography. This early nineteenth-century advance in technology proved crucial in opening the way for the wider distribution of cheap prints—including political prints featuring Brother Jonathan.[1]

Political Unrest and National Pride

The time, moreover, was ripe for political comment. Journalists writing in a 1980 issue of *Newsweek* reminded contemporary readers that, "Like any predatory species, editorial cartoonists multiply in proportion to their quarry: incompetence, folly, and hypocrisy."[2] The period following the War of 1812 saw more than enough of each of these qualities. At the same time a surge of egalitarian enthusiasm swept Jackson and his followers into power, while clashing domestically with republican traditions of constraint, checks and balances. Testy Americans labored on the international front to establish the country's cultural independence from England. In both skirmishes, the figure of Jonathan was engaged as a foot soldier and featured in the political caricatures of cartoons. Flat representation as he was of the ordinary American, the Jonathan of early nineteenth-century political caricature proved—to use Fredric Jameson's term—a useful ideologeme, "a symbolic resolution to a concrete historical situation."[3]

During the first several decades of the American republic, the masculine figures of Brother Jonathan and Uncle Sam partially supplanted first the Indian maiden and then the classical goddess used to depict America in the vernacular arts. Neither the European notions of America as an Indian princess or an exotic plumed goddess nor the genteel American depictions of America as a stately Liberty or Columbia captured the potentially explosive power, fickleness, anger, wisdom, or quiet strength of America's mass population. Brother Jonathan did. Until their integration sometime around the Civil War, Jonathan led a separate existence from the governmental Uncle Sam. Jonathan spoke in the popular media with and about a vernacular force, a kind of undisciplined joker that just might trump all of society's genteel aces.

The Yankie Doodles Intrenchments near Boston 1776. (*Courtesy of the British Museum, London.*)

Earliest Caricatures of America

Although America was commonly represented in political cartoons by feminine forms during the eighteenth century, as early as 1776 an English political cartoon showed Brother Jonathan defending the breastworks at Bunker Hill.[4] One of the few English caricatures hostile to the Americans during the revolution, this $8 \times 9\frac{5}{8}$ inch engraving, "Yankee Doodles Intrenchments Near Boston 1776" portrays a shabby group of defenders suffering in the cold and seemingly reconsidering their apparently religious fanaticism and enthusiasm for their cause. At least two of the stiff, awkwardly drawn figures wear the Genevan garb of a Calvinist minister. One of these shares his unease with the rest of the group, "I don't feel bold today" while the other urges the group to bravery, reminding them of the fight they are in, "Tis Old Oliver's [Cromwell] Cause no Monarchy nor Laws." Several of the patched and ragged soldiers wear liberty stocking caps with "Death or Liberty" emblazoned across the front.

These characters, however, worry lest the heat of battle should only too effectively warm their skins. Echoing the psalmist's warning "Unless the Lord build the house, he labors in vain who keeps it" (Ps. 127:1), the cartoon puns about General Putnam's labor. Since the cartoonist believed Putnam and his followers were pious frauds, the print implied that the ramparts' ragged defenders reflected an equally thin ethical defense for the revolution. The cartoonist argued, in effect, that the colonists' so-called religious motivation was a self-delusion; even their own historical precedents showed the wrongheadedness of their arguments. The cartoon's most prominent character stands on the breastworks and whines, "I swear its plaguy Cold, Jonathan; I don't think They'll Attack us, Now You." The rest of the rabble may be taken as Jonathan. They fly a banner that includes the liberty pine with a liberty cap[5]—or fool's cap—atop it; but on either side of the tree are gibbets, pointedly labeled "The Fruit."

This early collective representation of America as the Jonathan character is actually quite out of the ordinary. British caricaturists of the period— from whom American artists of the time lifted almost all of their symbols, figures, and even whole cartoons—preferred to depict America as an Indian. For at least the next twenty years, British caricaturists usually chose an Indian warrior or maiden to represent America. While some early departures from that norm do feature details (e.g., a whip, trousers made from the flag, America as a farmer)[6] that became standard American tags in later cartoons, America as an Indian maiden was more common than the Indian warrior. Unfortunately, though less threatening, she also made her opponents appear ungentlemanly. Using either a male or female figure, however, the British could feel superior to the savage people symbolized by half-clothed natives. Naturally, the savage Indian as a representation of America never enjoyed the same currency in America as it did in England. White Americans did not identify with either the Indians with whom their people were fighting on the frontier or with the disspirited native Americans whom they occasionally encountered in their towns.

Unlike the romanticized European version of America suggested by the caricaturized Indian maiden of political cartoons, the visual depiction of

Jonathan in "The Yankie Doodles Intrenchments" presents an early and clear illustration of Jonathan's primary identification with disruptive elements in American society. While one figure—the man at the far right in this print—questions the revolutionary cause, most of the ragged creatures in the print suggest a hord of disheveled malcontents. Certainly, their totality does not suggest a nation or a people capable of achieving community. Nor is the Jonathan they together represent a "noble savage." His creators instead envisioned him as an embodiment of the hoi polloi and of radical elements of the common herd. As the Jonathan figure became commonplace in nineteenth-century political caricature, some alteration occurred in his dress until his garb developed into the costume of today's Uncle Sam; but throughout the changes his potentially disruptive lower-class significance remained.

A second British print, "The English & American Discovery, Brother, Brother We Are Both in the Wrong," published by Matthew Darly in November of 1778 suggests a more pacific relationship: John Bull and Brother Jonathan as peers.[7] Actually, two Darly prints from the 1760s,

The English and American Discovery, Brother. Brother we are both in the wrong (1778). (*Courtesy of the John Carter Brown Library at Brown University.*)

now in the British Museum, No. 3884 and No. 3371,[8] had already used the phrase "Brother, Brother, we are both in the wrong," but these prints were concerned with satirizing Newcastle and Fox by associating them with scoundrels from *The Beggar's Opera*.[9] Belonging to an earlier development in political caricature, these prints alter the connotations of Jonathan's title. In these prints the title suggests complicity rather than kinship. The earlier prints also are tied to previous developments in English caricature. Some affected American caricature practice. Some did not.

During the 1750s and 1760s some artists, in particular Matthew Darly, his wife Mary, and George Townsend, published their political caricatures as small, $2\frac{1}{2}'' \times 4''$ pasteboard cards suitable for mailing.[10] This format encouraged a reduction in verbal text because these artists often made use of political rebuses. American caricaturists do not seem to have taken over either the use of rebuses or the small cards. But more significantly for American caricature, Darly and his colleagues absorbed into their visual caricatures the old symbols and allegories developed much earlier in political balladry.[11] Thus, for example, John Bull only appeared in visual caricature in 1757—almost fifty years after Arbuthnot's introduction of the character. John Bull's acceptance as an allegorical and comic symbol of England became common only during the 1760s when his possibilities as a figure of fun presented visual caricaturists with a more acceptable target than Britannia.[12] Given the usual pairing of John Bull and Brother Jonathan, the development of a visual representation for the former invited a similar development for the latter.

In Darly's "The English and American Discovery," neither John Bull nor Brother Jonathan are harshly satirized. The two sit together quietly smoking and drinking at a circular table set in front of a framed print of clasped hands. John Bull has his *Morning Post* and London *Gazette* on the table before him, while Brother Jonathan's Boston and another paper peek out from beneath the men's shared bottle. Neither John Bull nor Brother Jonathan speak, nor do their names appear. But Bull's rotund figure as well as Jonathan's lank hair and countrified clothes as well perhaps as his beady, rather mistrustful eyes provided adequate visual identifications. Dorothy George does not hesitate to identify the pair as John Bull and Brother Jonathan.[13] Underscoring George's point that the anger usually directed toward foreign enemies during a war was between 1775 and 1780 directed instead toward the British ministers in charge of the war,[14] the men in this print relax in one another's company as peers, and even as brothers.[15]

The Brother Jonathan of visual caricature does not commence his career in British caricature as only a figure of xenophobic distaste. Darly pokes fun at Jonathan in the same manner as he pokes fun at John Bull. The two figures remain, nonetheless, close relatives as well as rivals. (Until 1812, however, when J. K. Paulding began publishing his satiric allegories about John Bull and Bull's "son" Brother Jonathon, no one seems to have worked out a mythological background for Brother Jonathon as Arbuthnot had done for John Bull.) More than Yankee Doodle or Uncle Sam, Jonathan is clearly part of the British family. Later, American caricaturists also will assume this familial tie, though in their hands the figure develops in addition far greater class overtones—or at least (to use Fredric Jameson's phraseology again) a class relationship between dominant and aspiring groups.[16]

The Early Nineteenth Century

Until stage productions of the late 1820s and early 1830s gave Jonathan a particular visual definition, he appeared only occasionally in political cartoons. When he did appear, he most commonly functioned as a contrasting figure for John Bull. Thus in "Brother Jonathan's Soliloquy on the Times" (1812), "A Boxing Match, or Another Bloody Nose for John Bull" (1813), and "Brother Jonathan Administers a Salutary Cordial to John Bull" (1813), Jonathan was presented as a republican figure, the "neat but not gaudy" model citizen of virtuous restraint. He was the Colonel Manley rather than the Jonathan of *The Contrast*.

The first of these republican figures, the Brother Jonathan of "Brother Jonathan's Soliloquy on the Times" (1812), wears a frock coat, though his is in better condition than the one in "Yankie Doodles Intrenchments." And this figure muses on the state of the economy and the difficulty of adjusting to paper money.[17] Leaning on a fence that runs across the foreground and speaking language reminiscent of Shakespeare, Jonathan puzzles over the causes and solution for the economic distress pictured in the background. Houses and goods are being sold at a sheriff's auction. Rags are being reprocessed into paper money. Signs advertising "Notes Shaved" and "Peter Pillage," attorney and notary, proclaim the wreck of commerce. In the background looms the cold, ominous bulk of a jail. Jonathan knows that merchants dread taking paper bills; but on the other hand, the country does not have enough gold or silver for use as specie. Those countries with gold are unlikely to give it up. The only solution appears to be uncompromising economy.

The cartoon implies that Jonathan (perhaps like Brutus contemplating the murder of Caesar) would do well to weigh with more skepticism the urging of the newspapers, whose arguments may be inferred from the advertisements for "Homespun Essays" posted on the shed to the right. The first of these essays warns that "to pay the enormous tax of interest, levied by a monied Aristocracy on a fictitious Capital requires the whole of the agricultural productions of the country, combined with the collective industry of its inhabitants." Considering the economic chaos of war-torn 1812, Jonathan's confidence in simple economy and republican virtue sounds a bit hollow; yet he assures himself that, "Our credit it may fail! Commerce herself may be dumped and checked, but thou shalt flourish our beloved republic amidst the wars of Potentates, the wreck of Monarchies, and fall of Kings.''[18] In this 1812 cartoon by Thomas Kensett, Jonathan portrays the ordinary citizen, worried with good reason about business failures, high interest rates, and the lack of opportunity. His dress merely reflects the usual town costume.

Brother Jonathan Administering a Salutary Cordial to John Bull (1813). (*Courtesy, the Henry Francis du Pont Winterthur Museum.*)

A year later another cartoon, "Brother Jonathan Administering a Salutary Cordial to John Bull" (1813), produced by Amos Doolittle (who signed his work Yankee Doodle Scratcher) also shows Jonathan dressed in a relatively plain city dress. In the latter print, of course, Jonathan embodies American patriotism and not surprisingly looks young and vigorous in contrast with the bloated military figure of John Bull whom he is forcing to drink "Perry." The cartoon obviously commemorated Captain Perry's success against the British on the Great Lakes.

Born in Cheshire, Connecticut, and trained there as a jeweler and silversmith, Doolittle taught himself engraving. During the War of Independence, he gained wide recognition for four drawings of the battle of Lexington. Given the limitations of his expertise, one might assume that Doolittle copied and reversed somewhat in this print the idea from an eighteenth-century British print, "The Able Doctor, or America Swallowing the Bitter Draught" (1774). After all, Paul Revere had copied the print for an American periodical, so Doolittle might have recalled the concept and the phrase when he came to etch this cartoon.[19]

In still another print of 1813 "A Boxing Match, or Another Bloody Nose for John Bull," etched and printed by William Charles, Jonathan's dress once more stresses republican simplicity in contrast with John Bull's monarchical trappings—a crown on his head and fussy braid on his coat. Charles' print commemmorating the defeat of the British *Boxer* by the American frigate *Enterprise* and the Doolittle print as well are open and relatively simple in design, though Charles's drawing is better than Doolittle's. A contest between symbolic national characters often appeared in early nineteenth-century cartoons. A fist fight was one obvious choice while the countries were at war. Although Doolittle's John Bull is a caricature, these American cartoons and many like them are not true caricatures using comic exaggeration. In these cartoons commemorating naval victories, the backgrounds show ships blasting away at one another just in case the symbolic representation posed by the larger figures in the forefront is not entirely clear.

Illustrating both that during the first decades of the nineteenth century the Jonathan figure could be rendered in various visual forms and that British and American approaches to his visual rendition differed, a further print dealing with the War of 1812, a British engraving of "The Fall of Washington—or Maddy in Full Flight" (1814) presented an uninvolved Jonathan talking to two companions. Dressed as Quakers and using a quaint speech that might sound Quaker-like, neither Jonathan nor his companions appear overly disturbed by the burning capital or the flight of the government officials. One companion asks, "Jonathan where thinkest thou our President will run to now!" to which the other comments, "The great Washington fought for Liberty, but we are fighting for shadows, which if obtained could do no Earthly good, but this is the blessed effects of it."

During the nineteenth century, British visual caricatures of the American often lagged behind American usages.[20] In time, however, both British and American expressions of Jonathan became standardized; in particular the character became associated with the common man from the country rather than the city and with a rather quick irascible temper housed in a Yankee visage. Thus this British rendition of Jonathan as a comfortable Quaker burgher, unconcerned at the burning of the capital, strikes an anomalous note.

This, then, sums up Jonathan's early visual persona: he was envisioned as an American alter ego to John Bull; and American artists seem to have for the most part copied the ideas and practices of the British. Many American artists and engravers had emigrated, as a matter of fact, from England. American cartoonists of the first two decades of the nineteenth century did not yet show influences from the popular stage, the periodical press, or from political literature impinging on their portraits of Jonathan. In fact, according to William Murrell little political cartooning of any sort appeared in the United States during the second decade of the nineteenth century.[21] While Maureen O'Brien Quimby demonstrated in a 1971 *Winterthur Portfolio* article that Akin, at least, was active during this period,[22] neither the technological nor political impetuses of later decades were present to encourage extensive political caricaturing during the 1820s.

Although the Jonathan figure did not appear in separately published cartoons between the teens and the 1830s, the figure did appear in several engravings prepared to illustrate an American allegory meant to depict American history in relation to England. As part of the British-American paper war, J. K. Paulding's *Diverting History of John Bull and Brother Jonathan* went through five editions between 1812 and 1835. Several of these editions—i.e., those of 1813, 1819, and 1827—contained a set of four illustrations; not all copies of these editions, however, included these illustrations.[23] John Wesley Jarvis, the popular miniature engraver and portrait painter who was also responsible for bringing some of the oral humor associated with Jonathan to the attention of playwrights and actors, made these small ($3\frac{5}{8} \times 3\frac{3}{8}$ inches) engravings. One of the four, "Jonathan Throwing the Teakettle at Bulls Head,"[24] depicts a simply dressed young man swinging his lifted teakettle and about to throw it at a pugnacious fat man. Paulding's allegory at this point refers to the Boston tea party. While the Jonathan figure at this time was still drawn as an independent everyman, Paulding's tale makes him a farmer, so Javis dresses the cartoon character as a simple American farmer. In these illustrations Jonathan does not yet wear or carry any of the visual tags that later identified him on stage and in cartoons.

In any case, the fact that Brother Jonathan seemingly did not appear in political cartoons for fifteen years did not mean that he was not regularly presented in other media of the period. Moreover, the ways that he appeared in newspapers, for example, and on the stage influenced the visual expectations of media consumers. Thus the bumpkin who had appeared as early as Sarah Kemble Knight's 1704 *Journal*[25] proliferated in newspaper humor columns, which during the 1820s achieved "an emphatic native quality, which displayed localized characters and characteristics as well as various American social and political foibles."[26]

The Yankee was often named Jonathan and this identification grew during the 1820s and into the 1830s. The 1820s was also the decade that witnessed the rise of the stage Yankee to star status. The costume of stage Yankees—who often appeared in plays as Brother Jonathan—prefigured the costume that became Jonathan's until he was preempted by Uncle Sam.[27] The clumsy-sly bumpkin of stage and newspaper presentations thus had achieved recognizable form when cartoons returned to Jonathan as an American icon. Hence even though political cartoons had seldom featured Jonathan during the 1820s, his persona was altered during that period as political writers like J. K. Paulding, raconteurs like J. W. Jarvis, and stage personalities like Charles Mathews and James Hackett wove into the character of Jonathan humorous traditions about Yankee Doodle, the wily country fellow of most folk cultures and American folk exaggeration.

The Jacksonian Era

Brother Jonathan's reappearance during the 1830s was part of a response to dramatically changed social and political conditions. Not only did lithographic broadsides and occasional newspaper cartoons begin to appear, but political controversy became more heated as the voting franchise was extended but scandals proliferated during the Jackson administration. Especially during the financial crisis faced by Martin Van Buren's administration, the political opposition of old-time Whigs and Federalists was strengthened. A worsening economic situation further encouraged expressions of outrage in political cartoons. Some of the altered attitudes toward the people who had swept Jackson into office eventually found expression in the costume worn by Jonathan in this new spate of cartoons.

Only gradually during the 1830s did the visual caricature of Jonathan achieve clarification. During that decade, as the figure united in himself earlier traditions about Yankee Doodle, American humor, and the sly countryboy, he also took on a more lively personality and moved into a more overtly adversarial position. Stage productions and almanac humor undoubtedly influenced this radical alteration, but Jonathan's change during the 1830s probably indicated in addition some of the political and social ferments of the Jacksonian Era as pushing the frontier westward, trans-Allegheny settlers (roughly one-third of the total population) put into practice the democratic rhetoric of the Revolution. Men living in the West took for granted their place as voters and potential office-holders. Neither this mass of voters nor the new immigrants from Ireland, Scotland, and Germany, nor the Eastern craftsmen being squeezed by industrialization sympathized with the traditional Whig and Federalists leaders.

Brother Jonathan did not even have a visual representation in one prominent pamphlet using his name. When James Akin produced his anti-Jackson pamphlet *The House That Jonathan Built* (1832), he did not include one engraving of Brother Jonathan among his twelve wood engravings. Parodying the traditional English nursery rime "The House that Jack Built," Akin portrayed Andrew Jackson as a tyrannical plunderer of the nation's political heritage.[28] As illustrated by one of the later engravings in the pamphlet encouraging the country's "Yeomen" to "rouse for the contest"—reform—and suggesting that they constituted the true builders of the American edifice, the Jonathan of the pamphlet's title emerged as the responsible citizen.

For a time during the first half of the 1830s, Seba Smith's Major Jack Downing, another Yankee figure combining many of the same attributes as Jonathan, threatened to usurp Jonathan's function as a political observer. But in one cartoon, "The Vision" (1834) by Ezra Bisbee, the bloated figure of John Bull advises Americans as a group that, "Ha, ha, ha, Brother Jonathan might as well hang up his fiddle and not go bragging all over the world about his Freedom." This cluttered $9\frac{5}{8} \times 15\frac{1}{8}$-inch lithograph shows from the left across the upper half: the capitol burning, a rabble of "Kitchen Scallions & Pat-riots" cheering for Jackson, while Major Downing advises a crowned and ermine-robed Jackson that with a "leetle more Veto Resin" he can play Nero Doodle making the Constitution sing any tune he wants. Jackson responds with "Damn the Constitution." In the lower half of the cartoon, John Bull looks on from the left. Beneath eye level rests a tombstone commemorating Dame Freedom, while further to the right several prone officeseekers creep forward reaching for a brass studded chest labeled 30,000,000. In this cartoon Bisbee uses Jonathan's name much as later cartoonists used Uncle Sam's name; he is here a comprehensive representative of America, Americans, American pride, and even the government. In these and other cartoons opposing Jackson or Van Buren, political artists invoked Jonathan as the spirit of the American people. The political bias of the cartoonists, however, always makes the Whigs superior to the people, and almost invariably associates Jacksonian policy with demagoguery and the people with rabble.

By the 1830s Whig sympathies had undergone considerable metamorphoses since their wholehearted support of the American Revolution during the 1770s; these shifts in sympathy found some reflection in popular representations of Brother Jonathan. During the eighteenth century, English Whigs, actually members of various political and economic elites, made use of the language of the common man in their advocacy for change. In fact, they often wanted only to unseat those whom they considered unfair Tory rivals. Assuming a Masonic conspiracy that gave an unfair advantage to some ministerial groups, eighteenth-century Whigs used the rhetoric of revolution to lend weight to their own cause. (Eighteenth-century Masonic groups in England had been largely coopted by the royal family once the tradition developed that the grand master be a member of the royal family. Consequently, royalty's connections with masonry supported the popular sense that political decisions in England were influenced by a secretive cabal. A similar sense of aggrievement against secret patronage surfaced in New England during the 1830s when resentment against the Masons again became a political force.)[29]

Given English and American Whigs' early championing of the "common man," one might expect them to rejoice in the revolutionary changes made by the French during the 1790s, then by Americans under Jefferson and

Jackson. This was not so. Theirs had been a struggle by elites against elites. Many men who might have been Whigs in England became Federalists in America. In time that allegiance fell apart and then reemerged in the 1830s and 1840s as a Whig alliance; the latter party again had ties with anti-masonic, and then in the 1850s with, no-nothing groups. What in England had been the stewardship tradition of the Tories transferred to a variant stewardship tradition in the American South, while American Whigs became the entrepreneurs who supported urban industrialization. Neither group had any excess sympathy for the "common man" of antebellum America.[30]

A cartoon of 1832—"Confab between John Bull and Brother Jonathan,"[31] drawn by an artist who signed it Corkscrew, was typically

Confab between John Bull and Brother Jonathan (1832). (*Courtesy of the American Antiquarian Society.*)

critical of governmental policies under Jackson's administration. The lithograph shows a one-legged Jonathan wailing to John Bull, "I had a corn on my great toe . . . . I submitted it to the examination of Dr. Hickory, Dr. Kinderhook, and a few other quacks . . . . I suffered the limb to be lopped off, like a fool . . . . I wouldn't have suffered the operation, had not one of the quacks who was *bent on* amputation assured me that he had discovered a *specie*-fic . . . ." Typical of the period's humor, this cartoon puns on Benton's name, Jackson's nickname (in all the signs having to do with wood-working), and on specie. Another sign calls out, "Wanted; by more than Twelve Millions of People a Skilful Cabinetmaker" while still another implies imcompetence in the sort of person who would advertise together: "Jackson's Patent Safes, Kitchen Utensils etc." Torn and tattered, the one-legged Jonathan of this print wears his usual costume, although his pants are not striped. As usual, the figure is long and thin, particularly in comparison with John Bull's squat rotundity; but one of the oddities of this sketch is that the background looks like an English rather than an American street. Since many early American engravers had emigrated from Europe, the background may be an English street.

Who actually was hurt the most by Jackson's veto for the rechartering of the national bank in 1832? Philadelphia bankers, of course. Nonetheless, as universal white male suffrage was coming to be the norm in this period, opposition politicians strove to convince ordinary citizens that their interests were being dismembered along with the Jonathan of the cartoon.[32]

With the visual and iconographic Brother Jonathan newly reestablished, the figure flourished in a small flurry of cartoons published during the latter half of the 1830s. Attributed to Akin and probably published during 1835

A Kean Shave between John Bull and Brother Jonathan (1836). (*By permission of the Historical Society of Pennsylvania.*)

or 1836, a watercolored lithograph, "A Kean Shave Between John Bull and Brother Jonathan," vented American annoyance at the British condescension expressed in most English travel accounts. The immediate irritant seems to have been a published letter by Charles Kean criticizing uncouth American manners. Undoubtedly, Fanny Kemble's 1832–1833 *Journal* (published in 1835) also still rankled, for she is the ragged beggar pictured in the cartoon. As a young English star visiting America, Kemble had made a fortune before leaving the stage to marry Pierce Butler, a wealthy Philadelphian. Kemble's fastidious horror of American manners, coupled with the fact that her tour had singlehandedly recouped her family's bankrupt fortunes, especially piqued knowledgeable American readers. In addition, the print takes a swipe at Frances Trollope's *Domestic Manners of the Americans* (1833). The Jonathan figure in this print wears a costume like that of the later Brother Jonathan and Uncle Sam: high-water striped pants (but without the boot straps added later) and the long dark swallow-tailed coat that helps to identify Uncle Sam. On his head Jonathan wears an awkward low-crowned hat. He is a bumpkin, though he is definitely an American bumpkin. Jonathan's dress and dialect speech as well as John Bull's apologetic references to Edwin Forrest and George Hill, American stage stars who toured England without casting slurs on that country, encouraged readers to further connect the cartoon with the stage Jonathan.

The results of Jackson's dismemberment of the national bank and the country's financial disorders received regular satirizing in political cartoons that showed the country or government as ill, dismembered, or starving. One of the first of these cartoons, "Uncle Sam Sick with La Grippe" (1836 or 1838), overflows with national symbols in a riot of visual overkill. In what amounts to a throwback to the period right after the revolution when political cartoons tended to be packed with national symbolism,[33] this cartoon included both Uncle Sam—in buckskins beneath a dressing-coat made out of a flag, and a liberty cap—and Brother Jonathan, and a decapitated statue of George Washington on a pedestal (labeled, for the slow to comprehend, Peter Patrias) and an American eagle who is considering leaving for Texas. In addition, figures of Jackson as an eighteenth-century doctor, Thomas Hart Benton as an apothecary, and Van Buren as an old woman attend Uncle Sam. A list of bank failures slips to the floor from Uncle Sam's slack grasp. Outside the window Jonathan welcomes "Dr." Biddle who comes with his box of notes and bonds and the possibility of help from "Dr." John Bull. The very chair Uncle Sam sits in—an overstuffed one with a design of vines and flowers—may symbolize the American countryside.

Although Jackson managed to maintain political dominance through two terms, his destruction of the United States Bank and distribution of the Treasury surplus into "pet" banks left deleterious fiscal effects for his successor, Martin Van Buren, to deal with. Banks had issued their own, often unsound, currencies; using this inflated money, people speculated in land. Jackson attempted to stop the speculation by issuing the *Specie Circular* whereby (as of 15 August 1836) purchasers had to pay for government land in either silver or gold. The measure effectively burst the speculation bubble; but aided by crop failures, it also led to a severe depression, because banks whose specie supplies were depleted to pay for Western lands could not answer calls for specie payments demanded by British banks. By the summer of 1837 almost every bank in the United States had suspended specie payments. Many pet banks collapsed and the government lost the nine million dollars deposited in them.

For the most part, Van Buren did not deal with the panic that ensued. At this point in our political history, Democrats (called Republicans in the 1790s) objected to government interference in economic affairs. As Van Buren made clear in his message to a special session of Congress on 4 September 1837, he did not believe that government should encourage or limit foreign or domestic commerce. He believed that reestablishing a national bank would entail "blending. . . private interest with the operations of public business."[34] Instead of depositing government funds in private banks, Van Buren proposed an Independent Treasury bill, which however was not passed and signed until July of 1840. Even then it "made no fundamental contribution either to financial stability or to the search for a uniform currency."[35] Needless to say, the political cartoons during most of Van Buren's incumbency harshly condemned these policies that seemed to lead to nationwide financial chaos.

"Uncle Sam Sick with La Grippe" portrays Jackson, Benton, and Van Buren as antiquated quacks whose outdated nostrums have ruined the country's financial health. While business and banking interests would naturally welcome the return of Nicholas Biddle's National Bank, this cartoon shows the ordinary citizen embodied by Brother Jonathan joyously greeting Biddle outside the window. As a matter of fact, however, Biddle's own United States Bank of Pennsylvania collapsed in 1839—perhaps demonstrating that no private bank was immune to the economic stress. Lightly sketched in the background seen through the window at the right, Jonathan wears his by-now standard costume—top hat, swallow-tailed coat, and striped pants; Jonathan's speech also shows a standardization. He talks like a stage Yankee: "oh Doc Biddle I'm so glad you're come. Uncle Sam's in a darned bad way I guess, he's in kinder dwam like, I hope you'll ease him—" Jonathan is still beardless, while Uncle Sam the patient has the white hair and lined face of an old man. These circumstances lead to the assumption that Uncle Sam, a wise old man, represents the government of the country itself. Fundamental principles voiced by the Declaration of Independence and the Constitution as well as the ordinary folk sentiment represented by Jonathan have been endangered, according to this print, through the leadership of the Democrats.

In another cartoon critical of Van Buren's laissez-faire policy, an emaciated Jonathan pulls forward two equally starved female figures representing American credit and commerce. In "Brother Jonathan's Appeal"

Brother Jonathan's Appeal (1837). (*Courtesy of the New York Historical Society, New York.*)

(1837), Jonathan begs an obdurate Van Buren to palliate his hard money policy. While the Jonathan character in this cartoon does not speak in dialect, he does make the sort of comparison that we have come to associate with the stage Yankee and American humor. Jonathan warns Van Buren that he's "something like the man who tried how long he could live without eating, and just as he discovered he could go without for three weeks, he died. . . ." Jonathan's outfit does not differ much from that of other male characters, except that his is patched, torn, and battered. The cut of Jonathan's clothes recalls Uncle Sam's today. Jonathan, however, is young; his unkempt straight hair pushing out from beneath his battered top hat still suggests his country origins.

Jonathan growing into Uncle Sam also attends Van Buren in "Mr. Van Shuffleton and His Physician Sam" (1838). The doctor, Sam, sounds and looks like the stage Yankee, Jonathan, as he forces his patient to cough up promises, vows, and professions. Neither the drawing nor its idea gives this lithograph much distinction. Its publisher, H. R. Robinson of New York, the most prolific American publisher of political cartoons between 1831 and 1849, drew many of his own designs;[36] he may have drawn this one. Reminiscent of the stage Yankee's speech and the puns and the topics of other contemporary prints, this Jonathan-Sam exclaims, "Why! What an audacious heep of Cash the critturs thrown up!—he'll be much relieved—and then I'll whip this queer letter down his throat—it will be as good as a mint julep if he don't eat it kindly he shall lick all this here stuff up again." As long as the specie crisis continued, punning references to mint juleps and mint drops recurred regularly in cartoons.

Jonathan again has the look of ordinary simplicity in "A Dialogue Between two well known characters" (1837). Another lithograph published by Robinson, this print shows Brother Jonathan and John Bull chatting across a ditch labeled "Atlantic" about the current weathercock, Van Buren, atop Jonathan's liberty pole. Responding to John Bull's comment that he does not look well, Jonathan, who has a copy of the specie circular protruding from his pocket, explains,

> Why Mister Bull, you see, I planted this here pole in 1776, when I gave you that tarnation whipping Johnny, and since then I've had many good cocks on the top of it; all but the last, which was a contumaciously obstinate one, and never turned round at all,—however, as it always points to the *South-West*; I used to git up of a morning and think the weather was warm and comforting when it *war'nt*, and so I first of all cotched a *fever* and now I've got a chill,—and this here crittur as I've set up now, keeps *twisting about so*, that I guess I shall have to take it down again.

The somewhat ragged Jonathan of this cattoon leans on a long walking stick but looks young and agile enough to regain his strength; and in all of the speeches declaimed by Jonathan figures in these cartoons, he always seems to have control of his destiny. Regardless of the current crisis, the character still exudes confidence. In keeping with that confidence, a small pillared temple—symbolic of the Constitution or perhaps republican virtue—shines in the upper right portion of the sky like a beneficent god watching over Jonathan's best interests. In this and other cartoons, the Jonathan figure represents the ordinary citizenry, but the representation often condescends and suggests that if the people would just come to their senses and follow their rightful leaders everything would improve.

Another reference to Brother Jonathan—though lacking his actual appearance—occurs in an 1836 cartoon "The Heads of two great Nations . . ." This print presents Louis Philippe and Jackson as uncompromising billy goats with human faces who taunt one another in a contest neither is likely to win, since they are standing on a plank set across water. The cartoon refers to the controversy that evolved from the fact that the United States wanted twenty-three million dollars in reparations for French depredations on American shipping and property during the Napoleonic wars. France, for its part, was still trying to collect five million dollars for supplies sold to the colonies during the American Revolution. Through the good services of a series of American ministers, an 1831 treaty finally appeared to settle the mutual claims. The French government, however, refused to honor their own draft for the first payment of a million dollars because the Chamber of Deputies had not yet appropriated the money. During this contretemps, newspapers on both sides—signified by the men standing below the bluffs—encouraged the war talk of the countries' volatile leaders. In the background a jolly John Bull furthers the fight with, "Go it my Harties fifty to one on Brother Jonathan. Some one will profit by this, I don't say who!" Actually, the British Foreign Secretary, Lord Palmerston, helped to find a compromise that allowed both sides to retreat with honor; so the treaty was finally put into effect in 1836. Since Jackson is the combatant in this print, he may be thought of as the Jonathan John Bull is backing.

American international disputes also figure in "A general arguing of the Maine question" (1839). Jonathan figures in this Akin lithograph as a young sailor wagging his finger at a complacent Wellington, who in turn is urged on by a skeleton wearing a death's head helmet labeled "Waterloo." Although Wellington promises to repel any American forces sent to wrest control of northern Maine from the British, the nonchalant Jonathan quips, "I'll bet you a four pence you sarpet! *Uncle Sam*, will make you pay for every splinter on't. He can lick the whole grist of your Generals in no time *Pennsylvania & Porter* har. You foolish critur such a chebucco Boats staunch *Hull* you know—can slap a cod's stiff tail about your Lord's Royal chops, so slick." Jonathan has the codfish in his right hand ready to fulfill his pledge. Again Brother Jonathan is full of humor, a strong and able ordinary citizen. And in this cartoon, he speaks of Uncle Sam as a separate entity—doubtless the government and its force.

As illustrated by an election caricature of 1839 or 1840, the visual distinction between Brother Jonathan, the citizen, and Uncle Sam, the government, was not universal. "Uncle Sam's Pet Pups," has the Brother Jonathan figure chasing two dogs with the human faces of Van Buren and Jackson into a hard-cider barrel. A military figure, probably William Harrison, holds the barrel into which "Mother Bank" has already crawled. While the bold type refers to him as Uncle Sam, the youth of the figure on the left in this print and his function as the voice of the populace identify him as Jonathan.

Perhaps, however, in this print Jonathan and Uncle Sam's iconographic meanings merge. Eventually elected by the Whigs in 1840, Harrison campaigned on enthusiasm for his military reputation and his "plebean" background rather than on issues. Part of the Whig strategy to oust the incumbent included an attack on Van Buren's ostensibly luxurious tastes—thus the implication that Harrison's tenure would return the White House to an "honest" drink like hard cider in place of the decadence of a French wine.[37] Van Buren had called as well for a special session of Congress in 1837 where he proposed an independent treasury; this became the "Mother Bank" of "Uncle Sam's Pet Pups." During the session a concerted force of Whigs and conservative Democrats had sidetracked that legislation. Thus, this print may give an example of wishful thinking on the part of Whig leaders. Yet if the figure is really Jonathan, then he has been manipulated by the Whig emphasis on economic distress, for which the Whigs also bore some responsibility, and by their ability to focus on images like Harrison's log cabin—actually a commodious home set on his 2,000-acre farm near Cincinnati. On the other hand, if the figure is indeed Uncle Sam, he represents Harrison's Whig supporters who quite effectively buried the Jacksonian age in a barrel of hard cider. The Whigs did not associate themselves—except in rhetoric and iconography—with the plebians; they considered themselves the truly responsible citizens. Consequently, they would hardly sympathize with Jonathan's native rebelliousness.

During the 1830s and 1840s and even the 1850s, cartoons frequently put human faces on animal bodies. This cartoon has the vigor of a wood engraving but nothing much else in its favor. The figures are not particularly well drawn, and the humor is rather morose. Jonathan wears a rather diabolical smirk—as if he enjoys the thought of three scrappy animals forced to share cramped quarters.

Since the Jonathan of this chapter's cartoons sketches the outlines an ideologeme, his representation presents one means of tracing some fault lines in antebellum American culture. One such social stress line followed political loyalty. That, in turn, generally followed economic interest. Hence, Jonathan was a manipulated figure, as the printers who in concert with their political allies produced and distributed these cheap lithographs applied a kind of positive reinforcement in language and visual symbols to encourage "responsible" action on the part of a significant new mass of voters.

The original visual Jonathan had been a British invention, with at least one critical cartoon, "Yankie Doodles Intrenchments," emphasizing the character's provincial bumptiousness, while another, "The English & American Discovery," emphasized the character's ties with England. In the early nineteenth century, cartoons primarily depicted how the hoi polloi should think about the War of 1812, then about how they should view conflicts between Jackson's Democrats and their Whig opponents. The Jonathan shown in the cartoons, at first a city dweller and then a country-boy, was not a leader. Nonetheless, he was a commentator, the voice of the enfranchised worker, invariably worried about how events will affect his life. The cartoons strove, in fact, to tell him what his attitude ought to be.

5

The Cartoon Character: No Longer An Original

FOLLOWING A HIATUS DURING THE EARLY 1840S, THE CHARACTER CALLED Brother Jonathan resurfaced in political cartoons of the mid-decade. By the 1850s onward however, the same visual representation was frequently relabeled Uncle Sam.[1] In the process, a personality change also ensued. So except for occasional relics, Brother Jonathan practically disappeared from the American scene after the Civil War. Modern warfare and mechanization required a large population of team players. Jonathan was never that. His gradual adaptation to that role in the cartoons of the 1840s and 1850s trace, in fact, his decline as an American original. The populace may have come to realize that while Jonathan's country wisdom contributed useful criticisms of foreign aggression and destructive financial practices, the simplistic jingoism of his responses to expansionism during the forties and fifties did not answer to the period's complex economic and social questions.[2] Nor did Jonathan's satisfied self-sufficiency in confronting national divisions during the fifties and sixties serve the nation as a whole.[3]

The cartoon image of Jonathan belonged to the same nationalist impulse that produced the Jonathan figure for the stage and for other outlets of popular humor. Indeed, the surge of cartoons during the 1830s and 1840s paralleled a proud appropriation by Americans of all that it meant to be an American. The bumptious "warts and all" character of the Brother Jonathan who figured in cartoons defied European standards. What began as a foreign emblem of provincial ignorance characterized by colloquial speech and ill-fitting clothes developed instead into an American embodiment of literally "home truths," the honest and trustworthy figure associated with natural nobility "to be found in the isolated village and the countryside."[4] Although, as Joshua Taylor mentions, the glow of this romantic notion "has never wholly faded,"[5] it was tested severely during the last decades before the Civil War.

While the 1840s saw a spate of Jonathan cartoons published, they also witnessed a faltering in the iconography, as artists and publishers tried to agree upon both an immediately recognizable form for the figure and his significance. The first objective proved the easier to accomplish; the stage Yankee's tags eventually became the cartoon Jonathan's as well. The figure's purpose, however, got lost in disparate political and social agendas. "Everyone" claimed Jonathan; after a while he became "no one." More often than not, Jonathan was embroiled in political controversy in the cartoons of the 1840s; and because American comic periodicals did not achieve wide circulation before the 1850s, the overwhelming majority of Jonathan's portraits appeared in separately published lithographs.

The Whig Challenge

Although Whigs remained a potent force in national politics during the twelve years following Harrison's capture of the presidency in 1840, their party was united only in its opposition to Jacksonian Democrats in general and to Martin Van Buren in particular. While the Whigs feuded, the Democrats elected presidents. Two broadsides published in 1844, typical of the caricature style and political topics of the mid-1840s, feature Jonathan. The first of these lithographs, "Sale of Dogs," signed by H. Bucholzer and printed by James Billie of New York, presents human faces on animal bodies. In addition, the dog held on a leash by Jackson wears an identifying collar, "M v B." A man dressed in Brother Jonathan's striped pants and long-tailed coat offers Western candidates, Polk and Dallas, to Jackson and the party. Since the figure in striped pants has a genteel air and certainly does not talk like a stage Yankee, he may not actually be the Jonathan character even though he is dressed as one.

Another 1844 lithograph, "Annexation, or Sport for Grown Children," offers even stranger animal representations. The print shows two figures symbolizing John Bull. Two dogs, whose collars identify them as (the bloodhound) Santa Anna and (the bulldog) John Bull, yap at the heels of another dog, Jonathan, who has a kettle labeled Texas tied to his tail. Weitenkampf identifies the onlookers as Calhoun, Jackson, Polk, Van Buren, and John Bull. The dog Jonathan runs over a treaty between the United States and Mexico. In the background the human John Bull is, as commonly happens in an American cartoon, undecided whether to rush in to further his own self-interest or to assume a stance of moral superiority. At this point even a quick-footed mongrel defending himself in a dog fight was evidently acceptable as a pictorial representation of American feistiness.

Punch

With the establishment of *Punch* in 1841, British political caricature soon caught up with Jonathan's current costume and in time added fresh touches to the figure's delineation. Within decades, of course, the comic weeklies and more general illustrated journals would crowd out separately published cartoons; but in the 1840s *Punch* was a newcomer.

Perhaps influenced by the stage Yankee as English audiences saw him and, in any case, far less sympathetic to the ordinary American than American graphic artists were, *Punch* artists of the 1840s embodied what they perceived as the American spirit in a variety of forms. At first these characters were merely self-complacent clods, often termed "Yankee Noodle." But in time the same long-limbed, heavy-booted figure with lank hair hanging about his face was referred to as Brother Jonathan instead of Yankee Noodle. The untrimmed hair, in fact, along with a general air of careless dress often characterized the Jonathan figure in British cartoons. These traits appear in both the sly whip-toting young tough,[6] who looks as if he is never going to catch up with his own rapid growth, and the foreshortened, petty, and pugnacious character who is invariably bragging or fighting without adequate cause.

When the American comic weekly *Yankee Doodle* started publication in 1846, it quite naturally produced a long-legged character with the same costume worn by most previous Jonathan figures; but *Yankee Doodle* named this figure Yankee Doodle.

1840s: Manifest Destiny

Both *Punch* and *Yankee Doodle* were in print when "John Bull and Brother Jonathan," appeared in 1846. This Robinson lithograph, nevertheless, does not fit the usual visual patterns found in broadside cartoons or in comic weeklies. The Brother Jonathan of this print, disparaged by John Bull who calls him "Fellow—Yankee Doodle—Vile Dog" still appears to be the noble American farmer, the new man of Crevecoeur's *Letters*. He dresses in a genteel notion of the farmer's smock and hat and declaims with orphic certitude about his own innate virtue and future greatness: "I am the offspring of enterprise, intellect, virtue & courage, of the free spirits of old England, I arm not, I threaten not, Cousin be prudent, be peaceable, look to the shadow time throws before me: but a Hundred years, *and then*—I will protect you." Here Jonathan calls up the image of a WASP peaceable kingdom. This cartoon oracle is no stage Yankee truculently ready to fight over Oregon or some other bone of contention. The usual Brother Jonathan, for all his bragging, seldom exhibits such serenity. As with any oracular statement, the artist had a fifty-fifty chance of guessing right; still hindsight knowledge of World War II and the Falkland Islands armed conflict makes this a curious prophecy.

A far more characteristic Brother Jonathan appears in the visually busy and often reprinted "Uncle Sam's Taylorifics" (1846). Edward Williams Clay initialed this lithograph depicting Uncle Sam, dressed in the manner that had previously always distinguished Brother Jonathan, kicking a small Mexican military figure back across the Rio Grande. Uncle Sam talks like Jonathan too: "Why darn your eyes you bloody Mexican thief you come to steal my new Boot I'll discumgalligumfrigate you! I will be Jing!" Jonathan-Sam is in the process of cutting the ineffectual Mexican in two by means of a scissors whose blades are labeled "Volunteers" and "General Taylor." His sash reads "Union" while other parts of his clothing are named "Oregon," "Southern States," and so forth. "California" hangs, like a limp scarf, on a nearby tree limb as a bull in human clothing attempts to hook part of Oregon off of Jonathan-Sam's coattails. Also clothed in parts of his empire, John Bull puzzles, "Brother Jonathan's bait is very tempting. Egat I think I've got a bit! But it don't seem to make him any the less." So while the print's title refers to Uncle Sam, John Bull refers to the main figure as Brother Jonathan.

In "Uncle Sam's Taylorifics" Jonathan is a dapper parvenu, young and brash. His hair is combed but still long and dark. He puffs at a long cigarillo and wears a military plume in his top hat. His ruffled shirt and ostentatious stick pin suggest the stage presentations of Jonathan as a flashy "original." Apart from the different hats the two Jonathans wear and the two prints' opposing interpretations of America's "manifest destiny," this print and the *Punch* caricature of American society found in Richard Doyle's "The Land of Liberty" (1847),[6] contain strikingly similar Jonathans even to the elongated faces and pointed, slightly Roman noses. Clay's composition is, however, far more cluttered than Doyle's and Clay does not draw as well as Doyle.[7] The similarity, nonetheless, between British and American expressions of the American does suggest agreement on the part of the artists about a developing convention.

Aspects of this convention about Brother Jonathan's visual tags reappear in two cartoons published during 1848. Both "Whig Harmony," and "Coming to Terms," along with the vast majority of the cartoons we have seen thus far, agree that Brother Jonathan now dresses in a countryboy's idea of town clothes. Since this includes boots, a long-tailed coat, and a top hat, Jonathan wears these. He is also fairly young and rather casual about both dress and posture. Perhaps influenced by his country origins, his hair is shaggier than most townsmen's. Sometimes the physical and verbal tags of the stage Yankee also attach to Brother Jonathan. His dress is often more flamboyant than that of the other characters; often his striped pants and stars are reminiscent of the American flag.

The Land of Liberty. *Punch* 8 (1847): 215. (*Courtesy of the University of Iowa Libraries.*)

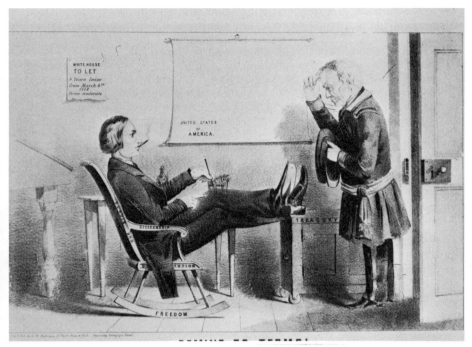

Coming to Terms! (1848). (*Courtesy of the Prints and Photographs Division, Library of Congress.*)

In the first of these two lithographs, "Whig Harmony," horses with the faces of Henry Clay and Zachary Taylor pull a two-wheeled cart in opposite directions. Horace Greeley and Jonathan drive the horses. Loaded with the issues of "bank," "tariff," and "internal improvement" the cart will clearly not go anywhere, even after a boulder signifying the Wilmot Proviso—which disallowed slavery in the new territories—has been removed. The Brother Jonathan of this print wears the boldly patterned waistcoat and pants of a stage Yankee. The whip suggests Jonathan's acceptance of slavery, and the character's support for a Southern military hero like Taylor is in keeping with his usual behavior. The character complains to Greeley in country lingo: "Do slack up a little there, Horace, till we get over a chock that some one has put before the wheel." The exaggerated dialect of earlier cartoons, however, is missing in Jonathan's speech.

As a matter of fact, Zachary Taylor did win the presidential election; and the other of these two prints from 1848 shows Taylor as a would-be office holder "Coming to Terms" with Brother Jonathan. In this Robinson lithograph Jonathan lolls in a rocking chair—whose supports include "our rights," "citizenship," "constitutions," and "freedom"—and rests his feet on a safe marked "treasury." Stirring his mint julep—his gin bottle close at hand—and smoking his cigar, Jonathan interviews an obsequious Taylor:

Ah! You're the Party that wants to Rent my Farm Eh!
Zach. If you please Mr. Jonathan sir. I'm an old Soldier sir. Served in the Mexican Campaign sir. [Jonathan.] Very well Mr. Taylor you can have it on one condition, that you offer no obstruction to the removal of the Subtreasury nuisance, so Detrimental to the River Currency, which as you know, sets all my Factories and Workshops a going.

Jonathan's relaxed pose and the map on the wall of the "United States of America"—actually embracing North and South America—offer evidence of an overweaning confidence. Actually, since Taylor came to the White House with a minimum of political debts to repay, he proved to be a fairly independent executive, and despite his Southern background, even supported the demands of California and New Mexico for statehood without slavery. The Brother Jonathan in this lithograph, however, depicts that portion of the population that was probably more worried about commerce than slavery or its abolition. He is perhaps supposed to indicate the ordinary farmer or workman, but actually he mouths the interests of Northern merchants and bankers.

1850s: Politics and Posturing

The expansionism implied by the map on the wall in "Coming to Terms" provides the theme for several of the cartoons of the early 1850s. A significant number of Americans hoped that the United States would acquire Cuba either through purchase or conquest. President Polk offered Spain one hundred million dollars for Cuba; and when this offer was refused by Isabella II, a filibuster—as the freebooters attempting to gain footholds in Latin America were called—and his supporters attempted to "liberate" the island through military means. The group was captured and most of the men executed in 1851.

Punch ran a couple of cartoons[8] during the first half of 1850 to celebrate American discomfiture at the failure of these diplomatic and military efforts. One *Punch* cartoon, "The American Rover-General Wot Tried to Steal a Cuba," pictures a Yankee getting booted out of a cigar store. The other, "Jonathan Tries to Smoke a Cuba," has two panels. In the first panel, a dapper youth attempts to demonstrate his worldly experience by puffing on a cigar labeled Cuba; in the second panel the youth looks headachy and sick to his stomach. The British, after all, also had interests in the Caribbean and did not rejoice at American expansion into that area. At least one American broadside, "Invasion of Cuba," challenged *Punch*'s derisive dismissal of the American efforts. Both panels in the American

MASTER JONATHAN TRIES TO SMOKE A CUBA, BUT IT DOESN'T AGREE WITH HIM!!

Master Jonathan Tries to Smoke a Cuba. *Punch* **18** (1850): 243. (*Courtesy of the University of Iowa Libraries.*)

lithograph depict a Jonathan determined to continue until he succeeds. After this, aside from a few minor tiffs, *Punch* cartoons show relatively little interest in American concerns until the onset of the Civil War. On the other hand, American lithographs during the 1850s closely follow American concerns—especially presidential politics.

An election broadside, "The Poor Soldier & His Ticket for Soup" (1852) shows a proud pug-nosed Jonathan explaining to Columbia that the pleading pensioner, Winfield Scott, who stands in supplication at the door of the Capitol has come for a handout. The artist who drew the lithograph argued that the White House was not a necessary prize owed to retired generals. Evidently the electorate agreed, since Franklin Pierce defeated Scott. This Jonathan has the round features and limbs of figures in Currier and Ives prints; in addition his body is foreshortened and his face resembles the young-old features of a cupid in a sentimental print or perhaps a della Robbia angel. His costume and long, straight hair nevertheless still fit the formula for Brother Jonathan. He wears boots, a beaver hat, and striped pants with boot straps. His long-tailed coat and vivid vest also fit the pat-

Invasion of Cuba (1851). (*By permission of the Houghton Library, Harvard University.*)

tern for Jonathan. And yet the differences do not serve any artistic or persuasive purpose. In fact the three figures in this broadside appear to be copied from three unrelated models. Published at the *Yankee Notions* office in New York, the lithograph was intended to influence voting. Those involved in its production probably had little interest in making the Jonathan figure's treatment wholly traditional.

Another topical lithograph apparently initialed by Edward Williams Clay is "John Bull's Fish Monopoly" (1852), which stays closer to the by-now-established pattern for the Jonathan figure. Close to the end of his long career as lithographer, Clay drew on conventions developed over the previous thirty years. The Jonathan in this print has the slight stoop and dialect speech of earlier characters. A variegated print handkerchief hangs from his back pocket; his tie hangs awkwardly from his throat. Despite the neatness and general air of prosperity that his clothes imply, the slightly outdated cut of his coat and shaggy length of hair in addition to his dialect definitely identify this figure as Jonathan. In this lithograph he confronts John Bull with the fact that the latter's refusal to allow American ships to fish in the Bay of Fundy is in violation of the Treaty of Ghent. Jonathan growls at John Bull, "Why consarn you, you tarnal old critter, looke'e here, you won't deny your own hand writin will you—And haven't we

The Propaganda Society (1855). (*Courtesy of the Prints and Photographs Division, Library of Congress.*)

been fishin in the Bay for thirty years without any muss—I want to know—Du tell?'' The other figures—John Bull, an elegantly genteel male personage, a frontiersman, and a little family group—also fit popular stereotypes.

A third broadside from this decade, "The Propaganda Society—More Free Than Welcome" (1855) uses Brother Jonathan to support nativist fears about Roman Catholic designs upon the spiritual and material welfare of the United States. A sentimentally portrayed child depicting Young America refuses the blandishments of the pope approaching with a sword and cross. In what amounts to a pun on the Native American Party's more common name, the child protests that he is "determined to *Know-nothing*" but the Bible that he holds in his hands.[9] Looking up, whittling and untroubled, Brother Jonathan warns the intruder, "No you don't, Mr. Pope! you're altogether too willing; but you can't put 'the mark of the Beast' on Americans." A flag above the pole that Jonathan leans against emphasizes his identification with patriotism. Although still a beardless youth, this character closely approaches the modern Uncle Sam. His long-tailed coat, for example, has become pointed; his long figure, fly-away hair, pointed nose, striped pants, boots and top hat all anticipate modern caricatures of Uncle Sam.

Currier and Ives

Although political cartoons furnished a relatively minor portion of Currier and Ives' lucrative print publishing business, their firm did publish broadside lithographs, including a number featuring Brother Jonathan. Their lithographs stand apart because, as Harry T. Peters remarks, Currier and Ives "had predecessors and competitors, but really no rivals"[10] in the production of lithographs. Through sheer numbers of individual prints as well as a consistent ability to gauge popular taste, Currier and Ives dominated broadside lithography during much of the middle and late nineteenth century.

The firm of Currier and Ives published at least seven thousand separate items—each with its own run—during the seventy years of the company's existence. Although the firm employed at least a dozen artists,[11] including Louis Mauer and Thomas Nast, their prints maintained a marked stylistic consistency. The artists were liable, in fact, "to have their work altered," and "were expected to produce stock work and collaborate on joint productions."[12] The main point, however, is that from 1834 when Nathaniel Currier established his own business through 1857 when he made James Merritt Ives his partner until their deaths in the last decades of the nineteenth century, the firm of Currier and Ives made profit their primary guide. Their prints gave the buying public what it wanted and thus provide remarkable indices of "the stock prejudices of Jacksonian common man"[13] as they ridicule the aspirations of women, blacks, and Catholics. Peters also credits their broadside cartoons with "a sincerity and wholesomeness, a simplicity and a Daguerrean sureness of detail."[14] When printing a potentially controversial political cartoon, however, they omitted their names.[15]

In 1851, before his partnership with Ives, Currier published at least one print with a Jonathan-like figure. "The Great Exhibition of 1851/American Department" appealed to American pride in its shipping. A young man, embodying American youth, vigor, and strength—providing a foil to John Bull's middle-aged limitations—points to an American clipper and a streamship; he tells John Bull that these, rather than the relatively small display of American manufactures at the Crystal Palace, are America's exhibition. Though this figure of the young man might be Brother Jonathan, he has lost much of his particularizing definition.

In two slightly later prints from the same company, "The Democratic Platform" (1856) and "The Irrepressible Conflict" (1860), the figure of Jonathan wears his standard garb and once again acts as the people's common-sensical commentator on the political scene. Yet the Jonathan of these prints is not labeled. He may have been too obvious to identify or he may already be merging with the figure of Uncle Sam. Perhaps, too, the always careful firm may not have wanted to identify itself with the political invective associated with the Jonathan figure from the Jacksonian Era. From the late 1820s through the early 1840s, Jonathan, though supposed to signify the American people's attitude toward contemporary affairs, often asserted the out-of-office party's positions—identified, of course, as Yankee common sense. In any case, only youth and the lack of a beard distinguish these Jonathans from the later Uncle Sam. In "The Democratic Platform" Jonathan warns the Southerner sitting with his black slave on the platform formed by Buchanan's prostrate body that the platform's kneeling supporters—Thomas Benton, Franklin Pierce, John Van Buren (Martin's son)—are apt to give way at any moment. An indictment of the Democratic Party's support of slavery, this print clearly distinguishes Jonathan from another sectional figure, the Southerner.

In "The Irrepressible Conflict" Jonathan stands on the shore commenting on the Republican convention that has chosen Lincoln as their nominee. While Horace Greeley and Francis Blair throw William Seward out of the running for the nomination because of his adamant insistence on the "irrepressible conflict" between slavery and freedom, Jonathan glumly advises, "You wont save your crazy old craft by throwing your pilot overboard; better heave that tarnal Nigger out." The regional dialect has almost disappeared from Jonathan's speech in this cartoon, and he is ripe for melding with Uncle Sam.

That the definition of Uncle Sam was not yet absolutely established by this point is clear from another Currier and Ives' print from the same presidential campaign. In "Uncle Sam making New Arrangements" (1860),[16] a clearly labeled Uncle Sam who looks like Benjamin Franklin takes down the "help wanted" sign from the wall outside the White House and explains to the defeated candidates that he has decided to leave "the management of my affairs" with Lincoln. Uncle Sam often took a more official role than Brother Jonathan. Considering his stage baggage as bumpkin and trickster, Jonathan may not have been considered dignified enough to usher a new president into the White House. On the other hand, the usual figure of Brother Jonathan might not have made the right visual contrast with the hayseed appearance of Lincoln in this print.

In Currier and Ives' "Reunion on the Secesh-Democratic Plan" (1862) Jonathan now represents the North alone. A Southern planter with a Lincolnesque face offers peace terms that amount to complete capitulation on the part of the North. Jonathan, burdened with both the Federal and Confederate debt as well as the figure of a manacled black man, agrees with a handshake. He concurs with the plan saying, "Anything my 'erring

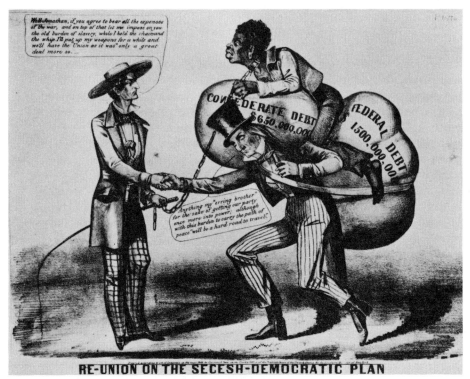

Re-Union on the Secesh-Democratic Plan (1862). (*Courtesy of the Print Collection, The New York Public Library, Astor, Lenox and Tilden Foundations.*)

The Stride of a Century (1876). (*By permission of the Bettman Archive, Inc.*)

brother' for the sake of getting our party once more into power; although with this burden to carry the path to peace 'will be a hard road to travel.'" Although this Jonathan is called by name and wears the regulation uniform, he does not speak in the typical dialect, nor does he act with Jonathan's characteristic braggadocio. Irony, understatement, hyperbole —all these belong to the Jonathan character's usual sense of humor. Sarcasm does not suit him as well. The pious phrasing he quotes may mock the argument of some Democratic politician or newspaperman.

In this and several other cartoons, the Jonathan character has clearly become localized and now refers to the North alone. He no longer includes all the people.

Some notion of how independent the Currier and Ives prints were of other streams of cultural iconography can be grasped from looking at "The Stride of a Century" (1876). Full of the youth and vigor of earlier Brother Jonathan figures, this lithograph figure celebrates American accomplishments during the century since the revolution. Both the tone of this lithograph and its visual tags agree with the early formula for Brother Jonathan, while most American periodicals had already ceased using the youthful figure ten years before.

Wood Cuts

Despite the continued popularity of separate lithographs and particularly of Currier and Ives' prints, by the 1850s the more common fount for cartoons satirizing political and social idiosyncrasies was the weekly illustrated magazine. Influenced by both the intense political agitation preceding the Civil War and by another technical innovation, an electrotyping process that allowed printers to run larger editions at a lower cost, newspapers and magazines increased significantly in number during the decade before the Civil War.[17] Of the fourteen new magazines to appear in 1846,[18] for example, three continued publication until at least the 1870s; of the thirty-two to begin publication during 1856,[19] eleven managed to continue for three decades.

Not all of these magazines were illustrated, of course, but many of the most popular were, e.g., Frank Leslie's publications. *The Illustrated Newspaper* in the fifties as well as the later *Harper's* and *Vanity Fair* featured illustrations that attempted reporting and satire. The popularity of cartoons in these magazines usurped the hegemony of the broadsides.

Illustrations in these magazines were run from woodcuts. The sharp black and white contrasts, the affinity of woodcuts for broadly conceived designs, and the dramatic quality of wood engraved illustrations—all of these characteristics made wood engravings well-suited to the needs of illustrated magazines bent on catching and holding the attention of mass audiences. In addition, since wood engraving was a relief process, the blocks could be simultaneously printed with movable type. Lithographic stones, in contrast, could not be integrated with movable type; and since the electrotyping process was the original innovation that encouraged the multiplication of periodicals, woodcuts rather than lithographs now dominated illustrations in magazines.[20]

American Comic Magazines

The Lantern (1852–1853) and *Yankee Notions*, (1852–1865) two new weeklies, plus a few broadside cartoons, continued to propagate the image of the Jonathan figure as the embodiment of the American. Yet a gradual hesitation in using the figure also shows up in the magazines. Could it be that as the United States progressed toward almost universal white male suffrage and—at least in the North—far more popular sense of participation in the national government's decisions during the last decade before the Civil War, citizens felt less need to voice their independence? Did cartoon-makers assume citizens no longer identified with Jonathan's oppositional style, except with regard to the aspirations of women, other races, Jews, and Catholics? During the last decades of the eighteenth century and the first several decades of the nineteenth century, for the most part Jonathan was pictured as an outsider demanding his rights. By the time he appeared in cartoons of the 1850s, he was an insider.

Yankee Notions uses almost the same figures for Jonathan and Uncle Sam. In addition, the *Yankee Notions* cartoons repeat many of the old chestnuts from jest books and stage comedies. If any distinction between the two figures exists, it may be that Brother Jonathan presents the more aggressively chauvinist front. *Vanity Fair* continues these confusions during the 1860s.[21]

Tensions between the North and the South may have helped to make Jonathan a less satisfactory national symbol because Jonathan always had strong sectional associations. The fact that nothing particularly new or vibrant was added to the stereotype may also have lessened popular interest.[22] The Jonathan figure of these cartoons does not have the necessary formulaic clarity that Uncle Sam's later caricatures possess. Nor do other elements in popular culture—such as plays, newspaper poetry or anecdotes, tall tales, or novels—appear to be augmenting Brother Jonathan's definition. The figure's diminishing popularity may be related to the lack of any new development, or just as possible, the same opposing attributes that provided a dramatic interest in the character on stage may merely have muddled his presentation in the literal black and white world of political cartoons.

One of the more popular of comic magazines, *Yankee Notions*, as well as more satiric periodicals like *The Lantern* and *Vanity Fair* (1860–1863), used the Brother Jonathan figure as a regular medium of satiric comment. The subtitle for *Yankee Notions* was *Whittling's of Jonathan's Jack Knife*; at times Jonathan became an editorial persona. One regular editorial feature of *Yankee Notions* was "Jonathan's Chip Basket," later changed to "The Chip Basket." The editor, T. W. Strong, and his staff apparently made a blunderbuss use of the Jonathan idea. In cartoons alone, the figure became the mouthpiece for both political and social satire. He remained also the traditional sly bumpkin of yore—the oddly victorious butt of humor—until the end of the decade.

A DECLARATION OF RIGHTS.

JONATHAN.—*Kin you endure ceremony?*

STRONG MINDED LADY.—*I can endure anything but the horrid slavery under which our sex at present groans. I can't endure nursing babies, mending clothes, darning stockings, rocking cradles, dabbling in wash-tubs, cooking victuals, or doing any kind of housework. I shall insist upon the largest liberty in action and speech, in my incomings and outgoings, and particularly in dress. I shall insist upon the bifurcated costume, and shall in all things expect the most implicit obedience from you, when we are united.*

JONATHAN.—*Guess you and I can't hitch together no how. You kin do as you're a mind to, but I'm darned if you ever git into my breeches.*

A Declaration of Rights. *Yankee Notions* 3 (1854): 271. (*Courtesy of the University of Iowa Libraries.*)

Many of the same controversial topics that appeared in broadside cartoons—such as American designs upon Cuba, presidential politics, nativism, and growing sectional tensions—also appeared in illustrated magazines like *Yankee Notions*. Nevertheless, in many of the cartoons that were more like today's comics than like real political cartoons, the magazine focused with deliberately blind concentration on domestic issues. With far less interest in abolition, expansionism, economics, or politics than in bloomers and the "woman's question," the Jonathan everyman of "A Declaration of Rights" (1854)[23] rejected feminism with the language of the stage Yankee and the sentiments of his male audience when he declared to the strong-minded woman in this cartoon, "Guess you and I can't hitch together no how. You kin do as you're a mind to, but I'm darned if you ever git into *my* breeches."

Also reminiscent of Yankee yarns and the stage Yankee's sly humor is another 1854 cartoon[24] that finds Jonathan replying to an English traveller's query as to how far he must go before reaching Hartford with, "Well, if you turn re nind [sic] and go 'tother way may be you have to travel about ten mile. But if you keep on the way you are going, you'll have to go about eight thousand, I reckon." Variants of this joke abound.

The Jonathan of such cartoons almost invariably wears the usual striped pants and boots, long-tailed coat, top hat, and has shaggy hair. But in keeping with new social facts, the Jonathan who generally depicts the ordinary American[25] in the pages of *Yankee Notions* now resembles Mose and B'hoy[26]—a familiar stage stereotype of the roughneck Irishman. In addition, a political figure could appear in the trappings of Jonathan. The same magazine printed a cartoon, "The Destiny of Young America,"[27] featuring a Jonathan figure astride a map of the world and bragging, "I am Master of all I survey." Beneath the cartoon, the caption reads, "As shadowed forth by Senator Douglas and the Democratic Review." Douglas, sometimes referred to as Young America,[28] is also associated with the people that Brother Jonathan represents.

The comments on domestic and social situations made by the artists employed by *Yankee Notions* were generally more pointed than its political opinions. Intended for a large audience, the magazine took care not to support unpopular causes that might alienate parts of its readership. The sardonic humor of "Scene—Ponchartrain Depot, New Orleans" (1856),[29] would however be acceptable in the Northern cities where most copies were sold. In a wry comment on Southern miscegenation, Jonathan tells his Polly Maria, "Yes, Polly, yaller sugars is the kind they mannerfacter down here, mostly."

Regardless of political consequences, however, expansionism was a popular cause. And so despite the failure of American freelance attempts to conquer Cuba, Strong still pictured on the March 1853 cover of *Yankee Notions*,[30] his rabble-rousing Jonathan sitting on the president's desk and promising support for still another expedition. "I an't no office seeker, Gin'ral, but I've come rite strate from hum to give yer a notion that if you realy want Cuby, why *me* an' a couple of *Clippers* will fetch her or dy." Popular sentiment may not have been as strong in favor of trying to annex Cuba as this cartoon implies; but following upon the United States success in Texas and the Southwest, many Americans must have believed almost any expropriation was possible.

A year later a more respectable Jonathan acts as personal barber to

FOREIGN IGNORANCE.

FOREIGNER, (just landed in New York.)—Sare, I've just 'rived in this counthry —I have von vish to reach New Orleans dis night. Vill you told me vat is de smallest vay, an' how much mile it is?

JONATHAN.—Wal, stranger; keep the SOUTH road arter you leave this ere place, an' if them spindle shanks o' yeour'n don't gin eout, you'll touch Orleans, I reckon, in abeout a MONTH!

Foreign Ignorance. *Yankee Notions* 2 (1853): 28. (*Courtesy of the University of Iowa Libraries.*)

Scene—Ponchartrain Depot, New Orleans.

Yellow chocolate dealer (to her young responsibility).—Go 'way FROM DE CARS, YOU LUMP O' SUGA'! DEM IRON HOSSES MASH YOU!"

Polly Muria (to her Jonathan)—DEW TELL! IS THAT 'ERE LITTLE MERLATTER A LUMP O' SUGAR?

Jonathan.—YES, POLLY, YALLER SUGARS IS THE KIND JBLY MANNEFACTER DOWN DERE, MOSTLY.

Scene—Ponchartrain Depot, New Orleans. *Yankee Notions* 5 (1856): 272. (*Courtesy of the University of Iowa Libraries.*)

Jonathan at the White House. *Yankee Notions* 2 (1853): 65. (*Courtesy of the University of Iowa Libraries.*)

JONATHAN MICAWBER

WAITING FOR SOMETHING IN THE SHAPE OF A PRESIDENT TO TURN UP.

Jonathan Micawber. *The Lantern* 1 (1852): 192. (*Courtesy of the University of Iowa Library Rare Book Collection.*)

politicians in "Political Shaving."[31] His straightedged razor at the ready, Jonathan gleefully prepares in another *Yankee Notions* illustration to work on a disconcerted Know-Nothing. He offers those in line the promise, "Wait your turn gentlemen, I'll shave you all in time. You can't be too barefaced for Politicians, I'll fix you all off presently. I've got the *Know Nothing* by the nose now, and you all have to stand on one side for him you know. More soap Sam." Once again Brother Jonathan functions in tandem with Uncle Sam. Actually, of course, no specific politician seems to have received any visible knicks from the political cartoons in *Yankee Notions*.

The shorter-lived illustrated magazine, *Diogenes hys Lantern*,[32] has been admired for its high level of wit and satire. Certainly one of the most original caricatures featuring Jonathan appeared in its pages when Frank Bellow drew a Humpty-Dumpty-like figure and titled it "Jonathan Micawber" (1852),[33] and subscribed the figure "waiting for something in the shape of a President to turn up." The cartoon comments all too well on that year's presidential elections that had put Franklin Pierce in the White House to replace Millard Fillmore. Both the drawing of Jonathan and the satiric idea are a cut above most cartoons that appeared, for example, in *Yankee Notions*.

Doctor (the Enthusiastic)/Jonathan (the Patient). *The Lantern* 1 (1852): 7. (*Courtesy of the University of Wisconsin Library Rare Book Collection.*)

CURE FOR IMPERTINENCE.

Uncle Sam. " Take yer papers, and start, darn yer pic-
ter."

Cure for Impertinence. *The Lantern* 1 (1852): 33. (*Courtesy of the University of Wisconsin Library Rare Book Collection.*)

During its short life, however, the *Lantern* did not make any clear delineation between the figures of Brother Jonathan and Uncle Sam. Even within the same volume,[34] the same figure could be used as Jonathan in one cartoon—to explain to the old military doctor who wanted to bleed him that, "My Old Doctor (Washington) thinks otherwise"—while in a smaller, later cartoon as Uncle Sam, the same figure kicks someone down the stairs because of a passport picture.

During the 1860s the Civil War naturally dominated political cartooning in the United States and even had an impact on *Punch*. *Vanity Fair* came on the scene at that time in the United States, and while much of its humor and drawing was derivative of the work found in *Punch*, during most of the three-and-a-half years of its existence, the magazine did provide a higher standard of satire than most American comic magazines.

Something of the earlier Jonathan's confident spirit as well as *Punch*'s influence on the drawing and the details of Jonathan's costume appear, for example, in Stephens's drawing of John Bull and Jonathan "Settling Vexation by Annexation."[35] When John Bull hints for help against the French,

SETTLING VEXATION BY ANNEXATION.

JOHN BULL.—My dear Boy, if it comes to the worst, you'll see your Old Dad out of this plaguy French bumboo, won't you?
JONATHAN.—Well—can't say without seeing the boys first; I tell you what though—s'pose we ANNEX you, that'll settle this bummers right away!

Settling Vexation by Annexation. *Vanity Fair 2 (1860): 105. (Courtesy of the University of Iowa Library Rare Book Collection.)*

Jonathan suggests, "Well—can't say without seeing the boys first; I tell you what though—Spose we *Annex* you, that'll settle this business right away!" The exaggeration must have made even Englishment laugh. A bust of a startled Louis Philippe looks down on the two characters from a relief pedestal on the wall behind them. In this as in other *Vanity Fair* cartoons, the Jonathan figure appeared in the conventional star-studded or variously striped costume developed for him by *Punch* cartoonists.

In the pages of *Vanity Fair* as well as in *Punch*, Jonathan appears as a fresh-faced young man, a contentious child, or, doubled as North-South brothers usually engaged in a fist fight. One out-of-the-ordinary cartoon, however, "The Political Invalid,"[36] depicts Doctor Jonathan, garbed in a physician's somber attire and with the receding white hair of a respectable old medical person, ministering to a politically sick Douglas.

Although Jonathan appeared in some *Vanity Fair* cartoons and Uncle Sam appeared in others, the latter gradually came to predominate. During the Civil War, the diffuse preferences of ordinary citizens and their rambunctious spirits gave place to the perceived need for a strong central government. In the middle of 1861, H. L. Stephens drew a cover "Fishing in

MORE FREE THAN WELCOME—A PROSPECTIVE FIX.

Nigger. " Now den, Massa Jonathan, what you goin' to do wid dis Child! Eh ! "

More Free than Welcome—A Prospective Fix. *Punch* **43** (1862): 160. (*Courtesy of the University of Iowa Libraries*.)

Abe Lincoln's Last Card: or Rouge-et-noir. *Punch* 43 (1862): 161. (*Courtesy of the University of Iowa Libraries.*)

Troubled Waters"[37] in which Uncle Sam as an aroused farmer warns off the tubby neighbor boy, John Bull, from fishing in his stream. By the end of the magazine's run, however, Jonathan appeared as another farm or working boy warning Fernando Wood, the Democratic mayor of New York during the 1863 draft riots, against preaching peace during wartime. In "The Repudiation of Aminadab Sleek,"[38] Jonathan growls at Wood (pictured as a Quakerish preacher), "Your peace preachin' don't seem to agree with Miss Columbia's turn of mind, it don't. No sirree! An ef you don't want to rile my fine temper, you'd best dry up, just and walk your chalks!" Jonathan, the democrat, typically suggested informal popular action for dealing with domestic threats;[39] while Uncle Sam, with the power of the government presumably behind him, dealt with official matters.

Punch vs. the Americans

Punch ran dozens of political cartoons commenting on the American Civil War, many of which featured a Jonathan character. Particularly in view of *Punch*'s influence on American drawing, of most interest was the addition of Lincoln's beard to the Jonathan figure. While an occasional cartoon had earlier put a beard on the Jonathan figure, during the early sixties, a gradual metamorphosis blended the caricature of Jonathan with Lincoln's rough features in political cartoons drawn by *Punch* artists. There is, for example, little difference between the Massa Jonathan, featured on page 160 of the 18 October 1862 issue of *Punch* and the caricature of Lincoln, featured opposite that cartoon on page 161. Actually John Tenniel gave both Lincoln and his Southern card-playing opponent Jonathan's striped pants while John Leech drew a so-called Jonathan who looks at first glance like the standard caricature of Abraham Lincoln.[40]

Less influenced by *Punch*, the American *Yankee Notions* continued to depict Brother Jonathan in its cartoons as the stereotypical bumpkin from the stage, the common-sense voice of the people, the irascible ordinary citizen ever ready to uphold his people's honor. A pair of cartoons,[41] for example, published in *Yankee Notions* dredges up essentially the same comic situations used in *The Forest Rose*, when Sally left the sleeping Jonathan cuddling a cat instead of her. In these cartoons, Jonathan's sweetheart has left him holding a butter churn. In addition to these similarities to earlier versions of Jonathan, a number of visual and verbal jokes rest on the Jonathan character's unparalleled gall—as when he all but forces a startled genteel theater-goer to lend him his opera glasses,[42] or when he assures John Bull that Strong's *Yankee Notions* "is a little ahead of all on 'em."[43] Despite Jonathan's boast, *Yankee Notions'* covers from the February and March issues of 1864 illustrate that the magazine's artists had begun by that time to follow *Punch*'s lead in mixing and merging the images of Brother Jonathan, Uncle Sam, and Abraham Lincoln.

The interchangeable characters of Brother Jonathan, Uncle Sam, and young Yankee Doodle continued to assert themselves in *Yankee Notions*, although Uncle Sam seems to have appeared most frequently.[44] After a few years the artists from *Yankee Notions* also began to make use of some of *Punch*'s conventions in depicting Jonathan or Uncle Sam. On the March 1864 cover of *Yankee Notions*,[45] for example, Uncle Sam wears the star-spangled shirt that *Punch* usually put on Jonathan's shoulders. Uncle Sam whittles away in this illustration at a secession rail with a sharp knife labeled Grant and calls out to Seward who is sharpening still another knife. "You needn't grind any more, Billy. I've got a blade sharp enough now to whittle this tarnal rail into a toothpick!" Though Uncle sam talks in Jonathan's dialect, he is clearly playing Lincoln's role by engaging in splitting—in a sense—rails.

By the end of the war, a woodcut in the same magazine features a dignified Uncle Sam, looking much as we know him today, resting in peace and security as he gazes off the right hand page into the future.[46] Here,

Uncle Sam and Wm. Seward. *Yankee Notions.* 13 (1864): 65. (*Courtesy of the University of Wisconsin Libraries.*)

Uncle Sam has taken over Jonathan's oracular role. The pumpkins the figure sits on might also associate him with the Yankee, but they also might be a substitute cornucopia. The rowdy Jonathan still showed up occasionally, however. He can be seen in this magazine, for example, "working" the Atlantic cable as a free-dealing entrepreneur;[47] and though labeled Uncle Sam, the figure in the double spread "Judgment of Solomon" deciding between the claims of the North and South is also clearly Brother Jonathan in all but name.[48]

The Civil War

CARTOONS

Although still beardless, the Brother Jonathan figure ages in Civil War cartoons. This slightly older figure appears in cartoons that almost repeat the designs of earlier cartoons. An untitled wood engraving from 1860,[49] for example, even brings to mind "Uncle Sam Sick with La Grippe." This print resurrects the image of an ailing Uncle Sam in a flag-like dressing gown and night (or liberty) cap sitting in an overstuffed chair. The American eagle stretches out its wings in defiance of Doctor South, a genteel-looking planter. Hanging from his back pocket is the label of his prescription, "Secession." Doctor South wants to amputate Uncle Sam's left hand. In fact, he already has a tourniquet in place and his bowie knife in hand. At the left Dr. North—a Jonathan figure practically identical with the figure glimpsed through the window in "Uncle Sam Sick with La Grippe"—also feels Uncle Sam's pulse. He observes that his vial of "Constitution" drops, rather than amputation, will provide a "capital remedy for an inflammatory State." The three figures in this print also seem to have been copied from other sources; yet in light of the triangle of tension often set up in stage comedies featuring the Jonathan figure, the opposition between the rumpled ordinariness of Brother Jonathan and the prosperous gentility of the Southern figure graphically embodies the social, geographic, and economic tensions implicit in the relationship between the wealthier plantation owners of the South and the wage-earners, small businessmen, and farmers of the North.

A serious, even vindictive, Jonathan appears in another cartoon from the early part of the war. In the lithograph "The Way to Fix 'Em" (1861), Jonathan roasts little human figures over the flames of Fort Sumter. In his traditional dialect he gloats, "So you will misbehave yerselves and go burning down forts and raising old Cain ginerally will yer? I'll jist give yer a roasting over the fire you have made, and'll see if you relish that you pesky varmints you." Weitenkampf[50] attributes the publication of this print to T. W. Strong, the publisher of *Yankee Notions*, and the humor is on a par

[Untitled] Dr. North—Uncle Sam—Doctor South (1860). (*Courtesy of the New-York Historical Society, New York City.*)

**Civil War envelope imprint (1861–1865) (Jonathan as North). (*Courtesy of the State
Historical Society of Wisconsin Iconographic Division.*)**

with what one would expect to find in *Yankee Notions*.

Equally cocksure and pugnacious, "5 to One," (1861), depicts an oddly weak-chinned Jonathan defending a hill labeled '76 with a Union flag stuck in it against five Southern soldiers running back to the palm trees behind them. The Capitol rises behind Brother Jonathan while several grotesque black figures, presumably black slaves, fiddle and dance in joy. A proud bantam cock holds center stage in this lithograph published by an Ohio printer.

Not all early war prints assumed such a confident air. "Wait 'Till the War Is Over" (1861) implies in two lithograph panels that any sharp Jonathan who trades with the South is unlikely to collect payment. Once again, the Southern terrain is indicated by a palm tree in the background as well as a "Mason and Dixon's Line" sketched between the panels. Feet up, whittling away in his storeroom, the Jonathan in the left panel belongs to a long line of shrewd Yankee traders. The lithograph was probably intended as a warning for traders who thought they could increase their profits by supplying the South as well as the North.

The British Lion heedless of the **Trap**,
The string of which is held by **Emp'ror Nap**,
Bent upon Cotton, boldly takes the field
Which simple **Jonathan**, he thinks, will yield.

Civil War envelope imprint (1861–1865) (Jonathan with Emperor Napoleon and British Lion). (*Courtesy of the State Historical Society of Wisconsin Iconographic Division.*)

The familiar lack of distinction between Brother Jonathan and Uncle Sam found in political cartoons evidenced itself as well on envelopes specially printed during the early years of the Civil War. Supporting the Northern cause and printed anonymously or by better-known firms such as S. C. Upham, Brown and Ryan, Baker, and J. R. Hall, these envelopes featured crudely sketched cartoons in the upper left-hand corner. Verse, puns, and unsubtle jokes often accompanied the cartoons. Although the American figure on some of these envelopes may be identified as either Uncle Sam or Brother Jonathan, he more closely resembles the latter.[51]

Post War

Postwar cartoons illustrate the point that the visual distinctions between Brother Jonathan and Uncle Sam took longer to sort themselves out in separately published cartoons than in periodicals. Two lithographs in particular manifest postwar dissatisfactions. "Jeff Davis, the Compromiser, in a Tight Place" (1865), features a rope-toting Uncle "Sammy" anxious to hang Jeff Davis, who has come to the Senate with a compromise solution only to be pinioned in a closing door by an armed Zouave. The drawing in this print is better than in the next. The design is better organized, and the idea supporting the design is fresher. But the Jonathan-Sam figures remain closely allied.

"The Reconstruction Policy of Congress, as illustrated in California" (1867) argues vehemently against universal male suffrage. Looking more like today's Uncle Sam than the figure in the last print—although both figures are still beardless—this Jonathan harangues the figure of a man who literally supports universal male suffrage. In a spirit similar to that of the nativist Jonathan portrayed in "More Free Than Welcome," this character warns his listener—and the rest of the country awaiting the Fifteenth Amendment to take effect in 1870—"Young Man,[52] read the history of your Country, and learn that this ballot box was dedicated to the white race alone. The load you are carrying will sink you to perdition, where you belong, or my name is not Jonathan." Extraordinarily vicious by today's standards, uncouth racial caricatures represent black, Asian, and Indian men pyramiding above the young white supporter; and another character suggests adding a monkey to their ranks. Jonathan holds his hand over the transparent ballot box set on a flag-draped base. Such heavy-handed use of Jonathan in some of these later cartoons recalls Samuel Johnson's quip about patriotism being the last refuge of scoundrels.

In separately published lithographs, the two previous cartoons featured the Jonathan-Sam figure that contemporary readers identify as Uncle Sam.

The Reconstruction Policy of Congress (1867). (*Courtesy of the Prints and Photographs Division, Library of Congress.*)

By the sixties, Jonathan, the sly countryboy only occasionally appeared in periodicals. In fact, from 1865 on American periodicals generally either used a figure with Jonathan's characteristics and called him Uncle Sam, or they did not name the figure at all.

By the end of the war, for whatever reason and despite occasional atypical appearances, the Jonathan figure had disappeared from American cartoons. These postwar lithographs shed some light on his disappearance. Both "Jeff Davis, the Compromiser" and "The Reconstruction Policy of Congress" deal with extremely emotional issues during the tense years right after the war. Davis, for example, eventually received an amnesty from Andrew Johnson as part of a blanket pardon at Christmas of 1867. This pardon included even those Southerners under indictment for treason or other felonies. Clearly, some unionists would gladly have seen Davis executed instead. Universal suffrage also remained controversial after the Civil War. Many of these prints illustrated prejudice against blacks. In 1868, blacks could still not vote in half of the Northern states. In dealing with such emotionally charged issues, both cartoons employ a hybrid Jonathan-Sam character who still looks like Jonathan but who has lost most of Jonathan's humor as well as his dialect. The character does, however, still have a sense of the rabble about him. As the Jonathan figure loses this sense of the joker and the rebel, he melts into Uncle Sam.

Jonathan worked well enough as the emblem of everyman during the democratic period of largely conforming originals. The Jonathan figure also aptly identified American differences in opposition to European figures. During the Jacksonian period—even though he was often utilized to mouth the opinions of genteel leaders—the Jonathan figure symbolized the ordinary American citizen. Nonetheless by the 1850s and 1860s the frontiersman was capturing the popular romantic imagination that had earlier adulated Jonathan. So many of the cartoons identify Jonathan as a Northerner in opposition to the Southern cause that this identification may have made the figure forever unacceptable to many Southerners and Westerners.[53] In addition to these difficulties, many of the cartoons during the 1850s increasingly used the Jonathan figure to make social rather than strong political or economic comments. Cartoonists and their audiences may have found Jonathan just too provincial and limited to comment on the larger issues of the post–Civil War world. Uncle Sam, on the other hand, was vaguer and hence a more durable figure. He symbolized the nation as a whole or its government. Lacking the symbolic sectional and social baggage of the Jonathan figure, the figure of Uncle Sam could more easily represent the industrialized power of the United States that developed after the Civil War.

6

Refracted Images in Occasional Verse

THE ORIGINAL BROTHER JONATHAN OF CARTOONS WAS A COUNTRYBOY EMBODY-
ing native simplicity and wisdom. His American admirers even insisted
that his intellectual and social limitations actually functioned as virtues.
Jonathan's lack of opportunity to obtain either academic education or social finesse, for example, encouraged him to develop instead his natural
wit. Moreover, because of his frequent recourse to native guile, in cartoons
as on stage, Jonathan's stratagems and comments flourished with original
and unexpected turns in an often barren imaginative landscape.

The Jonathan figure appeared almost everywhere in America's popular
culture during the first half of the nineteeth century. In addition to being a
staple of Yankee comedy and political and social cartoons, the figure
showed up in many popular artifacts: from the covers of cigar boxes to
music scores; as the name of steamships and locomotives; in magazine and
book titles; as the author of American, British, and European novels; as a
commentator on American or foreign manners, religion, and women; as
the butt of jokes found in occasional verse and prose pieces in newspaper
and other periodical literature as well as in almanacs and jest books; as the
heroic persona of young America in popular writing. Among these scattered references, however, the mass of American readers probably
bumped into the risible character of Jonathan most often in occasional
verses and in almanac, periodical, and joke book anecdotes. But while
literary efforts to mine the vein of Jonathan's perceived originality showed
alterations in the perception of the Jonathan character between the Revolutionary and Civil Wars, the Jonathan of occasional verse and humorous
anecdotes showed minimal progression beyond the sly bumpkin.

Broadsides

Although Jonathan made frequent appearances before the Civil War in

119

humorous verse and anecdotes, he neither developed his stage personality and nor did he change into Uncle Sam as he had in political cartoons. The many people who used the figure seemingly could not agree on its significance. Many of the earliest producers of the Jonathan figure perceived only the boorish country clown in him. The British and loyalists used Jonathan's name as a disparaging nickname for the rebels during the revolution. That, for example, was how the name was used in a humorous ballad, "Yankee Doodle's Expedition to Rhode Island," satirizing the combined forces of the French fleet under Count D'Estaing and the American troops under General Sullivan.

> From Lewis, Monsieur Gerald came,
> To Congress in this town, sir,
> They bow'd to him, and he to them,
> And then they all sat down, sir.
>
> Begar, said Monsieur, one grand coup,
> You shall bientot behold, sir;
> This was believ'd as gospel true,
> And Jonathan felt bold, sir.[1]

In a similar vein, "A Pastoral Elegy," a poetic dialogue between Jonathan and Isaac, satirically lamented the American rout at Camden, South Carolina, on 16 August 1780. In contrast to Gates's success at Saratoga, the elderly general's main distinction at Camden resulted from the speed and distance of his retreat.[2]

Charles Fessenden's American ballad "Jonathan's Courtship or The Country Lovers" depicted Jonathan as a cloddish plowman. Rewritten several times during the next twenty years after its first appearance as a broadside around 1795, and reprinted in anthologies, Fessenden's verse tale about a twenty-one-year-old Jonathan being pushed out by his mother so that he can court a girl who resembles Shakespeare's greasy Joan set the tone for much subsequent occasional verse featuring this comic character. Taught by his mother to make a bow, the Jonathan of Fessenden's poetic effort makes several. Each time he looks like "the cramp had caught him."[3] Nervous, he cannot summon any further social graces; Jonathan does not stand much of a chance, even with Sal who wears a shoe on one foot and a stocking on the other. When Jonathan lists a calf among the goods he would bring to their proposed marriage, her response is that Jonathan's father would "best by half/Keep his bull calves at home." Overcome with embarrassment, Jonathan starts to tremble. Assuming he is having a seizure, Sal dumps a bucket of water on him.[4]

Unfortunately, characteristic use of Yankee rural dialect sometimes was made to bear the full weight of authenticating the writer's message. The frame used by the versifier was often no stronger than the disembodied dialect voice of an unknown narrator. Hence, a broadside verse composed to be sung in celebration of the first half-century of American independence starts out:

Some years ago as father says, "For
Funnel Hull was rais'd
A mess of folks where Plymouth lays,
Stood on a rock amaz'd
And there they lean'd, and loll'd, and set,
All moping in the dumps;
Till fear of getting cold and wet,
Soon made 'em stir their stumps:

and the chorus rings in:

They built a house from iron free
'Cause wooden pins drove silently.[5]

Since the author of this fragment, "Jonathan's Account of the Pilgrim People," is not entirely sure whether to laugh at or to extol the simplicity of his narrator, his audience is also of two minds. The contrast between the implied praise of the intrepid pilgrims and the satiric debunking of their heroic stature leaves readers or singers unsure of the final effect. The rimes too are so strained that it is difficult to ascertain whether the versifier meant to be funny, perhaps could not think of a better rime, had some meaning that is no longer clear, or was unaware of the laughable entanglements of triple rimes. The conflict between the original purpose of Jonathan as a clear-cut comic figure and his evolution into a lively symbolic character apparently provided continuing difficulties for versifiers during the first decades of the nineteenth century. They often could not decide whether to poke fun at the countrified naiveté of the Jonathan figure or to sentimentalize his native virtue and common sense. Trying to do both at once, writers often produced verses that were diffuse and confusing in tone.

The Jonathan of the lyric about nation-building is an all-purpose countryman whose voice gives a sense of place and perhaps continuity to an historical celebration, but who lacks any further definiton. When writers tried to define the Jonathan character in verse or in the ephemeral anecdotes and tales of periodical and chapbook literature, Jonathan sometimes emerged as the inarticulate clod found in Fessenden's and in other very early nineteenth-century verse. Only gradually and occasionally did the "something extra" quality of the stage Jonathan also came to the fore in the verse presentations of the Jonathan figure.[6]

Newspapers

Newspapers also used Jonathan in order to make fun of bumpkins and to react to public events. The Charleston *City Gazette and Daily Advertiser* of 3 September 1795, addressed the populace as Brother Jonathan with a song set to the tune of Yankey [*sic*] Doodle. Since the ordinary citizens were incensed over Jay's treaty with England, the "wise" voice of the song cautions against precipitous action and for trusting leadership, in this case George Washington.

Brother Jon'than, what are you *'bout*,
What the nation ails you?
Why with treaty make such *rout*!
'Vow, your reason fails you.

Chorus—Yankey Doodle, keep it up,
Yankee Doodle, dandy;
Sure you've had a *pow'rful* cup,
'Lasses mix'd with brandy.

Sure, if treaty is not right,
Georgy will not sign it;
'Till't has teeth it cannot bite'—
To him then resign it.
Yankey Doodle, etc.[7]

Verses often depicted Jonathan and his girl in the stereotypical pastoral style of rude country lovers. A couple of pieces, for example, in *The Port Folio* of May and July 1802 presented a clod-like countryboy whose dialect, nevertheless, eventually begins to sound lively as well as risible. In a burlesque of Wordsworth's style, the Jonathan of the first selection declares his love to Jemima. Jonathan admits that he has watched in sick admiration as Jemima milked the cows.

Don't you remember t'other day,
When you was milkin in the piggin,
You had a straw hat on your head,
But on your neck there was no rigging.[8]

Depressed at what he fears must be an impossible suit, Jonathan despairs—and then reverts instead to the entirely practical character familiarly found in the comedies.

I thought you would not marry me,
You're so much prettier than I;
So I resolv'd to hang myself,
For still I thought that I should die.

I took a rope and went away. . . .
My heart was sorer than a bile. . . .
But when I got it round my neck,
I says, thinks I, it an't worth while.[9]

After he returns home, Jonathan's family cheers him up; so he comes back to propose again to Jemima.

The second selection from *The Port Folio* ran but six stanzas and featured a rustic dialogue between Jonathan and Jemima in imitation of the classical colloquy between Lydia and Horace. Although each has since declared love for another, Jonathan opens the way to reconciliation with these lines:

But Mima, if we both should wish
Again in love's horse-pond to fish,
Should I reject Chloe's dazzling charms
And press thee glowing in my arms.[10]

Though rather appalling poetry, the selections demonstrate two characteristic traits. First of all, in none of Jonathan's appearances does the character show any talent or skill in romantic dalliance. He is too immature and unformed to be anything but an inveterately awkward suitor. Secondly, in these verse pieces the writers pulled together traditional verse forms such as ballads and pastoral lyrics[11] in order to make fun of those whom they considered their social inferiors, but in so doing the versifiers also happened upon the dialect potential of Yankee speech that gives the selections whatever distinction they display. Metaphors like "fishing in love's horse-pond," are purposely homey and ludicrous yet somehow apt and certainly more vital than the pretentious and abstract poetry popular in genteel writing. The earthy language accurately reflects character. Though Jonathan is surely intended to be a figure of fun, he sounds real. That alone hands him a marked advantage over the air-drawn characters who float through other American poems of the period.[12] In errant pieces such as these selections from *The Port Folio*, the beginnings of a native American poetry appear, poetry written by people who no longer considered themselves British provincials but citizens of an entirely new nation.

During the latter part of 1823 and the first few months of 1824, Peter Force's Washington, D.C., *National Journal* published seven short ballads reprinted, for the most part, from other newspapers. In these verses another conventional form grew into recognizable shape and quickly disappeared. Though intellectually and artistically lightweight, these verses were American in diction and in attitude; and unlike the verses that first appeared with a Jonathan persona, these ballads seemed to show that Jonathan could provide social insights as well as laughs. Exhilarated with their attempts at using Yankee speech to express ideas and emotions, anonymous writers had the Jonathan persona exhibit joy in living, pride, naiveté, and that characteristic sly humor for which the Jonathan character came to be best known. All of the poems open with a conventional rhetorical question—either "Did you ever?" or "Was you ever?"; and like stage Yankees the narrators of each poem often lapse into the speech tags that generally identify Jonathan. "I guess," dialect words, and dialect spellings thread through the ballads. Jonathan is always the speaker.

The first two, "Jonathan's Visit to Uncle Sam's Thanksgiving," reprinted from the Brooklyn, Connecticut, *Observer*, and "Jonathan's Visit to the Steam-Boat," reprinted from the Providence *Journal*, express wholehearted contentment in being American. In the former piece, Jonathan gloats over the food and fun available at a communal Thanksgiving celebration. The eight stanzas of the poem tell of a slightly different "traditional" meal than we experience today and a village-wide rather than a familial celebration. Jonathan, however, cannot join in the dance, for, as with all things romantic, he is inept.

> Did you ever go up to Thanksgiving?
> I swaggers! what oceans o' cakes!
> Confounded fine lots o' good living!
> What a darnd sight o' *lasses* it takes. . . .
>
> And then there's the fiddling and dancing,
> And gals! all as cute as a whistle!
> The fellows are kicking and prancing,
> Their legs are as limber as gristle.[13]

Only five stanzas long, "Jonathan's Visit to a Steam-Boat"[14] relates Jonathan's amazed but accurate description of that mechanical wonder. The poem's interest during the nineteenth century as now lay in the perception of the naive observer viewing with fresh wonder the advent of a machine that was starting to transform transportation and commerce. Although nationalism is not explicitly expressed, the poem implies American pride in American achievements and in the technical progress symbolized by the steamboat.

As in the comedies, the Jonathan character was sometimes used to express sentimental nostalgia for the old homestead. "Jonathan's Recollections," eight stanzas reprinted from the New York *Statesman*, implies a contrast between rural simplicity and the complexity of urban life. Jonathan recalls the joys of home:

> There's the settle bench (next to the fireplace)
> that now's the dandy;
> It's th' old gentleman's place by good rights;
> But when you go sparkin it's handy
> To set on in cold winter nights.

and finally ends with an accepted sentimental comment:

> But this isn't half I'd remember,
> If I was'nt driv' so this noon,
> You'd best go up there in September,
> I shall, if I don't go in June.[15]

Although the Jonathan of "Recollections" seems to be yearning for "one girl that I know up yonder," the narrator of "Jonathan's Visit to a Wedding," reprinted from the Baltimore *Patriot*, is more true to his romantically inept form in that he complains, "I can't get a sweetheart— I've tried—."[16] In this five-stanza lament, the Jonathan narrator starts by telling his audience what fun weddings are, goes on to bewail his own apparent inability to take a leading role in such a production, but ends by consoling himself with the hope that if he stops chasing the girls, perhaps they will chase him.

Another eight-stanza poem entitled "Jonathan's Visit to the Museum, or Christmas Night" and reprinted from the Portland (Maine) *Statesman* probably began as a Christmas-New Year's poem but appeared in the same February issue of the *National Journal* as "Jonathan's Visit to a Wedding." "Jonathan's Visit to the Museum" resembles his "Visit to a Steam-Boat" in that it purports to express the simple countryman's amazement at a current wonder, a wax museum. Since he is only expressing pleasurable curiosity, the last stanza sums up Jonathan's attitude, "I swaggers! in all my born days,/I never seed such *curus* cheer—/'Twas real fine fun. . . ."[17]

Two weeks later the *National Journal* published "Jonathan's Visit to a Bowling Alley." These nine stanzas did not name a previous source of publication. They also lack the verve of the other verses and may have been written by some local admirer of the earlier verses. Touched by an implausibly genteel spirit, they outline a few experiences at an inn, including watching a skilled bowler knock down all his pins, and end with Jonathan's recollection that,

They [his companions] then halloo'd out for their bill,
I vow I'll knock under to that;
If that want a darn'd bitter pill,
I bet you my best Sunday hat.[18]

The diction here seems more awkward than usual; and in addition, neither the situation (sipping brandy at a commodious inn) nor the tone (of one who has been graciously included in leisured relaxation rather than of a touchy outside observer) quite fits the usual pattern for the early Jonathan character.

The closest approach of the Jonathan character to the stage comedies and oral tales of folk tradition appeared in the last of these poems, "Jonathan's Account of Commencement," reprinted from the New Hampshire *Patriot* and signed with the pseudonym Jock. Instead of being the butt of educated men's jokes, this Jonathan makes fun of the ceremony that sends the educated into the world. By implication, he makes fun of educated men who participate in such a ceremony.

Did you ever go in to Commencement?
    I swow! it beats goggle ey'd Lydd!
She never kno'd nothing what sense meant,
    By gorsh! and she always did.

Lor! you, there was a whole bunch o' parsons,
    And *purcessions*, long as your arm,
With trumpets, and two on 'em brass uns,
    They sounded, by jingo, like a charm.

The meeting house was as full as a tick,
    I *skace* could get in, I was 'fear'd
'Twas *consid'able snug*, 'twas so thick—
    I'll tell ye, now, some that I heard—

No kai non ditterottedon kai toe!!
    That's the Greek now I'll be butter'd
Say what you're mind to, 'bout larnin, Joe,
    'Tis as good Greek as Ev'rett utter'd.

Nunc nonne rides—now can't you see, thro'
    This ere latin what ar'nt hoggy?
Bera-o-shyth baw-raw-haw—Hebrew—
    Gazzaloot vaw nedai boggee—

Oh by the gracious! they mouth'd such lingo
    As a jackass, when he's braying,
Their English was so *chaw'd*—by Jingo!
    'Twas hard to tell what was saying.

It seem'd like this—man is a *crea-chure*,
    But he is so formed by *na-cher*,
That he will twist 'bout ev'ry *fea-cher*,
    When he chaws red hot *pota-cher*!!!!

'Twas the sweatingest day you ever know'd,
    I got *tired*, and dry as a husk—
So pull'd up stakes; took to the road,
    And got along home about dusk.[19]

The satire hardly soars into wit; yet this speaker making fun of the academic procession's pomp and pretension prefigures the malicious naïveté of the narrative personae who later enliven Mark Twain's *Innocents Abroad* and *Huckleberry Finn*.

The confusion as to how exactly the Jonathan name might be used—whether to signify a local or national figure, whether to identify the lower classes or all Americans, whether it included just farmers and peddlers or city people as well—still showed up in an anonymous verse letter (1852)[20] commenting on what Americans perceived as British posturing at the opening of the Grand Exhibition.[21] The writer's language combines a disconcerting mixture of genteel vanity with dialect misspellings. The twenty-five-page epistle opens, for example, with the inflated apostrophe,

> May syncophantic adulation
> To her, our honest parent
> Pass from a Freeman's contemplation.[22]

Later the same speaker of the poem refers to England's "sodger crew."[23] The language reflects a confused tone and perspective as the poem shifts from pride in American independence of mind and spirit to bragging about America's literary lights. The poem's speaker mentions the names of Percival, Bryant, Whittier, Holmes, Halleck, George P. Morris, Nat Willis, Ralph Hoyt, Lowell, Boker, and Stoddard. (The omissions here are as curious as the inclusions.) But the writer undercuts his own praise of American literary figures even as he has earlier glorified American shipping:

> But thrifty Yankees do not sit
> To muse the silly rhyming fit;
> Men on this shore, whose mother wit
>   Like lightning plays,
> Must find the meat or turn the spit
>   Before its blaze.[24]

> We've beat you, John, at all we tried,
> And though you have the fact denied,
> Have seen our ocean steamers glide
>   Right by your own,
> To mock your song-invented pride—
>   An ocean throne.[25]

In his defense of American superiority, the "Jonathan" persona of the author stoops to funny but graceless personal attacks on the British monarchy like the following:

> You warm your golden egg for years—
> Your Prince of Wales, whose baby tears
> Are wiped away by careful peers
>   And bishops holy;
> There's not a Yankee boy but sneers,
>   At such a folly.

> And yet you wish us to admire
> The joke, and kindle into ire
> Because you cannot coax or hire
>   Us to produce,
> By roasting over such a fire,
>   As great a goose.[26]

After insults like this and a reference to Queen Victoria as "Albert's wife,/ Stuck on a throne,"[27] the author proposes to finish his letter in harmony with England and offers:

> When the half-conscious hireling troop
> That gather round your ancient coop,
> May need some sticking in the croop,
>   Or shake their ears,
> Just clear the track and hear the whoop
>   Of volunteers. [presumably from America][28]

With so little definition or development of the Jonathan persona, the verses he appeared in were necessarily "occasional." A balladic dialect rendition in *Vanity Fair* (1860),[29] for example, asserts that Brother Jonathan would not have allowed himself to be overwhelmed by the laziness and impudence of Irish servants, which has happened to his city cousin 'Zeke. This Jonathan—in contrast with the immigrant workers and his cousin—clearly represents the rural solidity and simplicity assumed by the sentimental tradition. He is so well defined, however, that he is actually limited. Unlike the country Jonathans of earlier comedies, who managed to represent American aspirations and democratic ideals, this Jonathan is primarily associated with a limited, petty vision engendered by small-town living.

Just as British and continental graphic artists continued to use Jonathan in cartoons after Uncle Sam became the usual American icon for Americans, *Punch* continued to publish verse comments on the American Civil War. In these verses another "wise" persona expostulates over the taking of Fort Sumter, the sheer stupidity of civil war, and Jonathan's absurd behavior in threatening the British against taking sides.[30] As in British cartoons, the Jonathan of these verses evolved into a personification of the North alone.

Although verse uses of the Jonathan figure were far more limited than those of the stage or those in cartoons caricatures, these illustrations suggest that the varied authors who wrote the verses started with a country character most notable for his bovine density. Within a generation, however, the character's language had gained an importance and stature it had lacked earlier. Even when an author made fun of Jonathan, he usually gave him the best lines. Like the stage character, the Jonathan of verse spoke in dialect. After little development, the original metaphors and fresh combinations of words and ideas characteristic of Jonathan's dialect began to suggest an alert, if untutored, intellect. Mispronunciations were common, but they often cast opprobrium on someone else instead of the speaker. "Jonathan's Account of Commencement" illustrates these trends.

Later songs about Jonathan seem to be relatively scarce. Nevertheless in addition to Lowell's lyric (see chapter 8) and the 1826 one we have mentioned, the 1870 "Complete Catalogue" of the Board of Music Trade[31] still listed several song titles that suggest a continuing market for the Jonathan

The Carpet Bagger. (*Courtesy of the Levy Collection, Milton S. Eisenhower Library, The Johns Hopkins University.*)

Jonathan Puff. (*Permission of the Bettman Archive.*)

figure of broadside verse. Some song sheets covered by lithograph prints
pictured Jonathan. While the Jonathan figure of political caricature had for
the most part been subsumed by Uncle Sam, when Jonathan appeared in
music illustration, he had become the Simon Legree or Northern carpetbagger vilified in the popular mythology of the Reconstruction.

During the 1820s and 1830s the Jonathan of verse turned into a common-
sense commentator voicing public scruples. Jonathan's persona was not,
however, like a reasoned letter to the editor; his wisdom resembled the
conversation at the local Elks club, tavern, or gas station.[32] Just as on
stage, where Jonathan had been used as the primary defender of American
values, in later verses Jonathan defended America against British
braggadocio—as in "Brother Jonathan's Epistle to His Relations"[33]—or
against hypocrisy—as in "Jonathan to John."[34] But as in cartoons,

Jonathan also commentated on contemporary American manners, usually confining himself nevertheless to superficialities of the social scene. No Jack Downing,[35] Jonathan seemed only peripherally interested in politics. On closer examination, the Jonathan figure proves to be primarily an urban construct, a nostalgic recollection of rural simplicity, rather than dirt and sweat reality.

The authors seemingly lost sight of the fact that Jonathan's simplicity had traditionally been a ruse. The stage Jonathan at least told tales and anecdotes from oral culture and connecting him with his roots. These verse productions, however, kept the figure's speech tags and his country origins but lost most of the sly wit and the abrasive self-interest of the stage character. The Jonathan of these verses instead became, almost pitifully, nice.[36]

Refracted Images in Comic Anecdotes

ACTUALLY, JONATHAN'S APPEARANCE IN OCCASIONAL VERSE WAS PROBABLY less noticeable and culturally significant than his periodic appearances in other popular literary forms. For example, anecdotes told by and about Jonathan surfaced regularly in jest books[1] and in humorous almanacs and periodicals before the Civil War.[2] While chapbooks—including those that anthologized popular jests—were on the wane in America after the Revolutionary War,[3] almanacs and periodicals became increasingly more important. Even before the revolution almanacs had become, in Marian Stowell's apt phrase, "The Colonial Weekday Bible"[4] and the only nonscriptural "book" available in almost every American household. Quoting from an 1845 *Almanack de France*, Clarence Brigham reminds his readers that even generations later almanacs provided "the village library."[5] In addition to the almanacs' statistical tables and agricultural advice, proverbs and poetry reinforced the received moral code by encouraging frugality, temperance, industry, piety, and upright living. In the early nineteenth century, some almanacs also began to include other practical reference material such as court and legislative calendars, church-meeting dates, and eventually stage and then railroad schedules.

Almanacs

During the 1830s beginning with Charles Ellms' 1831 *The American Comic Almanac*, a new variety of almanac became popular. Because these were more apt to contain jests about the Jonathan character, comic almanacs pertain to this study. Comic almanacs enjoyed a notable vogue for about a generation. For example, more than thirty varieties of comic almanacs with varying names and imprints were issued in Massachusetts alone between 1830 and 1860.[6] Since almanacs were indispensable in most households, they probably had as great an influence as any popular medium in spreading Yankee anecdotes about Jonathan.

In almanacs as in popular verse, Jonathan's country bumpkin origins are easy to detect. Years ago, Walter Blair pointed out in *Native American Humor* that the *Columbian Almanac for 1801*, for example, merely added Yankee touches and substituted the name of Jonathan for a "vaguely sketched countryman"[7] when it resurrected an anecdote that had already appeared in a 1796 almanac. In a side-by-side comparison, Blair showed that aside from the switch from the name of Hodge to Jonathan and the addition of a few Yankee phrases, the two versions are identical, even to the punchlines. (In response to a haughty woman's curt explanation that her fashionable style of dress is referred to as a sack, Jonathan drawls, "I vow, I have heard of a big in a poke, but I'll swap it, if I ever saw a sow in a sack before.")[8] The character was known for the quickness rather than the tact of his rejoinders.[9]

As in other media, comic almanac writers sometimes used the name Jonathan merely for local identification: a multisyllabic, Biblical-sounding, typically New England name. A spoof on a would-be love letter written in legal jargon and found in an 1831 comic annual, for example, has been allegedly "Sealed and Delivered in the Presence of Jonathan Jocus."[10] In like manner, the villainous Mexican in an almanac tale about the Mexican-American War intends to kill "one dam Jonathan Doodle General asleep," the dastardly fellow thinks to "wake him up dead, wid a bullet in his brain pan."[11] This Irish bull emitted by an English-speaking Mexican is no stranger than the configuration of the name of "Jonathan Doodle General." This same use of the name Jonathan as a local referent was also prevalent in jest book humor.[12]

In the years before the Civil War, the Jonathan figure functioned in several ways. As a national figure, like Uncle Sam, he was usually a one-dimensional figure appearing in readily forgotten sketches and anecdotes.[13] Upon occasion, however, the national figure was incarnated as a local figure with sly Yankee humor and orneriness. A short sketch appearing in an 1836 almanac recounts a tale about a Yankee peddler who called out a bullying Scotch major in the British army stationed in Montreal about the time of the revolution. The major had asserted that all Yankees were cowards; so the Yankee showed up for their duel with a rifle and insisted that the major lay down the dueling pistols. The major huffed that no gentleman would use a rifle in a duel, but he still lay down the pistols. "Now," said Jonathan, "I'll deal fair with you; I have the pistols, and you shall have the rifle."[14] The gentlemanly Scot picked up the rifle, cocked it, and pointing the muzzle at Jonathan, pulled the trigger—only to discover that the rifle was not loaded, that Jonathan—since he had been willing to face loaded pistols with an unloaded rifle—could hardly be called a coward; and that, by his own definition, the Scot himself was no gentleman.

An allied twist occurred in an anecdote appearing opposite the March calendar of an 1846 almanac:

Complimentary.—A Yankee and an English captain, each in a schooner, tried their speed in Gibraltar Bay, when our countryman beat John Bull all hollow. They met on shore next day, the Englishman swore he had never been outsailed before, "Just like me," said Jonathan, "my Jemima never beat nothing before."[15]

As a local embodiment of America, the Jonathan figure continued to appear in comic anecdotes as the boorish countrybody and the sly trickster. As a boorish bumpkin, Jonathan often showed up in ludicrous courting scenes designed to accentuate his lack of gallantry and his essential inexperience. Perhaps the implied message was that no one this inept could possibly be a threat. Jonathan is so little conversant with graceful manners, for example, that he refuses to pay the one cent toll for his girl when they come to a bridge. As he explains to her, "you must pay your own toll, for just as like's not I shan't have you arter all."[16] In other anecdotes Jonathan compares his beloved to boiled beef and dumplings[17] as well as to the more hackneyed strawberries and cream.[18] One Jonathan is so suspicious of the girl who accepts his carefully worded and tentative proposal that he walks away complaining, "By hokey, Sal! you are too willing—there is some trick in this."[19]

Plenty of other anecdotes simply poke fun at Jonathan's simplicity:

(1836) *"Darn 'em,"* said Jonathan at the battle of Bunker Hill, "they're shooting bullets!" when one of them passed through the top of his hat.[20]

(1836) *Crying Oysters.*—An honest Jonathan, from Berkshire, on his first visit to the metropolis, was awakened one night by hearing the cry of "oysters! buy any oysters!" in the mellifluous tones of one of the venders of these luscious shell-fish, who was passing under the windows of the hotel. A noise so new to his ear, startled him, and he aroused his room mate to inquire what it meant. "They are only oysters," replied his fellow-lodger, pettishly. "Oysters!" exclaimed Jonathan, in astonishment, "and do *oysters hollur* as loud as that!"[21]

(1839) The Countryman and his Saddle of Venison.—The Exeter News Letter relates the following excellent anecdote:—'A Countryman from the Northern part of the state, once called upon Gov. Wentworth at Portsmouth, and begged his acceptance of a saddle of venison. The Governor loved venison, and smiled most graciously upon Jonathan as he accepted the present, and thanked him for so acceptable a mark of his respect. But the man hemm'd and scratched his head and was in no hurry to depart. This errand was but half done. His excellency inquired of him, if he could in any way be of service to him, when Jonathan informed him that there was no Ensign in the military company at _____ and he would be *dreadfully* obliged to his Governorship for a commission. The Governor would be very happy to oblige him if he had the proper recommendations; and asked if the company had elected him for their Ensign, or sent any evidence of their wish for his appointment? 'Why, no, may it please your Excellency's Honor,' said Jonathan, 'There are only two other men in the town but myself, and one of them is the Captain, and the other the Leftenant, and they exercise me and manoevre me so much that I am really afraid if I'm not made in Ensign pretty soon, they'll drill me to death."[22]

More than Jonathan's simplicity is involved in these anecdotes, of course. The 1839 anecdote, for instance, satirizes Americans' penchant for military titles.

At the same time that Jonathan appeared as a dullard, he also appeared in other anecdotes as a wandering trickster capable of matching wits with and fooling anyone—but having his best fun with strangers who mistake his simplicity for stupidity.

(1834) There is in famous Yankee land,
A class of men yclep'd tin-pedlars,
    A shrewd sarcastic Band
        Of busy meddlers.
They scour the country through and through,
Vending their wares,—tin pots, tin pans,
Tin ovens, dippers, wash bowls, cans;
Tin whistles, kettles or to boil or stew,
Tin cullenders, tin nutmeg graters,
Tin warming pans;—for your fish and 'tator.
        In short,
    If you look within
        His cart,
    And gaze upon the tin,
        Which glitters there
        So bright and fair,
There is no danger in defying
You to go off without buying.

One of these cunning keen eyed gentry,
Stopp'd at a tavern in the country,
        Just before night,
And call'd for bitters,—for himself of course,
—And fodder for his horse.
        This done, our worthy wight
Informed the landlord that his purse was low,
Quite empty, I assure you, sir, and so
        I wish you'd take your pay
        In something in My way.
Now Boniface suppos'd himself a wag—
And when he saw that he was suck'd
Was not dispirited,—but pluck'd
Up courage,—and his trowsers too!
Quoth he to himself,—"I'm not apt to brag

'Tis true,
But I can stick a feather in my cap,
By making fun of this same Yankee chap."

"Well, my good friend,
That we may end,
This troublesome affair,
I'll take my pay in ware,
Provided that you've got what suits,
              My inclination."
       "No doubt of that," the Pedlar cried,
              Sans hesitation.

Well bring us up a pair of good tin boots!"
"Tin Boots!"—Our Jonathan espied
       His landlord's spindle shanks,
       And giving his good Genius thanks
              For the suggestion,
Ran out,—returned,—and then—"By Goles!
—Yes, here's a pair of candle molds!
They'll fit you without question!"[23]

(1836)   A Yankee Trick.
An eastern pedlar lately desired accommodation for the night, at a
tavern in the southern part of Virginia; but from the prejudice frequently
existing against this class, our host for a long time refused. At last he
complied, on condition that the pedlar should play him a Yankee trick
before he left him. The offer was accepted. On rising in the morning,
Jonathan carefully secured the coverlid of the bed, which, amongst other
articles, he pressed the landlady to purchase. The low price of the coverlid operated at once upon the latter, who insisted that her husband
should buy it, adding, that it should match her's exactly. Jonathan took
his money, mounted his cart, and had got fairly under way, when our
host called to him that he had forgotten the Yankee trick he was to play
him. "O, never mind," said Jonathan, "you'll find it out soon enough."[24]

(1837) "Halloo, Mister!" cried a passenger in a stage coach, to a rough
looking pedestrian, "can you tell me what has become of those goslings
which were hatched last year on the top of that rock?" "Four of them are
dead, sir," returned Jonathan, "and the other, I presume, is a passenger
in the stage coach." The gentleman was used up.[25]

The Jonathan character was primarily known for his sly wit rather than
for the sort of delight in extravagant language that characterized the humor
of the old Southwest. From time to time, nevertheless, he could be used to
wed the period's newly discovered frontier language to any nine-day's wonder such as Davy Crockett's use of frontier brag in fighting with Britain
over boundary claims. Thus, the 1836 almanac persona of Gim Watson

attempts to outbluff would-be opponents in the language popularized by Crockett.

Crockett Outdone

I am a real ringtailed roarer of a jaw breaker, from the thunder and lightning, down east. I've been rowed up salt river seventeen times, and I'm not sil'd; I make my breakfast on stewed Yankees and pork stake, and by way of digestion, rinse them down with spike nails and epsom salts; I take dinner on roast goose stuff'd with wild cats and onions; I sup on nothing but wind; I can sneeze the coat off Colonel Crockett's back, from down east to Tennessee, by taking a pinch of the Gineral's snuff; I can lick my weight and the Gineral's in wild cats or racoons; I can grin steamboat machinery out of place, and snort Major Jack Downing from Washington to his uncle Jonathan's barnyard. I am just what you may call a real snorter and gaul buster. I can out eat, out drink, out work, out gun, out snort, out run, out lift, out sneeze, out live, anything in the shape of man or beast, from Maine to Louisiana.—Gim Watson[26]

For the most part the dialect of the Jonathan in these anecdotal monologues set the character off as a countryboy totally lacking urban polish, but the language of almanac and jest book Jonathans generally also lacked the liveliness of the stage Jonathans. Fresh new ways of expressing emotion, for example, seldom popped up in the speech of these characters. Nor did the Jonathans of almanac anecdotes take pains to speak in metaphors that were not hackneyed with repetition. Their language only occasionally stretched the imagination with its unexpectedness. In all probability, neither writers nor readers worried about character's dialect. The jokes most commonly revolved around the sense rather than the sound of Jonathan's speech. In contrast, stage Yankees built careers on their ability to accurately ape Jonathan's sound.

The dialect language of the Jonathan original at his best could be expected to deflate pretensions, to achieve down-home metaphors that made the listener recognize unexpected—and often absurd—similarities; it abounded in mispronunciations that made someone else look foolish. Whether Jonathan's lines were the laconic replies of the peddler dealing with the Scottish major bullying others into duels or rambling Yankee tales testing just how far the narrator could go, Jonathan was always taking the hot air out of someone's delusions. In "Crockett Outdone" for example, the inflated style of other popular characters was so effectively parodied as to make them smaller rather than a little larger than life size.

Jest Books

As the notes to this chapter indicate, much of the same humor about the

Jonathan figure that appeared in almanacs also appeared in jest books. From the first, the Jonathan in jest books showed himself to be much the same apparently ingenuous dolt appearing in other media. Jonathan might exercise physical courage as well, but he preferred using his wits. For instance, in an early jest book, Jonathan is gulled into playing a game of follow-the-leader, whereby several townsmen intend to force him to pay for their night out. Jonathan calls for a dentist to pull all the teeth in his mouth. The townsmen decide that they would rather pay his expenses as well as their own rather than follow his lead. Since Jonathan only has one tooth—and that a loose one—he is taking little real risk in order to win out over the others.[27]

Periodicals

Since American publishers of newspapers, magazines, almanacs, and chapbooks all felt free during this era to lift items from one another, the same jest or its first cousin may reappear in another setting. So the Jonathan figure played a similar role in comic periodicals to the one he played in almanacs and jest books. The joke about the soft-soaping Jonathan from *Elton's 1851 Almanac*, for example, reappeared verbatim a year later in the first volume of *Yankee Notions*.[28] However, since newspapers and magazines had more space than almanacs or jest books to amplify a sketch, they generally developed the Jonathan role more fully. At times this led to a pun-laden tale of Yankee ingenuity; at other times a folk exaggeration seemed to be reworked into a tale suited for popular consumption. At still other times, the Jonathan persona seems to be used as an all-purpose mask from which to satirize contemporary fashions and foibles. In this last situation, the Jonathan figure—with diminished craftiness, less country flavor, and fewer crotchets—subsided, apart from his dialect, into an almost genteel character. He thus was ready to blend into Uncle Sam, whose symbolic meaning contained no sharply obtrusive personality traits. The Jonathan of these anecdotes saved his criticism for safe targets: the clearly foolish stage passenger or clearly foppish dandy, the stuttering foreigner who foolishly took on a deceptively mild-looking Jonathan, the innkeeper who wanted to experience a Yankee trick. The audience could neither identify with nor take offense at jokes at the expense of such easy general targets.

The grasping entrepreneur of the comedies demonstrated many unlikable qualities, such as anti-Semitism and prejudice against the Irish and blacks. Unlikable as these traits were, nevertheless they saved Jonathan from an innocuous gentility. In almanac and jest books, however, the Jonathan character so blunted his criticisms that one senses only the slightest enmity even toward the wealthier, established groups in society.

ENGLISH TRAVELLER.—*Hi Say, Sir, Ham I on the right road to 'Artford.*

JONATHAN.—*Well, you be.*

TRAVELLER.—*How far shall I ave to go before I get there?*

JONATHAN.—*Well, if you turn reound and go 'tother way may be you have to travel abeout ten mile. But if you keep on the way you are going, you'l have to go abeout eight thousand, I reckon.*

English Traveller. *Yankee Notions* 3 (1854): 278. *(Courtesy of the University of Iowa Libraries.)*

Although some anecdotes exploited social and sectional tensions, they did so in such safe and general ways that they seldom exhibited any satiric bite.

In such anecdotes, Jonathan was a social commentator who no longer possessed a unique angle of vision. Variants still circulate, for example, of Jonathan's tale about a man who lent a neighbor an umbrella on a wet, nasty day only to be refused its return when he needed it on another day— because the borrower was using it.[29] In "Jonathan's Visit to the Opera," "Uncle" Jonathan complains that the audience seemed to spend more time spying out one another's attire through opera glasses than watching or listening to the performance.[30] Such comments could, of course, have been made by *Punch* or any other gadfly.

More of Jonathan's wickedly guileless approach to pretension appears in a pert little sketch in which Jonathan gloats over the way he put a congregation of fashionable big city hypocrites in their places:

Jonathan about Town

Jonathan.—Well, Aminadab, as I was telling you, I walked right down the middle of the congregation, a lookin right and left, to see if any of the folks would invite a feller to take a seat. But, darn my buttons, ef they wasn't all lookin at the parson jest as hard, eenamost, as a country school-boy at Barnum's new and improved petrified hoss. It made me feel like a strange pig in a pig-pen. But I kalkilate I got them for all that. Jest castin my eyes around, I seed a three-sided pin stick layin by the side of the stove, and permiscously takin it up, I walked back, right down in front of the parson, sot in one end, and squatted myself. Well, I had no more'n got my eyes on the preacher, when the pew doors began to open, and sitch an invitin to *kum in*, you never did see. But I determined to go in cahouts with the parson, and give 'em a double barrilled sermon on decency and perliteness. So I never, turned my eyes around, but sot there till the eend—then stuck the stick under my arm—walked back to the stove—laid it down—and then—walked out!

Aminadab.—I kalkilate that kongregation'll take a feller in the next time.[31]

A somewhat different use of Jonathan appears in a dialect editorial in the 1 May 1854 edition of *Yankee Notions*, which ends with a comic exaggeration that feels as if it has sprung from a folk saying. The editor —as Brother Jonathan—promises that the jokes in this and future issues will be funny enough to penetrate "the thickest skull. In fact those who believe that the Yankee notions ain't the funniest paper that ever was printed will be sucked as bad as aunt Aggy's cat." And then he recounts the fate of a cat that, evading his irate mistress, had fallen into a pan of milk so that when the frightened animal ran through the pasture, calves sucked him to death.[32]

Occasionally sketches of Jonathan's activities reflected the popular image of his indomitable ingenuity. An original tale by J. K. Paulding,

"Jonathan's Visit to the Celestial Empire," published in an 1831 issue of *The New York Mirror* belongs to this group. Long enough to be a short story, Paulding's tale recounts the absurdly exaggerated adventures of the young Jonathan, who in 1783 "fitted out his sloop, a tarnation clever vessel of about eighty tons, and taking a crazy old compass for his guide, his two cousins, one a lad about sixteen, and a great Newfoundland dog for his crew, and a couple of rusty revolutionary swords for an armament. . . boldly set forth on a voyage to the celestial empire."[33] Being Jonathan, he naturally overcomes all opposition and makes half a million dollars by being the first to sell ginseng to the Chinese after first convincing them that he is a poor, slow-witted countryboy ripe for fleecing. "A prosperous voyage ended in Jonathan's happy return to Salem," the tale finishes, "where he became a great man even to the extent of being yclept honorable. He lived long and happily, and his chief boast to the end of his life was that he had been the first of his countrymen to visit the celestial empire, and the only man that navigated with a Newfoundland dog for an officer."[34]

In this adept popular literary expression of a familiar figure, Paulding melded elements of the romance and the tall tale with a few touches of realism and put together an amusing early American example of wish fulfillment. Paulding's Jonathan is the American everyman, ready and able to take on the world. Cloaked in his Yankee dialect, he pretends to be taken in by the cunning orientals, but himself overcomes at last with his "infinite simplicity."[35]

Later newspaper anecdotes by or about the Jonathan character built anecdotes upon a single conceit. In one anecdote, for example, Jonathan tells about a Yankee who, in order to prove to his mother that the new parson's wife is not stingy, pretends to be a poor widow in need of help. He manages to get the woman to give away even her petticoat. Since the Yankee has bet the narrator that he can manage that feat, he also wins a bushel of corn for himself.[36] In another sketch "a trafficking Jonathan," piqued by the suspicious attitude of a Canadian customs officer, tricks the man into inspecting too closely the deep false bottom of his sawdust-laden wagon and then drives the hapless officer over three miles of a corduroy road. Finally the collector begs, "Oh, let me out!. . . You have pounded me on your wood-pile till my bones are almost broken, and if you will let me go, give me some water, and lend me a coat to wear home, you may smuggle if you like to all eternity, before I look at your traps again, only keep this exploit to yourself."[37] In the most satisfying of daydreams, the Jonathan figure could be downright malicious in obtaining vengeful satisfaction from authorities.

Unfortunately, these humorous anecdotes from jest books and almanacs and those later published in newspapers were often too succinct for the best expression of American humor. Or in straining to be popular, they failed to be trenchant. The best anecdotes, however, allowed the local character to mask his competence and national pride in a characteristically ironic brand of bragging, e.g., the sea captain who "never beat nothing before." As an ineffectual lover, tightwad, or trickster, Jonathan hardly differed from other similarly stereotyped figures. Yet when he was depicted as a local character with local traits, still intent on defending the national honor, the character same closest to being vivid and memorably funny.

While not entirely without development, the Jonathan of these anecdotes and short sketches remained primarily a "stupid" character whose main function involved making others appear intelligent. While J. K. Paulding and, later, J. R. Lowell, respected him, the bulk of the later short sketches show relatively little growth from the slighting 1780s references to Jonathan. Although the tradition that utilized Jonathan as the butt of humor died hard, when Jonathan was depicted as a national rather than a lower-class type, his laconic reactions masked sly wit.

As the next chapter demonstrates, some writers did attempt to develop the complexity implied in Jonathan's combination of inexperience and native wit. Even in longer works, however, writers continued to reinvent the one- and two-dimensional Jonathan of the humorous anecdotes.

8

Literary Development

IN LITERARY ATTEMPTS TO MINE THE VEIN OF JONATHAN'S PERCEIVED originality—as it was presented on the stage, in cartoon representations, and in anecdote humor—writers of fiction and cultural analysis eventually came to characterize the entire American nation under the pseudonym of Brother Jonathan. Jonathan thus altered during the period between the Revolutionary and Civil Wars and so did the favored means of representing his character. While late eighteenth-century references to Jonathan were still bound to the European traditional figure of the dull country lout,[1] J. K. Paulding gradually broadened and deepened the representation of America in his genially humorous explanation of the facts of American history. Retold in Paulding's tales and allegories during the 1810s and 1820s, Jonathan's history became part of a defense of American culture.[2] Finally, in his self-consciously American novel, *Brother Jonathan, or the New Englanders*, John Neal further developed what had been a minor stock figure to a full portrait of a complex character, an American Everyman.

Later workers in popular verse, fiction, and commentary continued to utilize the name of Jonathan; but the name and its significance flattened out. As in cartoons the eccentric costume of Brother Jonathan lingered on in Uncle Sam's form, although the latter figure was no longer an outsider. By the 1840s and 1850s Brother Jonathan often appeared in fiction and travelogues that retained his awkward turns of dialect speech and his country background but dropped his caustic outsider's insight and peremptory insistence on his own worth and dignity. A few British works allowed him some satiric bite; but for the most part by the Civil War the Jonathan character dwindled into genial obscurity. Yet before the eventual diminution of Jonathan into a nonentity, the character served during the antebellum period to enliven numerous anecdotes of American life. It also helped to provide a narrative frame for an array of primarily British and

American commentaries on American culture during the antebellum period.

Longer Nonfiction

In addition to overtly comic uses of Jonathan's name in anecdotes, nineteenth-century writers often employed the name to achieve a homey New England sound to their literary pseudonyms. When young Washington Irving, for example, first attempted the conventional "old bachelor" persona that he further developed in the Salmagundi Papers, he called his writer Jonathan Oldstyle. During 1824 after *The Sketch Book* and *Bracebridge Hall* had begun to establish a literary reputation for Irving, the nine letters on contemporary manners written and published in his brother's paper between 15 November 1802 and 23 April 1803 were published in pirated editions under the title of *Letters of Jonathan Oldstyle, Gent.*[3]

Irving made no explicit use in these letters of the Jonathan formula of character tags or vernacular language. It could be argued, in fact, that he had no conscious intent to connect his eighteenth-century epistolary efforts to the literary nationalism of the early nineteenth century. Nevertheless, Irving belonged to the same aspiring professional circles as did Paulding, and this group of friends consciously sought to develop distinctly American subjects and style in letters. Hence one might argue that Irving used the first name of Jonathan with the surname of Oldstyle to identify his narrative persona as an American belonging to the same tradition as Europe's literary gentlemen-bachelors. Irving, after all, always moved in elite circles in America and Europe and could be expected to want both his American and European readers to recognize that elite American and European culture had much in common. His choice of Jonathan as a name might, therefore, serve as a minor but explicit national identification tag.

GENTEEL ADVICE

The names of Jonathan, Brother Jonathan, even Uncle Jonathan and Grandfather Jonathan adorned a wide variety of personal commentaries and anecdotage by Americans and Europeans during the first half of the nineteenth century. Some wanted to praise American society. Others would gladly have buried it. Often these tales, sketches, and just plain ramblings by writers using the Jonathan persona had little to do with the developed character found in plays, cartoons, and anecdotes. Among other purposes writers used the persona as a mask behind which to preach their favorite gospels. A strange little homily, for example, on the text that "Man is born to sorrow" and illustrated with examples of the contrary fates of several men was entitled "Uncle Jonathan's Reflections" and reprinted in an 1806 collection of selections from contemporary newspapers.[4] The narrative frame provided a pipe-smoking Jonathan seated beside the hearth pensively administering advice to a young man. The homey rural pose fit Jonathan as he was known from other media, though this character lacked Jonathan's usual trenchant wit and irrepressible optimism.

In 1842 a retired editor, as he identified himself, put into print "Brother Jonathan's Wife: A Lecture," a sixteen-page paean to the American woman as an embodiment of the valiant woman of the thirty-first proverb. An odd combination of millenarian aspiration and the cult of domesticity, this piece assumed that American women already inhabited a paradise of sorts because, unlike all other women, an American woman was "free and independent as the wild winds of heaven." Examined more closely, however, her freedom consisted primarily in the "right of disposing of herself" in service to someone else.[5] But then the writer promised, "She spreads a paradise around her, and her warm and uncontaminated affections, enchant the soul. For kindness of heart, exceeding tenderness and high resolve, she has no superiors."[6] In this and other popular effusions, the author obviously hoped to catch the public's eye with the name of Brother Jonathan but used it for quite different purposes than the usual comic or patriotic ones.

HISTORY AS ALLEGORY

Beyond the common uses of Jonathan's name as mere catchword, stereotype, or persona, James Kirke Paulding further developed the concept of Brother Jonathan as an embodiment of America. He accomplished this primarily through allegories he wrote over a three-decade period starting in 1812. He began by using the Jonathan character as an allegorical representation of the entire United States in *The Diverting History of John Bull and Brother Jonathan*.

Paulding first published the *Diverting History* in September of 1812 but revised the text several times until the work was published in a fifth edition in 1835. This authorized text included a large section of satire on the comments of English travellers to America. While these latter chapters sound obscure and tiresome to contemporary readers, the early chapters on Brother Jonathan and John Bull are still sharp-edged and drolly amusing.

In Paulding's "history," the settlement of America, the American Revolution, the Napoleonic Wars and the eventual participation of the United States in the War of 1812 all dwindle into family and neighborhood activities and squabbles among the contentious people who have settled around the millpond sometimes referred to as the Atlantic Ocean. Paulding's strongly pacifist arguments here jar with his later sentiments as a committed nationalist who spent years as Van Buren's Secretary of the Navy. In his "history" Paulding argues by implication that for the most part the personnel and funds committed to war are so much waste, because they have to be taken from the country's productive capacity. According to Paulding, the strength of America is her peaceful attention to commerce and industry, at the same time that England wastes her substance in unnecessary and avoidable wars.

The John Bull of Paulding's history shows a mulish disposition to insist on his way even when he is clearly in the wrong. Since the neighborhood as a whole agrees only to "the famous statute of club-law"—meaning that the toughest bully with the biggest club wins—John Bull generally gets his way. Most complex and interesting, however, is Paulding's characterization of Brother Jonathan. Though clearly an allegorical representation, Jonathan conforms roughly to the character already familiar from other media:

> In a little time, Jonathan grew up to be large for his age, and became a tall, stout, double-jointed, broad-footed cub of a fellow, awkward in his gait, and simple in his appearance; but showing a lively, shrewd look, and having the promise of great strength when he should get his full growth. He was rather an odd-looking chap, in truth, and had many queer ways; but everyone that had seen John Bull saw a great likeness between them, and swore he was John's own boy, and a true chip off the old block. Like the old squire, he was apt to be blustering and saucy, but in the main was a peaceable sort of careless fellow, that would quarrel with nobody if you only let him alone. He used to dress in homespun trousers with a huge bagging seat, which seemed to have nothing in it. This caused people to say he had no *bottom*; but whoever said so lied, as they found to their cost whenever they put Jonathan in a passion. He always wore a linsey-woolsey coat, that did not above half cover his breech, and the sleeves of which were so short that his hand and wrist came out beyond them, looking like a shoulder of mutton. All which was in consequence of his growing so fast that he outgrew his clothes.[7]

When Paulding's awkward stripling as well as the country he represented had altered by around the time of the Civil War, Jonathan proved to be no longer an adequate American emblem. During these decades following the War of 1812, however, while the country was young, Jonathan still served as an excellent image of the young giant, growing into his strength, outgrowing his clothes and his earlier roles, awkward and bumbling as he tried to find his way, given to strategems and trickery to mask the limitations of his power.

In the *Diverting History* Paulding describes the different sections of the country as tenants from different areas; thus the tenants of each area retain a sectional loyalty to the Southlands, for example, the Middlelands, Down East, or the Far West. In explaining sectional distrust Paulding mentions that peddlers from Down-East regularly out-swap their neighbors to the south.[8] In fact, they have been known to engage in some very shady practices. And Paulding also tells about a tenant of John Bull called Oatlander having been stung in a horse swap with a "long-sided, rosy-cheeked, light-haired lad, who seemed as if he had just thrust his nose into the world. . . . This figure was learning over a gate, with one hand scratching his head, and supporting his chin with the other, in the true style of listlessness and simplicity."[9] In both instances, Paulding utilized the Yankee stereotype for New Englanders, while he used Brother Jonathan's name to signify the entire nation.

In addition to his book-length *Diverting History*, Paulding fired numerous shorter salvos against the British during the "paper war" that followed the War of 1812. In what a twentieth-century editor refers to as "perhaps the most temperate of Paulding's several replies by British critics of the United States,"[10] Paulding also published a satirical account of British-American relationships. This allegorical portrait of the "typical American," "Brother Jonathan" appeared in an 1825 issue of the *New-York Mirror*. Some elements of Paulding's analysis recall those of Crevecoeur and de Tocqueville. The Jonathan of Paulding's piece is a peaceful farmer, hard-working and confined by local interests. In addition, Jonathan's energies are taken up with practical matters; and while he is literate and devours periodicals and the Scriptures, he is "no great patron of literature."[11]

On the other hand, Paulding's portrait also resembles stage presentations of Jonathan in that Paulding consistently makes use of tags in his representation of Jonathan. Echoes of dialect, for example, remind readers of Jonathan's country speech when Paulding tells his readers that Jonathan was happy *"to do for himself,"*[12] that "he had yet some queer practical notions on the freedom of worship,"[13] and that he had no intention of being a mere tenant "at the time he settled down."[14] Paulding further explains that by the time of the Revolutionary War, "Jonathan had become a hard character."[15] And then after his independence Jonathan took the "notion"[16] to build a network of turnpikes. Jonathan is also accompanied by physical tags. For instance, he carries an axe and always has a pipe in his mouth.[17]

Poetry

Writers did attempt to raise the use of Jonathan to a somewhat higher literary plane than that of the occasional verses found in periodicals. And while the best of these efforts approach only the level of good comic verse, they indicate that the character had greater possibilities than those the occasional verses granted him. Vera Lawrence reprints from a 1862 collection a punning song about Stephen Decatur's squelching of the Algerian pirates in June of 1815. The poem may, of course, date from much earlier.

CARPE DIEM.—SEIZE THE DEY.

The Dey of Algiers, not being afraid of his ears,
Sent to Jonathan once for some tribute;
"Ho! ho!" says the Dey, "if the rascal don't pay,
"A caper or two I'll exhibit."

"I'm the Dey of Algiers, with a beard a yard long,
"I'm a mussulman too, and of course very strong;
"For this is my maxim, dispute it who can,
"That a man of stout muscle's, a stout mussulman."

"They say," to himself one day says the Dey,
"I may bully him now without reck'ning to pay;
"There's a kick-up just coming with him and John Bull,
"And John will give Jonathan both his hands full."

So he bullied our consul, and captur'd our men,
Went out through the Straits and came back safe again;
And thought that his cruisers in triumph might ply
Wherever they pleas'd, but he thought a big lie.

For when Jonathan fairly got John out of his way,
He prepar'd him to settle accounts with the Dey;
Says he, "I will send him an able debater;"
So he sent him a message by Stephen Decatur.

Away sent Decatur to treat with the Dey,
But he met the Dey's admiral just in his way;
And by way of a tribute just captur'd his ship;
But the soul of the admiral gave him the slip.

From thence he proceeded to **Algesair's** bay,
To pay his respects to his highness the Dey,
And sent him a message, decided yet civil,
But the Dey wished both him and his note to the devil.

But when he found out that the admiral's ship,
And the admiral too, had both giv'n him the slip,
The news gave his highness a good deal of pain,
And the Dey thought he'd never see daylight again.

"Ho! ho!" says the Dey, "if this is the way
"This Jonathan reckons his tribute to pay;
"Who takes it will tickle his fingers with thorns."—
So the Dey and the **crescent** both haul'd in their horns.

He call'd for a peace and gave up our men,

And promis'd he'd never ask tribute again;
Says his highness, the Dey, "here's the devil to pay
"Instead of a tribute; heigho, well-a-day!"

And never again will our Jonathan pay
A tribute to potentate, pirate, or Dey;
Nor any, but that which for ever is giv'n:—
The tribute to valour, and virtue, and Heav'n.

And again if his Deyship should bully and fume,
Or hereafter his claim to this tribute resume,
We'll send him Decatur once more to defy him,
And his motto shall be, if you please, **Carpe Diem**.[18]

Both the anapestic rhythm as well as the poem's internal rime and the puns reflect a notable sense of fun with language. In fact, the narrator is almost too urbane for the tradition in which Jonathan spoke for himself, deftly demonstrating as many failings as virtues. Yet "Carpe Diem" still belongs to the tradition in which Jonathan is the people and the people, the nation.

Even so well-known an author as James Russell Lowell utilized the Jonathan device upon occasion. His "Jonathan to John," (1862) demonstrates, in fact, the strengths and limitations of the Jonathan figure featured in all of these verses. Once again Jonathan is the poetic spokesman against British infringements—in this case, the British war material going to the South during the Civil War. Particularly in view of the high moral tone that the British press had earlier taken toward the institution of slavery in the United States, Lowell's Jonathan takes offense at the hypocritical turnabout that now allows the British to support the South in an armed conflict aimed at maintaining slavery.

Unlike most other versifiers mentioned, Lowell is in control of his material. Through his first series of Hosea Biglow papers, Lowell had already learned to control the dialect and persona featured in this poem. The Jonathan figure of this short poem seems, in fact, less truculent than the Hosea of the first series of papers. The Jonathan of "Jonathan to John" may be just as angry at the British who during the Civil War twisted the law and their commitments to suit their economic advantage as was the Hosea Biglow, who had no use for the recruiting sergeant seeking gun fodder during the Mexican-American War, but the author of both personae has better outward control of his anger in 1862 than he had in 1846.

"Jonathan to John" is a fourteen-stanza ballad-like poem, ostensibly by Hosea Biglow. The last section of the second part of this second series of his papers, the poem is framed and reframed by Hosea's musings as he walks on a moonlit night and dreams or hears the Concord Bridge and Bunker Hill Monuments discussing the perfidy of England's aid to the Confederacy. The entire paper is prefaced by a pseudo-erudite, pseudo-homey letter by Homer Wilbur, Hosea's pastor. Hosea's wise, homespun musings follow his pastor's letter. (His comment on people who try to prophesy when the war will end is that they resemble roosters who wake up the neighborhood at the wrong time because they confuse the full moon with the rising sun.)[19] Returning from his evening walk, Hosea "put some thoughts that bothered (him) in rhyme."[20] "Jonathan to John" is then the result of Hosea's[21] considerations.

In "Jonathan to John" a dialogue of sorts emerges as "Ole Uncle S." pipes in with an addendum in the second half of each stanza, in response to Jonathan's initial statement to John Bull. Ole Uncle S.'s "guess" is written in the same dialect as Jonathan's but usually adds something specific, an element of sagacity or worldly caution, as here:

> We ain't so weak an' poor, John,
> With twenty million people,
> An close to every door, John,
> A school-house an' a steeple.
> Ole Uncle S. sez he, "I guess,
> It is a fact," sez he,
> The surest plan to make a Man
> Is, think him so, J.B.,
> Ez much ez you or me!"
>
> We know we've got a cause, John,
> Thet's honest, just, an' true;
> We thought 't would win applause, John,
> Ef nowhereas else, from you.
> Ole Uncle S. sez he, "I guess
> His love of right," sez he,
> Hangs by a rotten fibre o' cotton:
> There's natur' in J.B.,
> Ez wal'z in you an' me![22]

And finally in the last stanza, Jonathan and Uncle Sam reassert their confidence in the rectitude of the Northern cause, which even "J.B." must, in time recognize.[23]

As popular verse, Lowell's poem is superior to most earlier uses of the Jonathan persona because Lowell had a topic that fired him with moral indignation, and he had considerably better control of the mechanics of his verse than had earlier producers of similar lyrics. Lowell's poem was popular enough, in fact, to be set to music by Francis Boott; whose title sheet was lithographed by Louis Prang, a German immigrant whose Boston presses produced the title pages for many songs during the Civil War.

Within a few years after the Civil War, Jonathan even appeared in a verse history of the conflict. Entitled *The New Yankee Doodle* (1868)[24] and

Jonathan to John (1862). (*Courtesy of the Levy Collection, Milton S. Eisenhower Library, The Johns Hopkins University.*)

authored by a woman who never publicly acknowledged that she wrote the book, this detailed account of events features a character called Old Jonathan. Distraught over the wretched condition of their grandson, a prisoner of war, Jonathan as Everyman and his wife Betsey Jane, complain to Lincoln about the South's treatment of Northern soldiers. Pertinent is Jonathan's aging. No longer Pauling's stripling, in *The New Yankee Doodle* Jonathan has evolved into a weary old man.

Longer Fiction

AMERICAN NOVELS

Fiction writers also wrestled with the idea of America as a gangling young giant. One of the best and worst of these writers was John Neal, who wrote an occasionally powerful but generally overstuffed three-volume novel called *Brother Jonathan or the New Englanders* (1825). Though just as impassioned a defender of American honor as Paulding, Neal treated the Jonathan character in an entirely different manner. Where Paulding gravitated toward the sparse forms of the classical tradition, Neal preferred the lush style and often fell into the worst excesses of the romantic tradition.[25]

In "The Colloquial Tradition in the Novel: John Neal," Harold C. Martin noted that Neal took full advantage of romantic poses. In Neal's life and personality as well as his writing, one finds "the arrogance, the sentimentality, the near-paranoia, the humanitarianism; the exuberance and the melancholy; the rage against order and frenzy in chaos"[26] that one associates with romanticism. Paulding, in contrast, always retained his greatest admiration for the English essayists of the eighteenth century. In his critical study of the *Diverting History*, Dennis Gartner contends that, "Addison, Goldsmith, Swift, Fielding, Dryden, and Pope were essentially responsible for the satiric vehicles of allegory, anecdotes, dialogue, dialect, parody, imagery, hyperbole, and character sketch which Paulding employed."[27] Thus a first, obvious, and essential difference between Paulding's and Neal's works was their form. While Paulding was following a satirical tradition established by Arbuthnot's *The History of John Bull* and Hopkinson's *Pretty Story*,[28] Neal was more immediately interested in creating an unequivocally American novel that might prove to be—as he expressed his preference—a "bad original" rather than a good imitation of someone else. Neal did produce a novel that was decidedly and properly American in character, language, and peculiarity.[29]

Critics who today mention John Neal's work generally connect his Gothic sensibility with Poe's, one of his early and most loyal admirers, and with Hawthorne's, who as a youngster devoured Neal's fiction; and with

Twain's, since Neal was an early practitioner of a consciously colloquial style. Melville, however, even more quickly comes to mind when one reads *Brother Jonathan*.[30] In this, Neal's sixth novel, his most persistent theme is a pervasive sense of mistrust and the absolute impossiblity of knowing anything for certain. Even toward the end, where Neal apparently is tying together the narrative threads and clarifying earlier obfuscations, his denouement feels as murky and questionable as any of the earlier explanations. But this sort of ending accorded with Neal's romantic sensibility. In defense of the bizarre and fabulous in his writing he editorialized,

> There is . . . a secret leaning toward the uncommon; a sort of appetite for the wonderful and extraordinary, in every human heart. This appetite *will* be fed—on garbage, if nothing better can be had. . . . Men feed upon falsehood, as they do upon opium. They begin with taking it in sport, perhaps; they continue till it becomes a thing, without which they cannot eat or sleep. So, too, in their fondness for the wonderful; they *must* have it, after a little time, to keep them alive. It is like flattery: nothing is too gross, nothing too abominable, for the appetite of him who has fed long upon it.[31]

Brother Jonathan does supply the reader's appetite for the wonderful and extraordinary. As in several of Melville's novels, the young hero in *Brother Jonathan*, Walter Harwood, makes a symbolic journey into the equivocal complexities of adulthood. Although brash and untutored, Walter is presented in the first volume as a young countryman whose person suggests future strength and wisdom:

> Walter Harwood, if one might believe his countenance, which was exceedingly fierce and beautiful, had somewhat within him which is not common with boys.
> He was tall—strong; well-proportioned; with a broad, clear, ample forehead; and a noble chin. His hair was parted before, like his father's; carried behind his ears; and let loose, below upon his broad shoulders, where, at every motion of his body, it played altogether in character, with his fine, large masculine head.[32]

A Connecticut youth, Walter has difficulty getting along with his strict deacon-farmer father and his vivacious cousin-sweetheart Edith Cummin. Given this uneasy contention in his childhood home, Walter's move to seek his fortune elsewhere follows logically.

In the second volume Walter takes a stage coach to New York. Off home ground and out of his ordinary clothes, his awkward country limitations are more evident than ever.

> Walter, unhappily, for him, was rigged out, in all his go-to-meetin' finery; unhappily, because, he never appeared so like a great, overgrown, awkward country boy, as when he was thus equipped; nor ever to such advantage, as in his old clothes; a striped woolen frock—or short

gaberdine; with his collar open;—his throat naked—and his rich, loose hair huddled about his neck.

He wore, now, a large brimmed, low crowned, wool hat—newly ironed up, for the occasion—you might have seen your face in it—"a leetle o' one side"—with a flaming brass buckle, in front; a dimity waistcoat—stiped with dark yellow—it had been a petticoat of his mother's—a part of her wedding dress—the flaps hanging half way down to his knees; cowhide shoes—newly greased with a famous preparation of the time, for keeping out water—which left a "smooch" upon whatever they came near; a pair of huge buckles in them, too;—his hair gathered in a club, and bound up, with a piece of skyblue "worsted ribbon"; a large, bright, silver brooch, firmly skewered into the bosom of a coarse, clean, good-looking shirt,—which it held, as it were, by the teeth—so that his white skin was visible above, and below it. His look was that of a lubberly country boy;—a "jinooine" Brother Jonathan—going forth, from his home.[33]

On the stage coach and later in New York, Walter experiences several types of fakery. With his dissipated friend (and perhaps half-brother) Harry, Walter gets drunk and visits a brothel. He experiences the sense of being a nonentity in New York crowds until taken into the employ of Ashley, a Quaker merchant. As a clerk in Ashley's employ, Walter learns something of sharp business practices. And scattered through these already muddled pages are letters from Edith and from one of the several men purported to be Walter's father. Each warns him—as has his friend, Nathan Hale—not to trust anyone else.

As if this did not supply enough confused action, in the third volume the American Revolution erupts. Amid battle scenes, the twin Savage brothers stalk one another. Spies prove to be double agents; a mysterious Indian who has saved the lives of several of the main characters is perfidiously destroyed by an old Indian witch bent on revenge. But before he dies, the Indian manages to wipe out the band that has captured him. His hound kills the witch. The war at last over, Walter and Edith are together again and happy; while Warwick Savage (also known at various times during the narrative as Robert Evans, George Savage, and Jonathan Peters), Walter's true father, "though not happy, was no longer bad, or foolish."[34] Like the nation, Walter has become presumptively free and independent—a young adult.

Reminiscent of Melville's *Pierre*, Neal's novel pairs several of its characters. George and Warwick Savage are twins, different as good and evil yet whose names, personalities, and actions have been taken over by one another in popular report. Harry and Walter share an affinity of spirit although their differences argue for the influence of different childhood environments. Edith, Walter's girl back home, and Olive, who bears his illegitimate daughter, also reflect a similar affinity.

Although Neal entitled his novel *Brother Jonathan* and gave Walter, his main character, many of the characteristics of the Jonathan figure, the novel's title refers to the American people and especially to New Englanders generally who in a sense came of age with the American Revolution. In addition to Walter, two other characters in the first volume are portrayed as quintessential New Englanders. The first is the protean Jonathan Peters, who "was an American; one of that singular people, who know a little, and but a little, of everything . . . he was a Yankee, the very character of whom is, that he can 'turn his hand,' as he says, 'to any thing.' This was the character of a New Englander, half a century ago: it is perfectly true of him, now."[35] The second character who captures the American personality is corporal Winslow, about whom another character observes:

> It is a common trick of my countrymen—I know that, very well;—a very common trick, when they have any object in view—to overreach other people, by their simplicity. . . . It is a kind of humor, that I like. It enables one to put almost any question; do almost any thing, without risk; and, in some cases, to set all wisdom and authority, at open defiance. In a time of trouble and warfare, it might be turned, I am sure, to good account.[36]

Later Neal as narrator reminds his readers that "Winslow, awkward as he was, and stupid, as he appeared . . . was one of the very men, who did the heavy business of the American Revolution."[37] Then, having shown Winslow in action, Neal digresses to what makes Winslow and his neighbors tick.

> It is amusing to see how adroitly; and for how long a time, a genuine Yankee will evade your question. Put it in what shape you may—though you believe it impossible for him to escape, he will either pass it over, entirely, without any question—urged in a serious, or pleasant, or droll manner, with singular promptitude, and a great show of simplicity. . . . This habit of evasion would seem to indicate a shrewd, conscientious, inquisitive people. Among the Brother Jonathans, however, it is a sign of something more; the sign of a suspicious—cool, keen, cyphering, thrifty temper; with little or no heart. Every thing is a matter of serious calculation with your genuine Yankee. He won't give away even his words—if another should have occasion for them. He will "swap" any thing with you; "trade" with you for any thing; but is never the man to give anything away, so long as there is any prospect of doing better with it. If you put a question, to a New Englander, therefore; no matter what—no matter why—beware how you show any solicitude. You will make a bad bargain, if you do. He is pretty sure to reason thus: generous and kind as he is, in some things.—"Now; this information is wanted. It must be of some value to him, that want it; else why this anxiety?—Of course, it would be of some value to *me*, if I knew how to make use of it, properly. At any rate (a favorite phrase, with him); at any rate, he wants

it; he knows the value of it; he can afford, of course, to pay for it; and will not give more than it is worth. Therefore I shall get as much as I can: if he gives too much for it; whose fault is that?—His; not mine. Therefore, he shall have it; if he will—*at any rate*."[38]

Neal's characterization sums up the reasoning behind much of the action of the Jonathan character seen on stage and in popular anecdotes.

Neal packed far too much into this novel he hoped would establish his reputation as a literary giant. Perhaps if, like Thomas Wolfe, Neal had been fortunate enough to find an expert and tactful editor, he might like Wolfe be remembered as something of a giant. He is not. Nonetheless, with *Brother Jonathan* Neal attempted, as no one before him had, to draw a broad and yet exact picture of both American society as a whole and of the individuals who gave it its flavor. Without insisting on allegorical exactitude, the novelist identified the young hero with the young country and suggested that his growth into maturity paralleled that of the country. Aside from the nationalist overtones, Neal's novel overflowed with a plethora of movements and characters. Neal's *Brother Jonathan* was not a successful novel; yet even in its failure, it was far more intriguing than later pedestrian attempts to make literary use of Brother Jonathan.

BRITISH NOVELS

British novelists also tried to pin down the American character by embodying it in a Brother Jonathan. No one who recognizes the name of Frances Trollope, for example, will be surprised to learn that in addition to her more widely known *Domestic Manners of the Americans* (1832), she also wrote a highly critical novel about American life entitled *The Life and Adventures of Jonathan Jefferson Whitlaw* (1836).[39] The title character, not however a New England Yankee, is the thoroughly self-serving son of a poor white settler in Mississippi. Both father and son are climbers who by means of hard work, some good luck, and implacable insensitivity toward the women and slaves who work for them, get ahead financially. In a melodramatic plot that mixes abolitionism, miscegenation, murder, and machination, Trollope depicts the moral bankruptcy of Jonathan.

Toward the end of her last volume, she has Jonathan murdered and secretly buried by four slaves. Before that well-deserved fate, though, Jonathan has been the motivating force behind a murder and a suicide as well as the expulsion from the country of a godly and civilized German family of non–slave owners. For Trollope the most evident quality of the Jonathan character, and perhaps of Americans as a group, was single-minded acquisitiveness.

Another British view of America and Americans appeared in an anonymous novel of 1841, *The Playfair Papers*. Pretending to be a travel account by a retired English naval officer who spends his days in leisurely travel, *The Playfair Papers* recounts this character's experiences in America and his encounters with all sorts of natives. The natives include, for example, a travelling preacher called Jonathan Lusts, who lives down to his bad name. The author subtitles his novel *Brother Jonathan, the Smartest Nation in all Creation*, and the several volumes express both admiration for the accomplishments of the young American nation and annoyance at the posturing, larceny, and hotheadedness of many of its citizens. The slave trade, for example, comes under criticism because its only justification is pecuniary.[40] That incentive, nevertheless, proves quite adequate for those citizens who underwrite the trade. Slavery itself comes in for repeated attack. *The Playfair Papers* includes abolitionist horror stories—such as one about Jefferson selling his mulatto daughter into slavery—as well as tales of religious intolerance.

Acquisitiveness seems to account for most of Jonathan's actions. One of the settlers attending a rabble-rousing political gathering at Liberty Hall in New York argues against fighting England over disputed Maine territory but concedes, "did ever any *crittur* know Jonathan to smell or snake after what wasn't of value? I guess!"[41] Like Neal's *Brother Jonathan, The Playfair Papers* uses Brother Jonathan's name to refer to all Americans; but unlike the earlier novel, *The Playfair Papers* does not develop any character or characters who embody the national spirit.

Several characters of extraordinary depravity illustrate most conclusively that Brother Jonathan's is neither the smartest nor the most ethical nation in all creation. But the writer also recounts stories of his various travelling friends and acquaintances who eventually pair off with the predictability of the last scene in a Shakespearean comedy. These characters, of course, belong to the same genteel social stratum as the narrator and those few Americans of whom he most approves.

This novel and later British novels such as *Jonathan Sharp; or the Adventures of a Kentuckian*[42] seem primarily intended to illustrate the moral and ethical inferiority of Americans, as scrutinized in light of the social codes assumed by genteel British writers. British novels thus utilized the Jonathan persona as a stick with which to cudgel wayward Americans. Outsiders, British writers were never able to crack the coded meaning that Jonathan had for many Americans. Even writers of superficial American fiction like Mrs. Stephens' *High Life* (1854)[43] came closer than any English writers to acknowledging the dualities in Jonathan. And though seriously flawed, Neal's *Brother Jonathan* was a full-scale attempt to explore the complexities of the American character. Neal's *Brother Jonathan* achieved a major development far beyond any other appearances of Jonathan. The eighteenth-century Jonathan of British cartooning, of almanac and jest book humor, of Aubury's letters, and of wartime balladry was discernible in yet superseded by Neal's character. The novel also progressed beyond Paulding's allegory and the stereotypical tag-characterizations of most stage comedies to an imaginative exploration of what it meant to be an American.

9

Conclusion

FROM OBSCURE ORIGINS IN SEVENTEENTH-CENTURY ENGLAND AND EARLY EIGH-
teenth-century America,[1] the Jonathan name and character first developed
in late eighteenth- and early nineteenth-century America into a low comedy figure who combined naïveté with a native shrewdness that became the
hallmark of his American origins.[2] In almanac and jest book humor, in
verse, visual caricatures, and on the stage this became the most popular
and sustained trademark of Jonathan. Particularly during the 1820s and
1830s, Brother Jonathan came to embody what Alfred Kazin refers to as
"that dearest of all American myths, the average man."[3] But for the entire
period between the Revolutionary and Civil Wars, Jonathan was an Amer-
cian character who, as Russel Nye says, "reflected something about the
American's vision of himself, as honest, shrewd, sentimental, independent, and possessed of a heart of gold."[4] Since the popular arts that
Jonathan appeared in aimed for realism, however, they also perhaps inadvertently showed that he was parochial, petty, anti-Semitic, racist, sex-
ist, anti-Catholic, and complacent.

Taken together the stories, jokes, and caricatures about Jonathan constitute an American myth sustained with increasing popularity and em-
bellishment through the first three decades of the nineteenth century but
then dwindling in popularity during the next three decades. Clearly during
the ascendant years of Jeffersonian and Jacksonian democracy, Jonathan
appealed to or reinforced the beliefs of popular culture consumers who
viewed the character as an American everyman. For a while, he did
indeed—as has the more recent western hero[5]—tell viewers about themselves and their society.

A folk creation, Jonathan was developed into a popular metaphor. He
seldom reached the complexity of a literary metaphor. Yet within the
limitations of this popular metaphor, artists in many media attempted to
"define something for which there was no dictionary meaning."[6] Their
metaphors indeed did try to create something new, since nowhere else did

such a vision exist.[7] In Brother Jonathan, popular artists in many fields worked to translate into the vernacular what it meant to be the "new man," "the democratic" and "common" man that foreign observers is particular found intriguing during the first quarter of the nineteenth century in America. While Jonathan never evolved into an imaginatively developed character with the amplitude or resonance of, for example, a Huckleberry Finn, his evolution in antebellum American folk and popular culture was part of what Peter Briggs calls the "subtle, ambivalent, and tortuous task of establishing . . . imaginative independence."[8] As Briggs explains, a nation needs an "imaginative context" of geographic, literary, and historical associations in which a literary piece can take root.[9] Jonathan's evolution provided part of the context out of which a Huck Finn could finally emerge.

By the 1850s and 1860s Jonathan had altered and in time he functioned only as a cultural relic. The country, the times, and the populace had all undergone massive changes. The figure of Jonathan had hardly altered to address or reflect these changes.[10] His exterior tags remained; but from being a symbol of radical change, the Jonathan figure came to be a fossilized shell whose only reference was to the past. From a folk character, Jonathan changed into a popular character who often—though not always—was manipulated by Whigs bent on controlling the language and meaning of the independent impulse Jonathan represented. Whig success, however, constituted his downfall, since to alter Jonathan's language and humor was to destroy him.[11]

Though still a predominantly rural country in the 1850s, the United States had withstood a crippling depression during the 1830s. Its population had pushed west and south during the 1830s and 1840s—in the process elbowing weak Mexican authorities out of disputed territories. Americans had faced off against the Russians and the English on the Pacific coast, and they were eyeing further expansions in the Caribbean and in South America. The cartoons best reflect the inadequacy of Jonathan's rural wisdom to comprehend the complexity of later decades. On the other hand, in later popular arts Jonathan was never a truly rural character but an urban construct. In contrast with this later innocuous character, the Jonathan of early stage depictions at least maintained ties with oral tradition.

The American populace changed as the country and times did. The 1830s witnessed the first of many waves of European immigration. Many of these newcomers settled in the cities. Few were in sympathy with the shuttered mentality of the Jonathan found in popular humor. City theatergoers, too, saw less to identify with in the Jonathan character of popular comedy. Immigrants, Westerners, and Southerners all had reasons to question Jonathan as the normative expression of America.

Once the bumbling comic figure who somehow triumphed over all adversaries, Jonathan underwent an internal change during the forties and fifties. No longer a clown or a gadfly, he broke apart, becoming an assortment of carefully genteel characters limited by their fear of offending.[12] These latter characters—the Jonathan, for example, who became Uncle Sam in cartoons or the Jonathan who become "no man" in fiction and travel accounts—signaled a decline in the earlier American vision of an independent everyman.

The alteration of Jonathan from eighteenth-century clod to early-nineteenth-century wily "simpleton" to mid-nineteenth-century nonentity offers "a given cultural configuration as it is found in a given time and place"[13] and one approach to better understanding that time and place. The Jonathan figure also offers a useful index of the cultural value system of antebellum America.[14] Unfortunately, the entirety of Jonathan's appearances still do not offer a consistent image that can be fully dealt with in terms of "conformity and variation alike."[15] Thus neither Hayden White's nor Frederick Jameson's theories can be used to develop a definitive comment about Jonathan's significance. Although Jonathan did achieve what appears to be a "classic form" during the 1830s, after that he was torn between the claims of increasing realism and a widening mass circulation of the sort that Hannah Arendt argues "consumes" cultural artifacts so that "they simply disappear."[16] Jonathan did disappear. For the most part, he disappeared into other American characters, but many of his idiosyncratic crotchets just disappeared altogether. Before melting into Uncle Sam and other stage Americans, however, Jonathan enlivened American culture through a multitude of humorous vignettes about typical Americans. In Jonathan the American's limitations were humorously noted; at the same time he also celebrated the quick intelligence of the American people. Jonathan's optimism, his capacity for wonder, his bedrock honesty and, above all, his youthful vigor made him a cultural icon for the American before the Civil War.

Appendix A

Yankee Doodle,
or
(as now christened by the Saints of New England)
The Lexington March

N.B. The words to be Sung thro' the Nose, & in the West Country drawl & dialect.

Brother Ephraim sold his Cow
   And bought him a Commision
And then he went to Canada
   To Fight for the Nation
But when Ephraim he came home
   He prov'd an arrant Coward,
He wou'dn't fight the Frenchmen there
   For fear of being devour'd.

2
Sheep's Head and Vinegar
   Butter Milk and Tansy,
Boston is a Yankee town
   Sing Hey Doodle Dandy:
First we'll take a Pinch of Snuff
   And then a drink of Water,
And then we'll say How do you do
   And that's a Yanky's Supper.

3
Aminadab is just come Home
   His Eyes all greas'd with Bacon,
And all the news that he cou'd tell
   Is Cape Breton is taken:
Stand up Jonathan
   Figure in by Neighbour,
Nathen stand a little off
   And make the Room some wider.

4

Christmas is a coming Boys
        We'll go to Mother Chases,
And there we'll get a Sugar Dram,
        Sweeten'd with Melasses:
Heigh he fer our Cape Cod,
        Heigh he Nantasket,
Do not let the Boston wags,
        Feel your Oyster Basket.

5

Punk in Pye is very good
        And so is Apple Lantern,
Had you been whipp'd as oft as I
        You'd not have been so wanton:
Uncle is a Yankee Man
        'I faith he pays us all off,
And he has got a Fiddle
        As big as Daddy's Hogs Trough.

6

Seth's Mother went to Lynn
        To buy a pair of Breeches,
The first time Nathen put them on
        He tore out all the Stitches;
Dolly Bushel let a Fart,
        Jenny Jones she found it,
Ambrose carried it to Mill
        Where Doctor Warren ground it.

7

Our Jemima's lost her Mare
        And can't tell where to find her,
But she'll come trotting by and by
        And bring her Tail behind her
Two and two may go to Bed;
        Two and two together,
And if there is not room enough,
        Lie one a top o'to'ther.

Appendix B

Comments on the Texts and Production History of the *Jonathan* Plays

- [Royall Tyler], *The Contrast*: A Comedy Written by a Citizen of the United States; performed with applause at the theatres in New York, Philadelphia, and Maryland; and published (under an Assignment of the Copyright) by Thomas Wignell (Philadelphia: Pritchard and Hall, 1790; reprinted New York: The Dunlap Society, 1887.) The American Company first performed the comedy on 16 April 1787, within a month of the John Street Theatre's opening. Walter Meserve, *An Emerging Entertainment*, 97, notes thirty-eight performances in New York, Baltimore, and Philadelphia between 1787 and 1804 by the Old American Company and by other companies in Alexandria, Georgetown, Fredricksburg, Norfolk, Boston, and Charleston. During this period the comedy was even made into a musical. But then it was apparently not produced until World War I and it was produced again during World War II. In 1972 a musical adaptation was produced in New York. This play's Jonathan character is named Jonathan.

- Joseph Atkinson's *Match for a Widow* (Dublin: P. Byrne, 1788), a three-act comic opera, was first performed at the Theatre Royal in Dublin on 17 April 1786. The play had a French source, *L'Heureuse Erreur* (1783) by Joseph Patrat; and an English analogue—in an only slightly altered version of Patrat's comedy—*The Widow's Vow* by Mrs. Inchblad. The English play appeared on a London stage during the same year as Atkinson's play appeared in Dublin. This play's Jonathan character is named both Jonathan and Jonathon.

- J. Robinson's *The Yorker's Strategem* (New York: T. & J. Swords, 1792). This play, written by a minor member of the Old American Company, was first performed in New York by that company during the spring of 1792 and was actually the only new "legitimate" afterpiece to be presented by the company while they were far below strength during the summer of 1792. This play's Jonathan character is named Jonathan Norrad.

- John Minshull's *Rural Felicity* (New York: the author, 1801). According to Grimstad, *Melodrama Unveiled*, 152, this play was performed three times. Reading the script, one wonders what the author did to bribe the performers. The play includes a very minor Jonathan character in a consistently dull plot that centers on the joys of a healthy diet. Nothing much happens in this pastoral. This play's Jonathan character is named Jonathan.

- L[azarus] Beach's *Jonathan Postfree* (New York: David Longworth, 1807). When Beach could not get this musical farce produced after writing it in 1806, he had it published; its subsequent production history was limited to an amateur performance by the students at Transylvania University in October of 1810 for the benefit of charity students at that university. This play's Jonathan character is named Jonathan Postfree.

- A. B. Lindsley's *Love and Friendship* (New York: D. Longworth, 1809). At nineteen, Lindsley, a member of Cooper's company playing at the Park Theatre, New York, saw his comedy produced there during the 1807–1808 season. This play's Jonathan character is named Brother Jonathan.

- General [David] Humphreys's *The Yankey in England* (1815) strictly speaking is not a Jonathan play, although Walter Meserve in *An Emerging Entertainment*, 235, does refer to the Yankee Doolittle as Jonathan; its relevance, however, stems from the fact that as Enkvist, *Caricatures of Americans*, argues, in 43n, Peake's *Jonathan in England* is "essentially an adaptation" of this play. Peake did lift some of his jokes and much of his American dialect from Humphrey's "drama." This play's Jonathan character is named Doolittle.

- J. K. Paulding's *The Bucktails* in *American Comedies* by J. K. Paulding and William Irving Paulding (Philadelphia: Carey and Hart, 1847) was written shortly after the War of 1812, perhaps in 1815, but it was not performed or published until Paulding added this comedy to several by his son in order to help launch his son's literary career. This play's Jonathan character is named Jonathan Peabody.

- Samuel Woodworth's pastoral opera *The Forest Rose* (Boston: William V. Spencer, 1855) was first produced at the Chatham Theatre, New York, on 6 October 1825 and published shortly thereafter. Along with *Jonathan in England, The Forest Rose* became a staple for Yankee actors and remained popular, even in the South, through the 1850s. This play's Jonathan character is named Jonathan Ploughboy.

- In *Trip to America* Charles Mathews played Jonathan W. Doubikins, opening at the English Opera House in London on 25 March 1824. This

production and his later *Jonathan in England* (which I refer to by its
later printed-version title of *Americans Abroad* in order to avoid the
common confusion between it and Hackett's play) capitalized on
Mathews's recent (1822–23) tour of America. According to the generally reliable Hodge, *Yankee Theatre*, 67, Mathews's original and fully
detailed version of *Trip to America* was never published. Some indications of Mathews's material, however, may be gleaned from *Sketches of
Mr. Mathews' Celebrated Trip to America* (London: J. Limbird, n.d.),
24. A Cruikshank engraving of Mathews's costume for the role of
Jonathan appears opposite the frontispiece of this text. This play's
Jonathan character is named Jonathan W. Doubikins.

- R. B. Peake's *Americans Abroad* (London: Dicks' Standard Plays, no.
589, n.d.) presents another British view of the "real Yankee" as the
dramatis personae identifies Jonathan W. Doubikins. This musical
farce, originally produced as *Jonathan in England*, is not at all sympathetic to the bragging comic American. The British comedian Charles
Mathews, who played Jonathan in the first production of the farce at the
Lyceum Theatre on 3 September 1824, had commissioned Peake to
write this play. An accomplished mimic, Mathews consciously gathered
material on his American tour. This visit and the material that he got
from John Wesley Jarvis probably influenced the fact that many of the
details of speech and action that one expects to find are present in this
Jonathan; nevertheless, Doubikins does not entirely follow the pattern
of Jonathan as that is generally found in plays written by Americans.
The Jonathans of Mathews's later "At Home" sketches, also written by
Peake and including "Jonathan W. Doubikins" and "A Trip to Natchidoches," are closely related to this loutish, slave-owning Jonathan.
Although the original version was entitled *Jonathan in England*, I refer
to the text by the published title so that I can avoid having this play
confused with the later comedy with the same title. This play's Jonathan
character is named Jonathan W. Doubikins.

- Practically every comic actor specializing in Yankee parts during the
several decades before the Civil War included the title *Jonathan in England* in his repertoire. Nevertheless, they were not all using exactly the
same material. Hodge, *Yankee Theatre*, 72–77, is obviously discussing the farce later entitled *Americans Abroad* when he writes about
the early version of *Jonathan in England*. This early play that Mathews
starred in is entirely different from James Hackett's 1828 alteration of
George Colman's 1805 comedy *Who Wants a Guinea?* (London: John
Dicks, n.d.). Hackett perhaps hoped to take advantage of the earlier
production by naming his work *Jonathan in England*. Solomon Swap,
the Jonathan of the title, though now a Yankee, greatly resembles the

Yorkshire Solomon Gundy in Colman's play. Colman, by 1832 the licenser of plays, had to pass on this version of his play before its first London production at Drury Lane on 17 November 1832, during Hackett's second attempt with London audiences. Having read the script, Colman sent a note to a friend in which he commented, "I have received the alterations made by Mr. Hackett (a very appropriate name for the purpose) and shall request the Lord Chamberlain to license the rubbish." Quoted in Enkvist, *American Caricatures*, 50.

The microprint and microfilm copies (both from the original listed by Samuel French, who became the dominant play publishing giant only in the late 1850s) in the University of Iowa Library probably belong to a period after 1859, since actors who starred as Solomon Swap through that year are listed before the playscript. The microprint of the copy in the Harvard University Library is said to date from 1828, but the copy itself is not dated and—apart from the list of characters (found in the microfilm but not the microprint)—it appears to be identical to the post–1859 copy. Hackett's first title for this play, incidentally, *John Bull at Home*, might have been altogether less confusing. Since all the Yankee actors freely took scenes and characters from plays such as these two titled *Jonathan in England* and since they developed monologues or skits patched together from their favorite acting vehicles, these two scripts may not indicate all that was presented under that title. Even after 1856 the copyright law that bad been passed to protect production rights in America was not enforceable; so actors with privately developed scripts often found it expedient to keep them out of print. As it was, Hackett, for example, strenuously objected without avail to Hill's appropriating *Jonathan in England* so that it became Hill's major vehicle. Fred Washington Atkinson in the catalogue of his collection of American plays at the University of Chicago, *American Drama in Atkinson Collection*, Part 1, 1796–1830 (unpublished MS. at University of Chicago, 1 March 1918), 60, mentions that though he had never been able to locate a copy, an edition of this comedy was supposed to have been published at Boston in 1828. Hackett's Jonathan character is named Solomon Swap.

- George Colman's *New Hay at the Old Market* (London: T. and W. Davies, 1795), later titled *Sylvester Daggerwood*, in *The Dramatic Works of George Colman the Younger*, 3 vols. (Paris: Baudry, 1827), originally had nothing to do with Jonathan. It is a short intermezzo first written for the reopening of Haymarket Theatre in London; but since this play within a play offers the opportunity for an actor playing an out-of-work actor looking for a job to demonstrate his histrionic talents—including his penchant for storytelling, many comedians seem to have melded Jonathan roles into the actor's repertoire. This play's Jonathan character is named Jonathan.

- Thomas Dibdin's *Banks of the Hudson, or the Congress Trooper* (London: John Cumberland, n.d.) was first produced on 16 December 1829 at the Colburg Theatre and published sometime between 1831 and 1835 in Cumberlands Minor Theatre Series. According to Allardyce Nicoll in *A History of Early Nineteenth Century Drama, 1800–1850* (New York: The Macmillan Company, 1930), 2: 476, this London theater had a reputation for producing under Moncrieff "melodrama of the most startling nature, performed for audiences of the 'lowest kind.'" According to Lawrence S. Thompson in *Nineteenth and Twentieth Century Drama* (Boston: G. K. Hall & Co., 1975), 72, this play was already an adaptation of an earlier work entitled *The Chelsea Prisoner*.

  The intriguing aspect of this play, however, is that the Jonathan character is a melodramatic villain; the heroes are British officers. The plot also has minor parallels with Cooper's *The Spy* (published in 1821 and dramatized by C. P. Clinch in 1822). This play's Jonathan character is named Jonathan Dobson.

- William Dunlap's *A Trip to Niagara* (New York: E. B. Clayton, 1830) included a diorama of scenes such as might be seen by passengers on a steamboat traveling up the Hudson River. The comedy was first performed in 1828. A character called John Bull, attempting to win over the heroine traveling in America with her brother, shows the absurdity of the brother's antipathy to all things American by assuming the stock roles of first a Frenchman and then a Yankee called Jonathan.

  Probably the most noteworthy element of Dunlap's production was a stage diarama of scenes encountered by passengers on their trip up the Hudson. Dunlap's diarama and its association with the stage Yankee of Dunlap's play might have suggested John Barnard's (1846) presentation in the United States and England of a ten-foot-high canvas that unrolled from cylinders twenty feet apart and presented a panorama of the Mississippi. According to the *Illustrated London News*, as quoted in Boorstin, *The Americans*, 238, Barnard sat on a platform and explained the localities as they passed before the audience and also reliev[ed] his narrative with Jonathonisms and jokes, poetry and patter, which delight[ed] his audience mightily." See Robert Wernick's "Getting a Glimpse of History from a Grandstand Seat," *Smithsonian*, (August 1985), 68–86, for more on the popularity of such visual shows. This play's Jonathan character is named Jonathan.

- Opening on 24 September 1827, *Uncle Jonathan; or Independence*, an operatic farce, ran until 12 October 1827 at the Sadlier Wells as a trailer to *Paul Jones*.

- A character called Jonathan Doogood appeared in an afterpiece entitled *Old Jonathan and His Apprentices*, written expressly for New York's Bowery Theatre and appearing there frequently following its first presentation in 1832. This play's Jonathan character is named Jonathan Doogood.

- George Lionel Stevens's wearisomely talky *The Patriot* (Boston: Marsh, Caper & Lyon, 1834) apparently was written in anticipation of an annual presentation on the Fourth of July; this comedy includes a seafaring Yankee named Jonathan Seabright.

- On 16 December 1837, James Hackett performed in a piece entitled *Jonathan Boobikins* at a theater in Mobile, Alabama. This play's Jonathan character is named Jonathan Boobikins.

- *Jonathan's Visit to Buffalo*. Odell, *Annals*, 3:476, lists this play. I find no other trace of it.

- *Tarnation Strange* by William Thomas Moncrieff (London: J. Limbard, 1842) was first performed at the New Strand Theatre on 3 August 1838. It was so successful that it ran for forty performances during the next two months. This play's Jonathan character is named Jonathan Jonah Goliah Bang.

- During the New Orleans' American Theatre's summer season of 1840, a piece called *Jonathan in Difficulty* shared the bill with *Mischief Making*. Since no major Yankee stars were in town at the time, some member of the company may have been trying to launch himself into such a role.

- A character called Jonathan Junks appeared in *Jonathan's Wedding* at The Astor Place Opera House on 27 September 1850.

- During the 1850s when people were expressing their amazement at the phenomenon called bloomers, one of the several plays on the subject was entitled *The Bloomer Costume* by Charles Somerset and contained an American cousin called Jonathan. It was first performed at the Grecian Salon in London on 13 October 1851. The University of Iowa has a negative microfilm copy of the British Museum manuscript copy. British Museum Add. MS43037. This play's Jonathan character is named brother Jonathan.

- *John Bull and Brother Jonathan* may have been just a conventional title for topical plays. Skits by that title appeared on 8 September 1851 at Brougham's Lyceum (where the alternate title was *Yacht Race*) and on 21 August 1858 at the Bowery Theatre (where the alternate title used was *On The Atlantic Cable*).

- James Pilgrim's 1858 comedy *Americans Abroad* playing at Burton's

Theatre included a character named Jonathan Baxter.

- Hitchcock's Concert Hall presented *Jonathan Doolittle* on 2 April 1859 with Jerry Merryfield playing the title role. There is some faint possibility, I suppose, that this was Humphrey's *Yankey in England*. Odell, *Annals*, 7:285.

- As late as 1877 William Busch published a two-act play titled *Brother Jonathan*. (St. Louis).

Appendix C

Brother Jonathan in Separately Published Cartoons

Note: In addition to separately published cartoons, Brother Jonathan appeared in large and small cartoons too numerous to enumerate in popular satiric periodicals such as *Punch, Vanity Fair, The Lantern, Harper's Weekly* and *Yankee Notions*, in some editions of Paulding's *Diverting History*, and on ephemera such as cigar box covers, music sheets, and Civil War envelopes. The bibliography contains complete citations for books listed as references or those containing reproductions.

1776
The Yankie Doodles Intrenchments Near Boston, 1776
    Engraving. 8 × 9⅝ inches.
    Reproduced: Matthews, "Brother Jonathan Once More."
    Copy: British Museum No. 5329.
    Reference: George, *Catalogue*, 5.

1778
The English and American Discovery: Brother, Brother We are Both in the Wrong.
    Engraving. Matthew Darly.
    Copy: John Carter Brown.
    Reference: Matthews, "Brother Jonathan Once More."

1812
Brother Jonathan's Soliloquy on the Times.
    Line Engraving: Thomas Kensett.
    Reproduced: Morgan.
    Copies: Harvard, American Antiquarian Society, New York Historical Society.
    Reference: Weitenkampf, 16.

1813
Brother Jonathan Administering a Salutary Cordial to John Bull.
    Line Engraving. Amos Doolittle.

Copy: Winterthur.
Reproduced: Murrell.
Reference: Weitenkampf, 17.
A Boxing Match, or Another Bloody Nose for John Bull.
Etching. 9½ × 3 inches. W. Charles.
Copies: Library of Congress, New York Historical Society, Historical
Society of Pennsylvania.
Reproduced: Lammon, Morgan.
Reference: Weitenkampf, 18.

1814

John Bull making a new Batch of Ships to Send to the Lakes.
Etching. Wm. Charles.
Reprod: New York Historical Society, Henry E. Huntington, Library of
Congress, New York Public Library.
Copies: Nevins and Weitenkampf, Maurice, Murrell.
Reference: Weitenkampf, 19.
The baker, John Bull, complains, "Ay? What-What-What! Brother
Jonathan taken another whole fleet on the Lakes—Must work away—
Work away—& send some more or He'll have Canada next."
The Fall of Washington—or Maddy in Full Flight.
Copy: British Museum No. 12311.
Reproduced: Lorant; *The Image of America*.
Reference: George, *Catalogue*, 9: 434–44.

1832

A general arguing of the Maine question, or John Bull's Bully trying to
frighten Jonathan out of Title and Timber.
Lithograph by James Akin.
Copy: Library Co of Philadelphia, Ridgeway Branch.
Reproduced: Murrell.
Reference: Weitenkampf, 28; Quimby, 107. A copy of this print appears
on page 135 of Murrell; the print is small, however, and indistinct. The
text fortunately is reprinted on page 107 of Quimby. Murrell dates the
lithograph 1832, Quimby 1839. Weitenkampf, 58, lists another print
"The *Maine* Question" (1839) on the same issue.

1834

The Vision.
Lithograph. 9⅝ × 15⅛ inches. By E. Bisbee.
Copies: American Antiquarian Society, Boston Public Library, Har-
vard, Library of Congress. New York Historical Society.
Reproduced: Lorant, Dickson.
Reference: Weitenkampf, 35.
John Bull says, "Ha, ha, ha, Brother Jonathan . . ."

Uncle Sam sick with LaGrippe.
   Lithograph signed C.
   Copies: Library of Congress, American Antiquarian Society, New York
       Historical Society, New York State Historical Association.
   Reproduced: Morgan.
   Reference: Weitenkampf, 36.

1836
Confab between John Bull and Brother Jonathan.
   Lithograph. Drawn by Corkscrew.
   Copy: American Antiquarian Society.
   Reproduced: Morgan.
   Reference: Weitenkampf, 40.
The Heads of Two Great Nations Have . . . !!!
   Lithograph.
   Copies: Library of Congress, New York Historical Society.
   Reproduced: Morgan.
   Reference: Weitenkampf, 42.
A Kean Shave Between "John Bull and Brother Jonathan,". . . .
   Lithograph. $9\frac{7}{8}'' \times 13\frac{7}{8}''$ By James Akin.
   Copy: Historical Society Pennsylvania.
   Reproduced: Murrell.
   Reference: Weitenkampf, 44; Quimby, 106; Murrell, 137–38.
   Quimby quotes the entire text.

1837
A Dialogue Between two well known characters.
   Lithograph.
   Copies: Library of Congress, American Antiquarian Society, Harvard,
       Henry E. Huntington, New York Historical Society, Museum of
       City of New York.
   Reproduced: Morgan.
   Reference: Weitenkampf, 48.
Brother Jonathan's Appeal!
   Lithograph. By John Childs.
   Copy: New York Historical Society.
   Reproduced: Morgan.
   Reference: Weitenkampf, 48.
The Smokers.
   Lithograph. [E. W. Clay].
   Copies: American Antiquarian Society, Harvard, New York Historical
       Society.
   Reference: Weitenkampf, 50, identifies as Jonathan what appears to be
   Major Jack Downing.

1838
Mr. Van Shuffleton and His Physician Sam.
  Lithograph. 11" × 17".
  Copies: American Antiquarian Society. Harvard, New York Historical
      Society, Museum of City of New York.
  Reference: Weitenkampf, 53.

1839
The *Maine* Question.
  Lithograph.
  Copies: American Antiquarian Society, Library of Congress, New York
      Public Library.
  Reference: Weitenkampf, 58.
  The advisor dragging Van Buren's ox away from a fight with England
  refers to the populace as "Brother Jonathan."

1840
Uncle Sam's Pet Pups! . . .
  Wood engraving.
  Copy: Library of Congress.
  Reproduced: Morgan.
  Reference: Weitenkampf, 68.

1844
Sale of Dogs.
  Lithograph. H. Bucholzer.
  Copy: Library of Congress.
  Reproduced: Morgan.
  Reference: Weitenkampf, 73.
Annexation or Sport for Grown Children.
  Lithograph. Sealsfield.
  Copies: American Antiquarian Society, New York Historical Society.
  Reproduced: Morgan.
  Reference: Weitenkampf, 76.

1846
John Bull and Brother Jonathan.
  Lithograph.
  Copies: New York Historical Society, Museum of New York City.
  Reproduced: Morgan.
  Reference: Weitenkampf, 87.
Uncle Sam's Taylorifics.
  Lithograph. E. W. Clay.
  Copies: New York Historical Society.
  Reproduced: Nevins and Weitenkampf, Maurice, Murrell, Morgan.

Reference: Weitenkampf, 88.

1848

Whig Harmony.
  Lithograph.
  Copy: Library of Congress.
  Reproduced: Morgan.
  Reference: Weitenkampf, 95.
Coming to Terms!
  Lithograph.
  Copies: Amiercan Antiquarian Society, Library of Congress.
  Reproduced: Morgan.
  Reference: Weitenkampf, 97–98.

1851

Invasion of Cuba.
  Lithograph. By A. W.
  Copy: Harvard.
  Reproduced: Murrell.
  Reference: Weitenkampf, 104.
The Great Exhibition of 1851. American Department.
  Lithograph.
  Copy: Library of Congress.
  Reproduced: Rawls.
  Reference: Weitenkampf, 104; Conningham, No. 2607.

1852

The Poor Soldier & His Ticket for Soup.
  Lithograph.
  Copy: Library of Congress.
  Reproduced: Morgan.
  Reference: Weitenkampf, 106.
The Fish Question Settled.
  Lithograph.
  Copies: American Antiquarian Society, Library of Congress.
  Reference: Weitenkampf, 106.
  The man at left might be Jonathan.
John Bull's Fish Monopoly.
  Lithograph.
  Copy: Library of Congress.
  Reproduced: Morgan.
  Reference: Weitenkampf, 111.

1855

The Propagation Society—more Free Than Welcome.

Lithograph.
Copy: Library of Congress.
Reproduced: Morgan.
Reference: Weitenkampf, 114; Conningham No. 4962 (dates 1853).

1856

The Democratic Platform.

Lithograph: (C. & Ives).

Copies: American Antiquarian Society, Boston Public Library, Harvard, Henry E. Huntington, Library of Congress, New York Historical Society, New York Public Library.

Reproduced: Lorant, American Caricatures of the Civil War, Bishop, Caricatures of the Civil War.

Reference: Weitenkampf, 117, Conningham No. 1551.

The "Mustang Team."

Lithograph: Louis Maurer.

Copies: American Antiquarian Society, Harvard, Library of Congress, New York Historical Society, New York Public Library.

Reproduced: American Caricatures of the Civil War, Bishop, Caricatures of the Civil War, Nevins and Weitenkampf, Murrell, Shaw 2.

Reference: Weitenkampf, 117; Conningham No. 4273. While Weitenkampf does not make this identification, the main tollkeeper holding up Fremont and his supporters from the press seems to be Jonathan.

The Great Presidential Stakes of 1856 Free for all ages, "go as they please"—another C & W print, Conningham No. 2641, Weitenkampf, 115–16—uses the same figures in this cart.

1860

"The Irrepressible Conflict," . . . Danger.

Lithograph. Louis Maurer.

Copies: American Antiquarian Society, Henry E. Huntington, New York Historical Society, New York Public Library.

Reproduced: American Caricatures of the Civil War, Bishop, Shaw 1, Wilson, Peters, Nevins and Weitenkampf.

Reference: Weitenkampf, 122, Conningham, No. 3134.

[No Title] [Dr. North and Dr. South].

Wood engraving.
Copy: NYHS.
Reproduced: Morgan.
Reference: Weitenkampf, 125.

1861

The Way to fix 'em.

Pen Lithograph. 10″ × 12″ Woolf.
   Copies: American Antiquarian Society, Boston Public Library, New
        York Historical Society, New York Public Library.
   Reproduced: Morgan.
   Reference: Weitenkampf, 126.
The Political Arena.
   Lithograph.
   Copies: American Antiquarian Society, Boston Public Library, New
        York Historical Society, New York Public Library.
   Reproduced: American Caricatures of the Civil War, Caricatures of the
        Civil War.
   Reference: Weitenkampf, 127–28.
5 to One.
   Lithograph. Signed *H.A.*
   Copies: American Antiquarian Society, Library of Congress.
   Reproduced: Morgan.
   Reference: Weitenkampf, 132.
"Wait till the War is over."
   Lithograph. Signed *Fris.*
   Copies: American Antiquarian Society, New York Historical Society.
   Reproduced: Morgan.
   Reference: Weitenkampf, 132.

1862
Re-Union on the Secesh-Democratic Plan.
   Lithograph.
   Copies: Henry E. Huntington, New York Historical Society, New York
        Public Library.
   Reproduced: Morgan.
   Reference: Weitenkampf, 134; Conningham No. 5132.

1864
The Clairvoyant's Dream.
   Lithograph.
   Copies: Library of Congress, New York Historical Society.
   Reference: Weitenkampf, 147.

1865
Jeff Davis, The Compromiser, in a Tight Place.
   Lithograph.
   Copies: American Antiquarian Society, New York Historical Society.
   Reproduced: Morgan.
   Reference: Weitenkampf, 147.
Uncle Sam's Menagerie.

Lithograph.
Copies: American Antiquarian Society, Henry E. Huntington, Library
    of Congress, New York Historical Society.
Reproduced: Maurice.
Reference: Weitenkampf, 151–52.

1867

The Reconstruction Policy of Congress, as illustrated in California.
Lithograph.
Copies: Library of Congress, New York Historical Society.
Reproduced: Morgan.
Reference: Weitenkampf, 154–55.

1869

Not "Love," but Justice.
Wood engraving. Terriel and Nast.
Copy: New York Historical Society.
Reference: Weitenkampf, 161.
Blood Will Tell!
Lithograph.
Copies: American Antiquarian Society, Harvard, New York Historical
    Society, New York Public Library.
Reproduced: American Caricatures of the Civil War, Caricatures of the
    Civil War.
Reference: Weitenkampf, 159.

1876

The Stride of a Century.
Lithograph. 11.15″ × 15.15″ (Currier & Ives)
Copy: Bettman.
Reproduced: Morgan.
Reference: Conningham No. 5843.

Notes

Preface

1. Toward the last chapter in *Capitalism and a New Social Order* (New York: New York University Press, 1984), 97, Joyce Appleby notes that during the 1790s "Self-interest—reconceived [by Jeffersonian Republicans]—turned out to be a mighty leveller, raising ordinary people to the level of competence and autonomy while reducing the rich, the able, and the well-born to equality." Brother Jonathan, the American antebellum everyman who grew out of Yankee Doodle, embodied that self-interest. Those who distrusted the increasing economic and political power of ordinary entrepreneurs—peddlers, small tradesmen, petty landowners—tended to disparage the Jonathan character. Those who trusted in America's abundance (Appleby, 100–101) tended to idealize the character.

2. The preface and first chapter of Orin E. Klapp's *Heroes, Villians, and Fools* (Englewood Cliffs, N.J.: Prentice-Hall, Inc., 1962) discusses the role of major social types serving as models in American culture. Klapp develops the notion that this typing process involves two strands: 1) a colorful personality penetrating the popular consciousness, and then 2) people refashioning that personality into someone who suits their needs. (12–13) As society undergoes the stress of changes, old types disappear and new ones emerge. (20) This appears to describe what is happening with the rise and fall of Brother Jonathan as a national icon.

3. *The National Union Catalog, Pre–1956 Imprints* (London: Mansell, 1979), 653: 251, lists a *Life of Washington* by Mason Locke Weems published at Georgetown in 1800. By 1806 the title and presumably the anecdotes had expanded to *The Life of Washington the Great*. Weems's numerous biographies of Washington appeared in new impressions throughout the nineteenth century.

4. The Fall 1985 issue of *The American Quarterly* has furthered discussion of what the term "republican" meant to Americans during the fifty to seventy-five years following the Revolutionary War. The Brother Jonathan character belonged to the "many" according to the early, Macchiavelian, analysis of republican politics. Initially, the character was rooted in the country and clearly in sympathy with the "country" as opposed to the "court" faction even in his later migrations to the city. Finally, Brother Jonathan belonged to the company of "'owners of small and moveable property'" who found appealing Locke's emphasis on an economically productive citizenry. See Linda Kerber, "Republican Ideology of the Revolutionary Generation," *American Quarterly* 37 (Fall 1985): 489.

5. John Cawelti, *Adventure, Mystery, and Romance* (Chicago: the University of Chicago Press, 1976), 38.

6. Constance Rourke, *American Humor* (New York: Harcourt, Brace and Company, 1931), 3–32.

7. Jennette Tandy, *Crackerbox Philosophers* (New York: Columbia University Press, 1925), 1–42.

8. Kenneth Lynn, *The Comic Tradition in America* (London: Victor Gollancz, Ltd., 1958), xi.

9. Walter Blair, *Native American Humor* (New York: American Book Company, 1937), 17–27.

10. Jesse Bier, *The Rise and Fall of American Humor* (New York: Holt, Rinehart and Winston, 1968), 32–51.

11. Walter Blair and Hamlin Hill, *America's Humor* (Oxford University Press, 1978).

12. David E. E. Sloane, *The Literary Humor of the Urban Northeast, 1830–1890* (Baton Rouge: Louisiana State University Press, 1983).

Chapter 1. Jonathan's Territory

1. Sallie McFague TeSelle, *Speaking in Parables* (Philadelphia: Fortress Press, 1975), 39.

2. Albert Matthews, "Brother Jonathan," *Publications of the Colonial Society of Massachusetts, Transactions*, 8 (1901): 99–100.

3. Albert Matthews, "Brother Jonathan Once More," *Publications of the Colonial Society of Massachusetts, Transactions*, 32 (1935): 374.

4. Matthews, "Brother Jonathan Once More," 379, n.1.

5. Matthews, "Brother Jonathan Once More," 383–84.

6. Matthews, "Brother Jonathan Once More," 380–83.

7. See Appendix A for the song's lyrics. This text, with the spelling modernized, is reprinted from a facsimile version found in Vera Brodsky Lawrence, *Music for Patriots, Politicians, and Presidents* (New York: Macmillan Publishing Co., 1975).

8. Walter Blair, *Native American Humor* (New York: American Book Company, 1937), 22.

9. Walter J. Meserve, *An Emerging Entertainment* (Bloomington: Indiana University Press, 1977), 71.

10. Meserve, *Emerging Entertainment*, 51.

11. Kent G. Gallagher, *The Foreigner in Early American Drama* (The Hague: Mouton & C., 1966), 31.

12. J. A. Leo LeMay. "The American Origins of 'Yankee Doodle,'" *William and Mary Quarterly*, 33 (1976): 437.

13. Daniel F. Havens, *The Columbian Muse of Comedy* (Carbondale: Southern Illinois University Press, 1973), 31.

14. Oscar George Theodore Sonneck, *Report on "The Star-Spanguled Banner," "Hail Columbia," "America," "Yankee Doodle"* (Washington: Library of Congress, 1909; reprinted New York: Dover Publications, Inc., 1972), 97, 114.

15. LeMay, "Yankee Doodle," 438, 441.

16. [Samuel Foster Damon,] *Yankee Doodle* (Providence, Rhode Island: Bibliographical Society of American, 1959), 11.

17. LeMay, "Yankee Doodle," 435.

18. F. O. Matthiessen, *American Renaissance* (London: Oxford University Press, 1941; reprinted 1974), 640.

19. When Constance Rourke subtitled *American Humor, A Study of the National Character* (New York: Harcourt Brace Jovanovich, Inc., 1931; reprinted 1959),

she was, of course, implying that humor derives from the deepest sources in character. I realize I am belaboring her point, but this is especially true of the Jonathan character because many other ways of approaching the figure as a symbol of America also exist. (That is, Jonathan was part of a continuum of American icons. At any one period he had rivals and analogues as "the American." Jonathan also changed as the political winds altered and as he appeared in various popular media.) One can pile up details about what the character looked like, how he spoke or acted; his origins, relationships with different parts of the country and populace; but his humor sets Jonathan apart and offers a most rewarding approach to why he mattered to the Americans who made him widely popular.

20. Blair, *Native American Humor*, 17.

21. Alton Ketchum, *Uncle Sam* (New York: Hill & Wang, 1959), 40.

22. E. McClung Fleming has published three useful articles demonstrating the early predominance of the Indian Princess, her transformation into Miss Liberty or Columbia, the country's preference after 1815 for male images, and the eventual transformation of Jonathan into Uncle Sam. "The American Image as Indian Princess, 1765–1783," *Winterthur Portfolio*, 2 (1965), 65–84; "From Indian Princess to Greek Goddess: The American Image, 1783–1815," *Winterthur Portfolio*, 3 (1967), 37–66; "Symbols of the United States: From Indian Queen to Uncle Sam," in *Frontiers of American Culture*, edited by Ray Browne et al. (Purdue University Studies, 1968), 1–24.

23. In any case, the Indian Maiden, Liberty, and Columbia—in whatever media they appeared—were more likely to stand for America rather than for Americans. Besides, as Alan Leander MacGregor demonstrated in "Tammany: The Indian as Rhetorical Surrogate," *American Quarterly*, 35 (1983): 391–407, the American Indian in particular functioned as a complex symbolic character for Americans. Particularly during the 1790s the Indian's rhetorical significance was specifically revolutionary rather than national. The Uncle Sam of political cartoons as well as the three feminine figures represented the government of the nation rather than the people.

24. Coincidentally, from time to time cartoons featured the figure of Uncle Sam in the Quaker garb identified with Benjamin Franklin. See, for example, "A Boston Notion of the World's Fair" (1844), "Stephen Finding 'His Mother'" (1860), and "Uncle Sam Making New Arrangements" (1860).

25. The phenomenon of the countryman or boy who uses apparent ineptitude for protective coloring is not limited, of course, to American culture.Thus, for example, a line from a contemporary Japanese novel echoes a sentiment with which Europeans and Americans might concur: "The wisdom of the peasants shows itself in their ability to pretend they are fools." Shusaku Endo, *Silence*, translated by William Johnston (Tokyo: Sophia University Press, 1969; reprinted New York: Taplinger Publishing Company, 1980), 72.

26. "Yankee Ingenuity," *Yankee Notions*, 2 (1853): 285.

27. J. K. Paulding, *The Bucktails*, in *American Comedies* by J. K. Paulding and William Irving Paulding. (Philadelphia: Carey and Hart, 1847), 35.

28. The cartoon Jonathans on successive covers of *Yankee Notions*, e.g., the frontspieces of successive issues during 1853 illustrate the character's truculence. See *Yankee Notions*, 2 (1853): 33 and 65.

29. Neil Schmitz, *Of Huck and Alice* (Minneapolis: University of Minnesota Press, 1983), 11.

30. Schmitz, *Huck and Alice*, 11.

31. Diane Skaar, untitled position paper (Sinsinawa, Wisconsin, 1982).

32. Quoted in Vera Brodsky Lawrence, *Music for Patriots, Politicians, and Presidents*, 132.

33. Rourke, *American Humor*, 10–11.

34. Kathleen Smith Kutolowski, "Freemasonry and Community in the Early Republic: The Case for AntiMasonic Anxieties," *American Quarterly*, 34 (1982): 561.

35. J. K. Paulding, "Jonathan's Visit to the Celestial Empire," *The New York Mirror*, 8 (June 1831): 393.

36. "The Propaganda Society—More Free Than Welcome," a separately published cartoon listed in Frank Weitenkampf, *Politically Caricature in the United States* (New York: The New York Public Library, 1953), 114.

37. *Punch*, 43 (1862): 160.

38. In *The Forest Rose* (1825), for example, Jonathan made fun of a black woman. In *Love and Friendship* (1809), he loathed blacks and Jews.

39. In *Cartoons of the War of 1898* (Chicago: Belford, Middlebrook & Company, 1898), 70.

40. In Roger Butterfield, *The American Past*, (New York: Simon & Schuster, 1947), 66.

41. Thus, for example, Richard M. Rollins in "Words as Social Control: Noah Webster and the Creation of the *American Dictionary*," in *Recycling the Past*, edited by Leila Zenderland (University of Pennsylvania Press, 1978), 50–65 outlines the shift in Webster's sympathies from a revolutionary to a reactionary as demonstrated by Webster's definitions and his choice of literary authorities.

42. Washington had been welcomed to New York in 1789 with an "Ode" by Samuel Low. A facsimile of the broadside published at that time appears on p. 117 of Lawrence *Music for Patriots*, with a second verse that starts, "Thrice blest Columbians hail!" During the same year Oliver Holden's "Ode to Columbia's Favorite Son" greeted Washington in Boston. After Washington's death, saddened Columbias such as the one reprinted on p. 159 of Lawrence also adorned the elegiac music and verse published in honor of Washington.

43. *Vanity Fair*, 4 (December 1860): 285.

44. Dixon Wecter, *The Hero in America* (New York: Charles Scribner's Sons, 1941), 106.

45. Seymour Martin Lipset, *The First New Nation* (New York: Basic Books, Inc., 1963), 18.

46. According to Lawrence, *Music for Patriots*, 155, the nation's "orgy of mourning" for Washington found an outlet not only in simulated funerals conducted in churches and theaters throughout the country but also in "universal tributes in prose and verse, unlimited varieties of memorial objects . . . turned out by artists and artisans, from paintings and sculpture to ceramics and mourning jewelry. Little girls executed apotheoses in needlework; memorial wallpapers were hung; and floods of odes, elegies, monodies, threnodies, psalms, anthems, and dead marches were composed, published, and performed everywhere."

47. Jay B. Hubbell, *The South in American Literature* (Duke University Press, 1954), 232.

48. James D. Hart, *The Popular Book* (Oxford University Press, 1950; reprinted Berkeley: University of California Press, 1963), 49.

49. Wecter, *The Hero*, 132.

50. While Brother Jonathon receives treatment in this work as a separate type, the names and characteristics of Jonathan and Yankee Doodle often were used interchangeably. See, for example, cartoons in the short-lived *Yankee Doodle*, 1 (1846): 55, 78, 103, 159; 2 (1847): 125, 155, 215, as well as *Punch*'s "Yankee Doo," 6 (1844): 18.

51. Mary Boykin Chesnut, *A Diary from Dixie*, edited by Ben Ames Williams (Boston: Houghton Mifflin Company, 1949; reprinted Cambridge, Massachusetts: Harvard University Press, 1980), 18.

52. Lumping together everyone from the North continues today. For example, since I was born and raised in Chicago, when I moved from South Dakota to Dallas in the late 1960s, I felt the incongruity of the Yankee label; but my friend from Fort Worth whose ancestors had fought for the Southern cause during the Civil War considered it entirely appropriate.

53. See, for example, Lawrence, *Music for Patriots*, "Yankee Song" (1788): 106–7; "Yankee Frolics" (1812), 197; "Yankee Thunders" (1812), 194; and "Constitution and Guerrierre" (1812), 195. See also George Stuyvesant Jackson, *Early Songs of Uncle Sam* (Boston: Bruce Humphries, Inc., 1933). This collection, dealing with songs of a later generation, shows songs continuing to identify Americans as Yankees during the 1830s and 1840s, for example, "Uncle Sam's Song to Miss Texas," 36, reprinted from *Rough and Ready Songster*; "The Tear Tax," 46, reprinted from *Everyday Song Book*; "Yankee Notes for English Circulation", 48, reprinted from *Diprose's Comic Song Book*; and "Sam Slick, the Yankee Pedlar," 49, reprinted from *Elton's Illustrated Song Book*.

54. Francis Hodge's *Yankee Theatre* (Austin: University of Texas Press, 1964) provides a thorough introduction to the Yankee on American stages from 1825 through 1850.

55. J. O. Bailey, *British Drama of the Nineteenth Century* (New York: The Odyssey Press, 1966), 194. Though written by a Briton and first produced in England, *Our American Cousin* achieved popular success only after Laura Keene brought the play to New York and gave the part of Asa Trenchard to a "Yankee character" actor, Joseph Jefferson, and the role of Lord Dundreary to the comedian Edward Askew Sothern.

56. Milton and Patricia Rickels, *Seba Smith* (Boston: Twayne Publishers, 1977), 9–10.

57. Rickels, *Seba Smith*, 37.

58. Rickels, *Seba Smith*, 14–16.

59. Rickels, *Seba Smith*, 24.

60. Albert Matthews, "Uncle Sam," *Proceedings of the American Antiquarian Society*, New Series 1 (1908): 21.

61. Ketchum, *Uncle Sam*, 70.

62. Ketchum, *Uncle Sam*, 80 and 86.

63. Chesnut, *Diary*, 19.

64. See, for example, 14 and 276, Bill Mauldin, *Bill Mauldin's Army* (New York: William Sloane Associates, Inc., 1949.) In the latter cartoon, GIs pelt officers with rotten fruit during a liberation parade.

65. Henry D. Thoreau, for example, in his 1854 *Reform Papers*, edited by Wendell Glick (Princeton, New Jersey: Princeton University Press, 1973), 174, used "Jonathans" as a synonym for provincials. *The Illustrated London News* also referred to a performer relieving his narrative with "Jonathanisms." Quoted in Daniel Boorstin, *The Americans* (New York: Vintage Books, 1965), 2: 238. In Irving's "Rip Van Winkle," Rip returns to find his comfortable village inn now a scene of angry political dispute with a sign over the door painted "The Union Hotel by Jonathan Doolittle."

66. Lipset, *The First New Nation*, 1 and 101.

67. Richard Bridgman, *The Colloquial Style in America* (New York: Oxford University, 1966), 9.

68. J. A. Leo LeMay in *The Frontiersman from Lout to Hero* (Worcester,

Massachusetts: American Antiquarian Society, 1979) traces the shift from the sixteenth-century perception through eighteenth-century perception of the frontiersman as "a shiftless outcast, a lout tending to criminality, a villain too lazy or too stupid or too vulgar to exist in society, and a traitor to the culture," to a nineteenth-century cultural hero, 187. A similar shift occurred in society's perception of Jonathan.

69. Alan I. Marcus, "National History Through Local: Social Evils and the Origin of Municipal Services in Cincinnati," *American Studies*, 22 (Fall 1981): 27–28, "While in the early nineteenth century, the city was a collection of individuals who gathered simply to pursue the civilizing endeavors of commerce and manufacturing, it had become by 1840 a place in which groups, each of which was composed of members defined only by their behavior, interacted."

Chapter 2. Brother Jonathan on the Stage

1. Candour, "Royall Tyler's *The Contrast*," in *The American Theatre as Seen by its Critics: 1752–1934*, edited by Montrose J. Moses and John Mason Brown (New York: W. W. Norton & Company, Inc., 1935), 193, 25.

2. Royall Tyler, *The Contrast* (Philadelphia: Pritchard & Hall, 1790; reprinted New York: The Dunlap Society, 1887), 52. All in-text page numbers refer to this edition.

3. Cawelti, *Adventure, Mystery*, 13.

4. Cawelti, *Adventure, Mystery*, 18.

5. Rourke, *American Humor*, 11.

6. Mark Twain [Samuel Clemens], *How to Tell a Story and Other Essays* (New York: Harper & Brothers, 1897), 8. Havens, *The Columbian Muse*, 50, also refers to Twain's predilection for the naive incredulous mask in his personal and narrative personae.

7. See, for example, the discussion of Havens, *The Columbian Muse*, 16–30; 43, 50.

8. (Lincoln: University of Nebraska Press, 1977), 39. A favorite for me among Mrs. Malaprop's verbal manglings is the way she brags about her own "nice derangement of epitaphs" in place of "arrangement of epithets." (Act 3, scene 3) With invincible conceit to match her ignorance, Mrs. Malaprop has unconsciously chosen exactly the right words.

9. Flannery O'Connor, *The Habit of Being*, edited by Sally Fitzgerald (New York: Farrar, Straus, Giroux, 1979), 138.

10. A. B. Lindsley, *Love and Friendship* (New York: D. Longworth, 1809), 29.

11. J. K. Paulding, *The Bucktails* in *American Comedies* by J. K. Paulding and William Irving Paulding (Philadelphia: Carey and Hart, 1847), 90.

12. James Hackett, *Jonathan in England* (New York: Samuel French, n.d.), 22.

13. Samuel Woodworth, *The Forest Rose* (Boston: William V. Spencer, 1855), 13.

14. Lindsley, *Love and Friendship*, 10.

15. George Lionel Stevens, *The Patriot* (Boston: Marsh, Caper & Lyon, 1834), 34.

16. Stevens, The Patriot, 83.

17. Mathews, *Dictionary of Americanisms*, 453, gives as a primary definition "especially attractive, dainty, artful." The 1838 illustration from a Jonathan anecdote illustrates this definition; "sharp," as in acute, is considered rare.

18. Hackett, *Jonathan in England*, 5 (unnumbered).

19. Woodworth, *The Forest Rose*, 29.

20. J. Robinson, *The Yorker's Strategem* (New York: T. & J. Swords, 1792), 7.

21. L[azarus] Beach, *Jonathan Postfree* (New York: David Longworth, 1807), 24.

22. See *The Forest Rose*.

23. See *The Yorker's Stratagem* and *A Trip to Niagara*.

24. R. B. Peake, *Americans Abroad* (London: Dick's Standard Plays, no, 589, n.d.), 6.

25. Hackett, *Jonathan in England*, 18.

26. Woodworth, *The Forest Rose*, 20.

27. Woodworth, *The Forest Rose*, 31. Coming at a time, 1825, when Americans were smarting under the criticisms of foreign travellers to America, this line from the comedy's transparent villain must have received an appreciative response from American audiences.

28. According to Humphreys' "Sketches of American Characters," a prefatory note to *The Yankee in England*, visitors should expect to encounter three distinct types of American characters: 1) A group who "will not . . . in their general deportment and manners, or in their conversation or style, in many instances, suffer by a comparison with men in the first circles of society in other countries" (12). 2) Those who have had a secondary school education. "They are competent to perform the high duties of useful citizens, or hold important offices under our representative government, with credit to themselves and advantage to the community" (13). 3) Those who have attended public primary schools where they received instruction in "English grammar, geography, and several other branches of practical knowledge. . . . They not unfrequently add much afterwards to their original stock, by their own judicious observation, in mixing with mankind; as well as by the help of books, whenever their avocations allow them time for reading" (13–14).

Chapter 3. Sources of the Stage Jonathan

1. Royall Tyler, *The Contrast*, 61.

2. The Yankee actors who popularized the character on the stage maintained strong audience support in the South as well as the North. Three of the most prominent of these actors—Hill, Marble, and Silsbee—also became important on the Southwest circuit during the 1830s before their major success in the large cities of the Northeast. Francis Hodge, *Yankee Theatre* (Austin: University of Texas Press, 1964), 284–85.

3. A political and literary Whig, as a young man Tyler had partnered Joseph Dennis in satirizing a Republican—thus plebian—congressman from Vermont. Tyler's Whig preferences were further demonstrated in a "Federalist Convival Song" (1799) praising Washington, Columbia, and John Adams. Vera Brodsky Lawrence, *Music for Patriots*, 138 and 154.

4. Hodge comes to this conclusion in *Yankee Theatre*, 48, from examining Dunlap's print of the last scene.

5. Blair, *Native American Humor*, 3.

6. Theorists of comedy and humor, in turn, frequently base their explanations of humorous or comic responses on the playful. See for example, Robert M. Torrance, *The Comic Hero* (Cambridge, Massachusetts: Harvard University Press, 1978), viii; Elder Olson, *The Theory of Comedy* (Bloomington, Indiana: Indiana

Univerity Press, 1968), 40; George McFadden, *Discovering the Comic* (New Jersey: Princeton University Press, 1982), 6; Max Eastman, *The Enjoyment of Laughter* (New York: Simon and Schuster, 1936), 163ff.

7. Roberta F. S. Borkat, for example, in "Lord Chesterfield Meets Yankee Doodle: Royal Tyler's *The Contrast*," *The Midwest Quarterly*, 17 (1976): 436–39, has traced the comedy's ties to the sentimental tradition; and as early as 1941, Arthur H. Nethercot in "The Dramatic Backround of "Royall Tyler's *The Contrast*," *American Literature*, 12 (1941): 435–66 had already demonstrated Tyler's clear debts to the eighteenth-century English stage conventions he was familiar with from his reading. Donald T. Siebert, however, in "Royall Tyler's 'Bold Example': *The Contrast* and the English Comedy of Manners," *Early American Literature*, 13 (1978): 3–11, insists that the play's structure implies that the author is freely using a valued inherited theatrical tradition and consciously exaggerating elements in that tradition in order to encourage independence of thinking in the audience.

8. Candour, in Moses, *The American Theatre*, 25.

9. Thomas, for example, who is the coachman of Sir Anthony Absolute, and David, Bob Acres's man in Richard Brinsley Sheridan's *The Rivals* (1775); reprinted in *Three English Comedies* (New York: Dell Publishing Co., Inc., 1966) belong to drama's crowd of awkward country servants. Acres himself, though supposedly a country squire, has much of the yokel in him. Acres's explanation to Sir Lucas in act 5, scene 3, as he tries to back out of the proposed duel with Ensign Beverly (Captain Absolute's assumed name) sounds much like the Boston Jonathan who later appears in a 1776 cartoon: "I-I-I don't feel quite so bold, somehow, as I did" (207). Oliver Goldsmith also makes use of comic country servants in *She Stoops to Conquer* (1773), reprinted in *Three English Comedies*, when Mr. Hardcastle attempts to train his men to serve their expected guests. Harcastle's stepson, Tony Lumpkin, plays the uncivilized squire.

Even before these better-known plays saw production, theater-goers would be familiar with the comic country type perhaps from having seen Richard Cumberland's popular comedy *The Brothers* (1769); reprinted in *The British Theatre*, vol. 18, edited by Mrs. Inchbald, (London: Longman, Hurst, Rees, and Orme, 1808). Scene 4 of Act 2 in that comedy begins with a scene (28–30) that illustrates the brash self-will of a servant called Jonathan who matches the self-serving ineptitude of Colman's Solomon Gundy and Hackett's Solomon Swap. Reminded that he is being called for by the master of the house Jonathan replies, "Ay, ay, 'tis only my master; my lady tells the servants not to mind what Sir Benjamin says, I love to do as I am bid" (29).

Finally, Richard Steele's trend-setting sentimental comedy *The Conscious Lovers*, 3d ed. (London: J. Tonson, 1730) included in Act 5 a country servant named Daniel who has been recently introduced to town ways. This character is also a clown but shows a distinct inclination to quickly acclimate himself to his wicked new environment.

10. Hodge, *Yankee Theatre*, 48.

11. John Bernard, *Retrospections of America* (1887; reprinted New York: Benjamin Blom, 1969), 39.

12. Bernard, *Retrospections*, 286–87.

13. Richard M. Dorson, *American Folklore* (Chicago: The University of Chicago Press, 1959), 66.

14. Quoted in Willard Thorpe, *American Humorists* (Minneapolis: Univesity of Minnesota Press, 1964), 5.

15. H. E. Dickson, in "A Note on Charles Mathews' Use of American Humor," *American Literature*, 12 (1940): 78–83, shows Mathews's debt to an American wit and raconteur, John Wesley Jarvis, for at least part of his American sketches. Joseph John Arpad, "David Crockett: An Original," unpublished M.A. thesis, University of Iowa, 1965, 36–39, further notes the close ties that several influential popularizers of the Jonathan persona, including Hackett, Hill, Dunlap, and Paulding, had with Jarvis. Since they apparently took many of their anecdotes from him, he was a primary link to the oral traditions about Jonathan.

16. Jerome J. Sommers, "James H. Hackett: Profile of a Player," Ph.D. dissertation, University of Iowa, 1966, 154.

17. Sommers, "James H. Hackett," 147.

18. [George H.] Yankee Hill, *Scenes from the Life of An Actor* (New York: Garret & Co., 1853), 74.

19. Delineating the connection between the special character of the stage Yankee and the actors who enlivened the roles, Jonathan Curvin in "Realism in Early American Art and Theatre," *The Quarterly Journal of Speech*, 30 (1944), 455, speaks of nineteenth-century audiences' identifying the "roles with the particular mannerisms of the actors." It seems that the tags may have taken precedence over the plays. Certainly, as Arthur Hobson Quinn comments in *A History of the American Drama* (New York: Harper & Brothers, 1923), 302, the Yankee was the only "real character" in these plays. Quinn's succinct summation of the plays' importance is worth quoting:

> Trivial and conventional as the 'Yankee Plays' are, they were important in several ways. First, . . . they contained one real character, and drama . . . becomes significant only in proportion as it develops character. Second, this character was native and was usually portrayed by native actors. Third, it grew up from the roots of our own drama, . . . Fourth, it led forward to the work of James A. Herne, and Uncle Nat of *Shore Acres* is a descendant of Jonathan. Fifth, it brought to foreign attention a school of American playwriting, which would probably have had little notice given to it, had it not been caricature. Hackett in 1833, Hill in 1836, Marble in 1844, and Silsbee in 1850 captivated London, and Hill even went to Paris (302–3).

20. W. K. Northall, ed., *Life and Recollections of Yankee Hill* (New York: W. F. Burgess, 1850), 19. Two tales from this collection suggest the flavor of Hill's performance. Dan Marble's tales appear in [Jonathan] F[alconbridge Kelly], *Dan Marble: A Biographical Sketch* (New York: DeWitt & Davenport, 1851).

21. Stuart M. Tave, *The Amiable Humorist* (Chicago: The University of Chicago Press, 1960) shows how conventions in comic theory and criticism altered from the sixteenth to the nineteenth century. During the early period laughter represented a "Scornful expression of superiority at a deformed thing" while later comic works presented "amiable originals, often models of good nature, whose little peculiarities are not satirically instructive, but objects of delight and love." (46). (Jonathan belonged in part to both traditions.)

In his discussion of changes in nineteenth-century speech, Bridgman, *The Colloquial Style*, 41, notes the tension between the valued romantic individualism of originals and the perceived "vulgarity" of their utterances.

Joan Shelley Rubin's tracing of the cult of "personality" in the twentieth century suggests the persistence of "originality" in American popular sentiment. See " 'Information Please': Culture and Expertise in the Interwar Period." *American Quarterly*, 35 (1983), 499–517.

22. Arpad, "David Crockett," 12.

23. Appleby, *Capitalism and a New Social Order*, quotes someone writing in the 11 April 1784 *Freeman's Journal* who started with a sarcastic reference to "our present state of imaginary republican equality" and then went on to complain of plays that, by making fun of "'a sneaking subservient tradesman and a dirty blundering Plowman' lead ordinary people to join in the laughter and thereby 'learn gradually to despise themselves'" (71).

24. H. W. "Yankeeana," *The London and Westminister Review*, 32 (1839): 138.

25. H. W., "Yankeeana," 140.

26. Most of this group of theorists—as, for example, Martin Grotjahn in *Beyond Laughter* (New York: McGraw-Hill Book Company, Inc., 1957)—have at least been influenced by Freud's theories on laughter. Freud declares, for instance, that "by making our enemy small, inferior, despicable or comic, we achieve in a round-about way the enjoyment of overcoming him—to which the third person, who has made no efforts, bears witness by his laughter." Sigmund Freud, *Jokes and Their Relation to the Unconscious*, translated by James Strachey (New York: The Norton Library, 1963), 103. Following Freud's lead, Langer insists "Laughter always—without exception—betokens a sudden sense of superiority." Susan K. Langer, *Feeling and Form* (New York: Charles Scribner's Sons, 1953), 339.

27. Robert Sklar, "Humor in America," in *A Celebration of Laughter*, edited by Warner M. Mendel, M.D. (Los Angeles: Mara Books Incorporated, 1970), 14.

28. Sklar, "Humor in America," 13.

29. *Political Satire in the American Revolution* (Ithaca, New York: Cornell University Press, 1960), 1.

30. Stow Persons, *The Decline of American Gentility* (New York: Columbia University Press, 1973), 16–17.

31. Bier, *The Rise and Fall*, 1.

32. The catalog of the Franklin J. Meine collection as shown at The Newberry Library in Chicago in 1939 offers a quick and useful means of identifying the variety of forms taken by nineteenth-century popular humor. The Meine collection now resides at the University of Illinois, Champaign-Urbana.

33. The authors do not, however, equate reputable with literary humor nor subversive with popular humor. Thus, for example, Blair considers both the literary J. R. Lowell and the popular Seba Smith "reputable." See Blair and Hill, *America's Humor*, 176.

34. See Northrop Frye, *Anatomy of Criticism* (Princeton, New Jersey: Princeton University Press, 1957), 40 and 172; Walter Blair, "Americanized Comic Braggarts," *Critical Inquiry*, 40 (Winter 1977): 331–49; Aristotle, *Nicomachean Ethics*, translated by D. P. Chase (1847; reprinted London: The Walter Scott Publishing Co., Ltd., n.d.), 126–28, end of chapter 9, book 4.

35. Langer, *Feeling and Form*, Two pages later Langer further explicates what she sees as the role of the buffoon.

In comedy the stock figure of the buffoon is an obvious device for building up the comic rhythm, i.e. the image of Fortune. But in the development of the art he does not remain the central figure that he was in the folk theater; the lilt and balance of life which he introduced, once it has been grasped, is rendered in more subtle poetic inventions involving plausible characters, and an *intrigue* (as the French call it) that makes for a coherent, over-all, dramatic action. Sometimes he remains as a jester, servant, or other subsidiary character whose comments, silly or witty or shrewd, serve to point the essentially comic pattern of the action, where the verisimilitude and complexity of the stage-life threaten to obscure its basic form (344).

Jonathan's long dominance of the American comic stage answered a cultural need but opposed the usual dramatic tide.

36. When one looks at the "rube" found in "Toby" sketches, one sees an illustration of a decayed Jonathan figure. For an example, see the "Interruption Scene," 81–85, in *American Popular Entertainments*, edited by Brooks MeNamara (New York City: Performing Arts Journal Publications, 1983). This text carries sketches in use between 1850 and 1930.

Chapter 4. The Cartoon Character: Beginnings and Heyday

1. Anyone interested in a readable but far more inclusive introduction to early lithography would do well to refer to Peter C. Marzio's "American Lithographic Technology Before the Civil War," in *Prints in and of America to 1850* edited by John D. Morse, (Charlottesville: The University Press of Virginia, 1970), 215–56.

2. Jerry Adler et. al., "The Finer Art of Politics," *Newsweek*, 13 October 1980.

3. Fredric Jameson, *The Political Unconscious* (Ithaca, New York: Cornell University Press, 1981), 87 and 117.

4. Mary Dorothy George, *Catalogue of Political and Personal Satires: Preserved in the Department of Prints and Drawings in the British Museum* (London: Printed by Order of the Trustees, 1935), 5: 218, lists this print, No. 5329, "Yankie Doodles Intrenchments Near Boston 1776."

5. Actually, however, given the widespread use of the Phygian liberty cap in political graphics during the 1770s, the artist may not even have considered a fool's cap. As Lawrence, *Music far Patriots*, 24, notes, the cap was close to omnipresent in cartoons of that decade.

6. See "Jack England Fighting the Confederates," British Museum No. 5828; "Blessed are the Peacemakers," No. 6174; "Proclamation of Peace," British Museum No. 6267. All three are reprinted in my dissertation, Winifred Morgan, "An American Icon: Brother Jonathan in the Popular Media between the Revolutionary and the Civil Wars," University of Iowa, 1982, 82, 83, and 85.

7. The original for this reprint is in the John Carter Brown Library, Providence, Rhode Island.

8. Copies of both prints appear among the illustrations at the back of M. Dorothy George, *English Political Caricature to 1792*, vol. 1. (Oxford: At the Clarendon Press, 1959).

9. George, *English Political Caricature*, 116.

10. George, *English Political Caricature*, 116, 118, 147. Given the provincialism of North America during the eighteenth century, a time lag occurs before any similar alterations arise in New World iconography.

11. George, *English Political Caricature*, 118.

12. George, *English Political Caricature*, 117.

13. George, *English Political Caricature*, 156.

14. George, *English Political Caricature*, 152.

15. Darly's line from Gay's *Beggar's Opera*: "Brother, Brother, we're both in the wrong" became a cliché of popular visual caricature, trotted out to refer not only to the political opposition between Newcastle and Fox in the 1760s but also to Queen Victoria and the Russian czar for their domination of Ireland and Poland. See *Punch*, 6 (1844): 255.

16. Jameson, *The Political Unconscious*, 83.

17. The United States actually led the way in the use of paper money. In addition to the impetus of limited specie, an American, Jacob Perkins, had devised in 1810 a means of substituting steel for copper in engraving banknote plates. This and a series of other mechanical improvements made the production of paper money cheap and efficient in the United States. David McNeely Stauffer, *American Engravers Upon Copper and Steel* (New York: The Grolier Club, 1907), xxviii.

18. The program finds an echo in that of John Taylor, a Virginia Republican: "Return to frugality; restore a free trade; abolish exclusive privileges; retract unjust pensions; surrender legislative patronage; surrender, also, legislative judicial power; and vindicate the inviolability of property, even against legislatures, except for genuine national welfare." Quoted in Arthur M. Schlesinger, Jr., *The Age of Jackson* (Boston: Little, Brown and Company, 1946), 24, from *Tyranny Unmasked* (Washington, 1822), 100, 346.

19. George C. Groce and David H. Wallace, *The New York Historical Society's Dictionary of Artists in America, 1564–1860* (New Haven: Yale University Press, 1957), 183; J. S. Bratton, *The Victorian Popular Ballad* (Totowa, New Jersey: Rowman and Littlefield, 1975), 22; Nils Erik Enkvist, *Caricatures of Americans on the English Stage Prior to 1870* (Helsingfors: Societas Scientiarum Fennica, 1951), 60; George, *English Political Caricature*, 150.

20. George Cruikshank, for example, was still using a red Indian wearing feathers and war paint to represent the United States as late as 1815 in his print "Twelfth Night, or What You Will." Mary Dorothy George, *Catalogue* (London: Trustees of the British Museum, 1949), 9: 491, No. 12453. And still later, one of *Punch*'s first "pencillings"—"Fair Rosamond; or the Ashburton Treaty" (1842), 3: 203, depicted America as an Uncouth Indian woman with, however, a flag for a skirt and "slavery" engraved on her girdle. Perhaps moving toward the Yankee as the American, the artist has the misspelling "Deplomacy" inscribed on the background between his figures of America and Britannia.

21. Murrell, *A History*, 97.

22. Maureen O'Brien Quimby, "The Political Art of James Akin," *Winterthur Portfolio*, 7 (1971): 66.

23. Dennis D. Gartner, "A Critical Edition and Study of James Kirke Paulding's *The Diverting History of John Bull and Brother Jonathan*," Ph.D. diss. University of Wisconsin, 1972, 204, 207.

24. Copies of this print appear in both Murrell, *A History*, 104 (no. 96), and Gartner, "A Critical Edition," 205 (illustration 2).

25. Sarah Kemble Knight, *The Journal of Madam Knight* (New York: Peter Smith, 1920; reprinted 1935), 42. Written in 1704, Knight's journal was not published until 1825.

26. Walter Blair, *Native American Humor, 1800–1900* (New York: American Book Company, 1937), 38.

27. A sampling of the stage Yankee's costumes and the likelihood of its having determined the alterations in the cartoon figure's dress can be discovered by examining Charles Mathews's *Mathews in America* (London: Hodgson & Co., n.d.) whose frontispiece shows Mathews's usual costume for six of his 1820s characters, including Jonathan; Montrose J. Moses's *The American Dramatist* (Boston: Little, Brown & Co., 1925) where the frontispiece shows George Hill as he appeared in Yankee costume for a comedy in 1836; and [Jonathan] F. [Kelly's] *Dan Marble*, 97, which shows a slightly later character still wearing essentially the same costume as earlier stage Yankees had regularly worn.

28. These engravings are reprinted in Quimby, "The Political Art," 73 to 78, and also in Stephen Lorant, *The Presidency* (New York: The Macmillan Company, 1951), 124–26. The latter series, however, are rather small and indistinct.

Most American illustrators and engravers of the early and mid-nineteenth century copied the ideas and style of George Cruikshank, who eventually worked as Dickens' illustrator. When Cruikshank illustrated *Sketches by Boz* (1839), his name was actually far better known than that of Charles Dickens. An earlier political rejoinder, Cruikshanks's illustration of William Hone's *The Political House That Jack Built*, was published in 1819. See Deborah Reilly, *Eminent Irreverie: The Work of George Cruikshank, Illustrator* (Madison, Wisconsin: The University of Wisconsin—Madison Libraries, 1984).

29. In the Winter 1982 issue of *American Quarterly*, 34: 543–61, Kathleen Smith Kutolowski, through a study of Genessee County, New York, demonstrated that the popular perception of Masons' helping one another was not all paranoia because during the 1820s Masons collectively did wield considerable political—though not necessarily economic—influence.

30. I owe much of my synthesis of the material in the foregoing paragraphs to the tutelage of my friend and colleague, Esther Heffernan. Useful readings in this area, however, might include: Stanley Brodwin, "Strategies of Humor: The Case of Benjamin Franklin," *Prospects 4* (1979): 121–67. Drawing upon the research of John K. Alexander's, "Philadelphia's 'Other Half': Attitudes Toward Poverty and the Meaning of Poverty in Philadelphia, 1760–1800," Ph.D. diss. University of Chicago, 1973, Brodwin makes a strong case for the wealthy class's fear of demogogic manipulation of poor people during the last quarter of the eighteenth century in English-speaking North America, 139.

In addition, as Alexander Saxton demonstrates in "Problems of Class and Race in the Origins of the Mass Circulation Press," *American Quarterly*, 36 (1984): 234, such conflict continued into the 1830s, 1840s, and 1850s as egalitarian rhetoric originating with artisans had a way of being preempted by the established oligarchy against whom it had been turned. For a fairly straightforward description of the shifting Whig position, see Butterfield, *The American Past*, 103.

Emory Elliot, in *Revolutionary Writers* (New York: Oxford University Press, 1982), outlines the unease felt by the literary elite during the first several decades of United States history:

> For many of the clergy and for most of the men of letters who lived in America during the last decades of the eighteenth century, the American Revolution seemed to involve a betrayal. As the most perceptive writers and the ministers realized, the changes being brought about were only signs of a radical shift of attitude within the American populace that could constitute a serious threat to traditional religion and intellectual authority (36).

Sacvan Bercovitch, "The Rites of Assent: Rhetoric, Ritual, and the Ideology of American Concensus," in *The American Self*, ed. Sam G. Girgus (Albuqueque: University of New Mexico Press, 1981), 5–42, argues that the Whigs employed the rhetoric of a continuing revolution for their own ends. Then, however, they had to find a way of endorsing individualism without endorsing anarchy. To do so, they used the concept of "representative selfhood." "Independence became the norm of representative selfhood: independence of mind, independence of means, and these twin blessings, sacred and secular, the mirror of a rising nation—what could better demonstrate the bond of personal and social identity?" (13). These are the qualities that Jonathan as a national icon will also develop.

31. The print for this illustration from the American Antiquarian Society does not include the two columns of text quoted by Weitenkmpf, *Political Caricature*, 40–41.

32. In much the same manner, Jay "Ding" Darling of the *Chicago Tribune* used John Q. Public in support of his paper's opposition to the policies of Franklin D. Roosevelt.

33. E. McClung Fleming, "From Indian Princess to Greek Goddess: The American Image, 1783–1815," *Winterthur Portfolio*, 3 (1967): 38.

34. Glyndon G. Van Deusen, *The Jacksonian Era, 1828–1848* (New York: Harper & Row, 1959; reprinted Harper Torchbooks, 1963), 121. The text of Van Buren's Special Session Message is reprinted in Robert V. Remini, ed., *The Age of Jackson* (University of South Carolina Press; reprinted New York: Harper Paperback, 1972), 122–27. Van Buren argued that

> it was not designed by the Constitution that the Government should assume the management of domestic or foreign exchange. It is indeed authorized to provide a general standard of value or medium of exchange in gold and silver, but it is not its province to aid individuals in the transfer of their funds otherwise than through the facilities afforded by the Post-Office Department (124).

35. Remini, *The Age of Jackson*, 129.

36. Stephen Hess and Milton Kaplan, *The Ungentlemanly Art* (New York: The Macmillan Company, 1968), 73; Helen Comstock, *American Lithographs of the Nineteenth Century* (New York: M. Barrows and Company, Inc., Publishers, 1950), 86, credit Robinson with giving political lithography direction because of his sensitivity to the possible connections between news subjects and caricature.

37. Thus, for example, did Harrison supporters chant this doggeral in praise of their own Cincinnatius:

> No ruffled shirt, no silken hose,
> No airs does Tip display;
> But like "the pith of worth" he goes
> In homespun"hodden-grey."
>
> Upon his board there ne'er appeared
> The costly "sparkling wine,"
> But plain hard cider such as cheered
> In days of old lang syne.

Quoted in Samuel Eliot Morison, *The Oxford History of the American People* (Oxford University Press; reprinted New York: New American Library, 1972), 2: 201. And, of course, the Democrat-sponsored jib about a barrel of hard cider and a hefty pension in a log cabin satisfying the old soldier just as well as the White House did not help Van Buren's campaign.

Chapter 5. The Cartoon Character: No Longer an Original

1. *The Image of America in Cartoon and Caricature* (Fort Worth: Carter Museum of Western Art, 1975), 3, credits H. R. Robinson, referred to by the author as a "prolific Whig lithographer" as probably the first American artist to use—in the early 1830s—Uncle Sam in graphics. Given the eventual triumph of Uncle Sam over Brother Jonathan, a curious detail was that during the 1850s the Know-Nothings called themselves "Sams." Lawrence, *Music for Patriots*, 330. It is

not surprising, however, that Brother Jonathan remained dominant throughout the 1830s and 1840s because as Alton Ketchum notes in *Uncle Sam: the Man and the Legend* (New York: Hill & Wang, 1959), 66, until the 1860s Uncle Sam remained primarily a verbal tradition.

2. The white villages in New England's heyday of water power were another attempt at grafting rural and urban traditions. They too succumbed to the advantages of large-scale steam-operated machines during the 1850s.

3. The individual did find scope in the newly opened Western plains. While Uncle Sam took over as an embodiment of the national response, by the last decades of the nineteenth century, the American cowboy had replaced Jonathan as the American original in popular mythology.

4. Joshua Taylor, *The Fine Arts in America* (Chicago: The University of Chicago Press, 1979), 722.

5. Taylor, *The Fine Arts*, 722.

6. "The Land of Liberty," *Punch*, 9 (1847: 215. Critical as this caricature of American society is, it is no harsher than Doyle's cartoon summations of other societies—such as France. Having freed its West Indian slaves in 1833, Britain considered the United States barbaric for still allowing its citizens to own slaves. References to slavery and to the violence of American society frequently reoccurred in British prints. British artists depicted a lawless American society. Jonathan's whip associates him and all American citizens with the South's "peculiar institution."

7. Clay could neither draw nor design as well as Doyle. Clay, after all, for all that he worked much of his adult life as an artist and had studied for a while in Europe, primarily was trained and qualified as a lawyer. Groce and Wallace, *The New York Historical Society's Dictionary of Artists*, 131.

8. *Punch*, 8 (1850): 243 and 247.

9. Although they used the rabble to achieve their ends, the Know-Nothings had close ties with the Whig establishment—electing a Harper from the publishing firm as mayor of New York in 1844 and having a hand in the elections of seven governors and a president as well. Butterfield, *The American Past*, 127.

10. Harry T. Peters, *America on Stone* (New York: Doubleday, Doran and Company, 1931), 11.

11. Harry T. Peters, *Currier & Ives*, (Garden City, New York: Doubleday, Doran & Co., Inc., 1942), 33.

12. Celina Fox, "Patriotism Through Prints," rev. of *The Great Book of Currier and Ives' America*, by Walton Rawls, *Times Literary Supplement*, 27 November 1981, 1389.

13. Fox, "Patriotism Through Prints."

14. Peters, *Currier & Ives*, 33.

15. Peters, *Currier & Ives*, 34.

16. Weitenkampf, *Political Caricature*, 125. This Franklinesque Uncle Sam was hardly original, of course; E. W. Clay's "A Boston Notion of the World's Fair—A New Cradle of Liberty" (1844), for instance, already had presented a visually almost identical Uncle Sam. For a reprint and commentary on Clay's print, see Joseph Bucklin Bishop, *Our Political Drama* (New York: Scott-Thaw Co., 1904), 100 and 119.

17. Irving Garwood, *American Periodicals from 1850 to 1860* (Macomb, Illinois: Commercial Art Press, 1931), 377.

18. Frank Luther Mott, *A History of American Magazines, 1741–1850* (New York: D. Appleton and Company, 1930), 808.

19. Frank Luther Mott, *A History of American Magazines, 1850–1865* (Cambridge, Massachusetts: Harvard University Press, 1938), 560.

20. George T. M. Shackleford, *Nineteenth Century American Prints from the Dartmouth College Collection* (Hanover, New Hampshire: Dartmouth College, 1977), 10–11. The introduction to this catalogue presents clearly and exactly the advantages of one type of print production over another; the introduction also explains how each process works.

21. See, for example, *Vanity Fair*, 1 (1860): 387; 3 (1861): 263; 7 (1863): 46.

22. Cawelti shows how popular literary successes have created interest in an old formula either by varying the formula, by working with it in unexpected ways, by reversing it, or by working off of it in some way.

23. *Yankee Notions*, 3 (1854): 271.

24. *Yankee Notions*, 3 (1854): 218.

25. *Yankee Notions*, 1 (1852): 285.

26. *Yankee Notions*, 2 (1853): 28; *Yankee Notions*, 3 (1854): 23.

27. *Yankee Notions*, 1 (1852): 309.

28. Generally, of course, Young America represents the youth (and by extension the future) of the United States.

29. *Yankee Notions*, 5 (1856): 272.

30. *Yankee Notions*, 2 (1853): 65. (frontispiece).

31. *Yankee Notions*, 3 (1854): 381.

32. *The Lantern* lasted only eighteen months from the beginning of 1852 and half way through 1853.

33. *The Lantern*, 1 (1852): 192.

34. *The Lantern*, 1 (1852): 7 and 33.

35. *Vanity Fair*, 2 (1860): 105.

36. *Vanity Fair*, 1 (1860): 387.

37. *Vanity Fair*, 3 (1861): 263.

38. *Vanity Fair*, 7 (1863): 46.

39. Alexander Saxton's tracing of ideological shifts in the life of a nineteenth-century journalist makes an interesting parallel, see "George Wilkes: The Transformation of a Radical Ideology," *American Quarterly*, 33 (Fall 1981): 437–58.

40. Hess and Kaplan, *The Ungentlemanly Art*, 36, and Stephen Becker, *Comic Art in America* (New York: Simon and Schuster, 1959), 291, also refer to Lincolon's influence on caricature. Becker is more interested in the fact that Lincoln was such a good subject for caricature; Hess and Kaplan note that *Punch* gave "the visage of the bewhiskered Abraham Lincoln" to Uncle Sam.

41. *Yankee Notions*, 9 (1860): 210–11.

42. *Yankee Notions*, 9 (1860): 258.

43. *Yankee Notions*, 9 (1860): 306.

44. Taking on a mythic quality, Abraham Lincoln by 1862 already was being referred to as "Father Abraham" in popular music. Lawrence, *Music for Patriots*, 364.

45. *Yankee Notions*, 13 (1864): 65.

46. *Yankee Notions*, 15 (1866): 287.

47. *Yankee Notions*, 15 (1866): 291.

48. *Yankee Notions*, 15 (1866): 304–5.

49. Weitenkampf, *Political Caricature*, 125.

50. Weitenkampt, *Political Caricature*, 126.

51. The Historical Society of Wisconsin, Madison, Wisconsin, Iconographic Department, has a relevant article clipped from the Chicago Sunday *Intelligencer*, 19

(25 May 1890): 62, on these "war envelopes." As one might expect, the article mentions that the envelopes enjoyed a greater vogue earlier than later in the conflict.

52. The "Young Man" is George C. Gorham, who ten years later became secretary of the Senate. Stanley P. Hirshon, *Farewell to the Bloody Shirt* (Bloomington: Indiana University Press, 1962), 34. In 1867, Gorham, one-time editor of the Washington *National Republican*, was the Republican candidate for governor of California until another convention chose another nominee. See *The Image of America*, 83.

53. The South of the 1840s and 1850s apparently came to see Jonathan primarily as a sectional figure. To illustrate, the *Rebellion Record* (1860) ran the lyrics of a song "Carolina's Farewell to Brother Jonathan," indicating that the local populace envisioned the latter figure as belonging only to the North. Ketchum, *Uncle Sam*, 32.

Chapter 6. Refracted Images in Occasional Verse

1. Frank Moore, *Songs and Ballads of the American Revolution* (1855; reprinted Port Washington, N.Y.: Kenniket Press, 1964), 232.

2. Perhaps printed first as a broadside, "A Pastoral Elegy" appeared in the *Royal Gazette* on 27 September 1780 and later in the *South Carolina and American General Gazette* (Charleston). Lawrence, *Music for Patriots*, 84, reprints the seven stanzas.

3. [Thomas Green Fessenden], "Jonathan's Courtship or The Country Lovers," New Haven? 1795? Broadside. Evans microprint copy No. 47420 of the American Antiquarian Society holdings.

4. Fessenden belonged to the same literary group and the same Whig-Federalist establishment as Royall Tyler. The group's satiric poems about country lovers were widely published in late eighteenth-century New England newspapers. Tandy, *Crackerbox Philosophers*, 7. In writing comic poems like "Jonathan's Courtship," this group was following a clearly defined tradition. See, for example, "The Taylor's Courtship" reprinted on pp. 68 and 69 in Robert Collison, *The Story of Street Literature* (Santa Barbara, California: ABC–Clio Press, 1973). Peter M. Briggs makes an articulate case for the relative literary value as well as the inherent limitations of satiric poetry in the English tradition. "English Satire and Connection Wit, " *American Quarterly*, 37 (1985): 13–29.

5. Robert Stevenson Coffin, The Boston Bard, "Jonathan's Account of the Pilgrim people or the Natural Free Masons," broadside, (Boston: G. Graupner, 1826).

6. As William Chauncy Ford points out in the introduction to his compilation, *Broadsides, Ballads etc.* (Boston: The Massachusetts Historical Society, 1922), viii, broadside songs as a group decreased sharply in influence and thus in cultural importance after 1800. Occasional broadside newspapers bearing the title "Brother Jonathan"—such as the eight-page broadside portfolio "Brother Jonathan" (1856) listed in the Library of Congress Catalogue of *Broadsides in the Rare Book Division*, vol. 4, (Boston: G. K. Hall & Co., 1972), 557, or the 1840 issue found in Indiana's Lilly Library—are more properly thought of as periodicals.

7. Quoted in Lawrence, *Music for Patriots*, 132.

8. "Jonathan to Jemina," *The Port Folio*, 2 (15 May 1802), 152.

9. Ibid.

10. "Rustic Dialogue," *The Port Folio*, 2 (10 July 1802), 216.

11. The fact that these early poems appeared in periodicals suggests that they were unusually popular. In late eighteenth-century America, broadsides or broadsheets were the usual modes for publishing songs. Street ballads had been a familiar part of urban life for centuries in England and remained so until cheap newspapers and music halls undercut the need for them. Printers did not need to include music because the public easily supplied popular tunes for the lyrics. Actually "Jonathan to Jemina" and "Jonathan's Courtship" are extant as broadsides.

12. This poem of David Humphreys, for example, is fairly representative of the period's prosody.

        "On the Prospect of Peace"
E'en now, from half the threaten'd horrors freed,
See from our shores the lessening sails recede;
See the proud flags that to the wind unfurl'd,
Waved in proud triumph round a vanquish'd world,
Inglorious fly; and see the inglorious crew,
Despair, shame, rags, and infamy pursue.
Hail, heaven-born peace! Thy grateful blessings pour

On this glad land, and round the peopled shore;
Thine are the joys that gild the happy scene,
Propitious days, and happy nights serene;
With thee gay Pleasure frolics o'er the plain,
And smiling Plenty leads the prosperous train.

13. "Jonathan's Visit to Uncle Sam's Thanksgiving," *The National Journal*, 17 December 1823.

14. "Jonathan's Visit to a Steamboat," *The National Journal*, 17 December 1823.

15. "Jonathan's Recollections," *The National Journal*, 28 January 1824.

16. "Jonathan's Visit to a Wedding," *The National Journal*, 14 February 1824; quoted in George Stuyvesant Jackson, *Early Songs of Uncle Sam* (Boston: Bruce Humphries, Inc., 1933), 47–48.

17. "Jonathan's Visit to a Museum," *The National Journal*, 14 February 1824.

18. "Jonathan's Visit to a Bowling Alley," *The National Journal*, 28 February 1824.

19. "Jonathan's Account of Commencement," *The National Journal*, 27 March 1824.

20. "Brother Jonathan's Epistle to his Relations," (Boston: White and Potter, Printers, 1852).

21. This same sense of American pique at British posturing self-congratulation over their own accomplishments regularly surfaced in the political cartoons of the period as well. See, for example, "The Great Exhibition of 1851/American Division" by Currier.

22. "Brother Jonathan's Epistle," 3 (unnumbered).

23. "Brother Jonathan's Epistle," 12.

24. "Brother Jonathan's Epistle," 13.

25. "Brother Jonathan's Epistle," 7.

26. "Brother Jonathan's Epistle," 11.

27. "Brother Jonathan's Epistle," 22.

28. "Brother Jonathan's Epistle," 25.

29. "Jonathan on Biddies," *Vanity Fair*, 1 (1860): 86.

30. All three poems "Ink, Blood and Tears," "Ode to the North and South," and "A Warning to Jonathan," are reprinted in William S. Walsh, *Abraham Lincoln and the London Punch* (New York: Moffat, York and Company, 1909), 28, 30, 32; 24, 26; 46, 48.

31. Board of Music Trade of the United States of America, *Complete Catalogue of Sheet Music and Musical Works, 1870* (1871; reprinted New York: Da Capo, 1973), 67. As the introduction to the 1973 reprint notes, this catalogue never was "complete"; it is, nonetheless, the most complete single listing of nineteenth-century sheet music. The catalogue lists "Jonathan's Appeal to Caroline" (perhaps having to do with North-South tension?) and "Jonathan to John" (U.S. and Britain); both of these were published by Root & Cady of Chicago. The third listing is "Jonathan, What Say," published by Oliver Ditson & Co. of Boston.

32. See, for example, "Jonathan to Adalina" in *Momus*, 3 (May 1860): 3. In this thirteen-stanza verse monologue, Jonathan praises the singing of a popular chanteuse. See also "Jonathan to the Japanese" in *Momus*, 1 (June 1860): 88, in which Jonathan advises the visiting delegation from Japan.

33. "Brother Jonathan's Epistle."

34. James Russell Lowell, *The Complete Poems* (Boston: Houghton, Mifflin Company, 1896), 238–39.

35. Constance Rourke, *American Humor*, 23, refers to Jack Downing as a Yankee oracle. Under the pseudonym of Jack Downing, Seba Smith, a Maine editor, wrote dialect monologues for his newspaper for a period of twenty years. In time these were collected under the title of *My Thirty Years Out of Senate*. As Downing, Smih effectively satirized the political chicanery of the 1830s and 1840s. Smith's outstanding success led to his being imitated by other writers.

36. "Brother Jonathan and John Bull," for example, perhaps a Fourth of July verse from the late 1830s, brags about American Revolutionary War exploits "some sixty years' ago" but sounds like a memorized recital rather than a personally realized tradition. The song is reprinted from the *Universal Songster* in *Uncle True Songster* (Philadelphia: Fisher & Brothers, n.d.), 140–41. Fisher & Brothers were active during the early 1850s

Chapter 7. Refracted Images in Comic Anecdotes

1. Chapbooks never had the same popularity in America that they enjoyed in England. See Harry B. Weiss, "Chapman Witcomb, Early American Publisher and Peddler of Chapbooks," *The Book Collectors' Packet*, 3 (1939), 3. The humorous jest books that form a small part of this larger source of American artifacts get short shrift in my study. A Jonathan anecdote, of course, might be "borrowed" from another publication and appear as a filler of white space at the end of even a British chapbook. Thus it happened that "Jonathan's Hunting Excursion"—a slightly smoothed out British version of Jonathan's tale in *A Trip to Niagara*—appeared in a chapbook with seven other anecdotes following the "Tragical History of Jane Arnold, commonly called Crazy Jane." This version is reprinted in Collision, *The Story of Street Literature*, 23–24. The tale was further "borrowed" for *Crockett's Yaller Flower Almanac for '36* (New York: Elton, 1836), 17–18.

By the 1850s hardbound joke books had become popular. Many of the most popular anecdotes about Jonathan were reprinted in these joke books. In addition, new anecdotes about the character were also appearing in these joke books. In any case, the anecdotes found in the earlier chapbooks and in the later joke books tended to be either duplicates of the anecdotes found in the almanacs or analogues in theme and structure. *The American Joe Miller*, for example, (Philadelphia: Daniel and Getz, 1853), 95–96; 182–83 reprints one of Jonathan Jonah Goliah Bang's comic illustrations from *Tarnation Strange* and an almost-identical version of the "Tin Boots" narrative found in *Hoods Komick Almanack, 1834*.

2. Rob Sagendorph, *America and her Almanacs* (Dublin, New Hampshire: Yankee, Inc., 1970), 29, asserts that 1740 through 1840 was the "great age of almanacs." After this date, almanacs become specialized.

3. Harry B. Weiss, *A Book About Chapbooks* (Trenton, New Jersey, 1942; reprinted. Hatboro, Pennsylvania: Folklore Associates, Inc., 1969) 124, offers a couple of possible reasons for the relative scarcity of chapbooks in America after the Revolutionary War: i.e., magazines and newspapers were more plentiful than in England; in addition, the American reading public had become slightly too sophisticated for the "elementary tastes and child-like intelligence required for the enjoyment of chapbooks."

4. Marian Barber Stowell, *Early American Almanacs* (New York: Burt Franklin Publisher, 1977), x, "The Bible took care of the hereafter, but the almanac took care of the *here*."

5. Clarence Brigham, "An Account of American Almanacs and their Value for Historical Study," *Proceedings of the American Antiquarian Society*, New Series, 25 (1925): 196.

6. Charles L. Nichols, "Notes on the Almanacs of Massachusetts," *Proceedings of the American Antiquarian Society*, New Series, 22 (1912): 38.

7. Blair, *Native American Humor*, 18.

8. Ibid., 18–19.

9. What has happened in this instance and at least one other is that the stereotypical role of the British North countryman Hodge had been appropriated by the Jonathan character with little or no alterations beyond the addition of a few dialect words. The conceit that the Jonathan of *The Contrast* does not know that the raising of the stage curtain signals the start of a play also appears in a closely variant form as a jest book anecdote about Hodge and his companion, *The Merry Fellow's Company* (Philadelphia: M. Carey, and W. Spotswood, 1789), 74. The similarity between these two versions accords with Weiss's contention in *A Brief History of American Jest Books* (New York: The New York Public Library, 1943), 11, that only later, i.e., during the 1830s and 1840s, were almanac jokes to revolve around American customs, ideas, politics, and happenings.

10. Henry J. Finn, *American Comic Annual* (Boston: Richardson, Lord & Holbrook, 1831), 166.

11. *Fishers Comic Almanac 1851* (Philadelphia: Fisher & Brothers), 21.

12. See "The Black Bull," *Collection of Funny, Moral, and Entertaining Stories and Bon Mots* (New Haven: D. Bowen [1787]), 14; and *Chaplet of Comus* (Boston: Monroe and Francis, 1811), 215; and especially *The Merry Fellow's Companion*, 7–8.

13. Examples of this use can be found in *Finn's Comic Almanac, or United States Calendar for 1835* (Boston: Marsh, Capeu & Lyon), 13 (unnumbered); *Fisher's Comic Almanac 1844 for the Middle Southern and Western States* (New Orleans: H. A. Turner), 21 (unnumbered); *Elton's Comic All-My-Nack, 1848* (New York: Elton, Publisher), 3 (unnumbered); *Fishers Comic Almanac, 1850* (Philadelphia: Fisher & Brothers), 12 (unnumbered).

14. *Crockett's Yaller Flower Almanac for '36*, 29; another sly upholder of national pride appears in "A Stretcher," a jest book anecdote, in Sam Slick, Jr. [Samuel P. Avery], *Laughing Gas* (New York: Garret & Co., 1854), 28.

15. *Elton's Funny Almanac 1846* (New York: [Elton]), 9 (unnumbered). Since the front cover of the copy I examined at the Lilly Library, Indiana University, was missing, my pagination may not be exact.

16. *The National Comic Almanac, for the year 1836* (Boston: The President of the American Eating Club 1836), 26. Jest books also pictured Jonathan as a romantic boor, e.g., *The Comic Token for 1835* (Boston: Charles Ellms), 31; S. F. Avery, *Mrs. Partington's Carpet-Bag of Fun* (New York: Garrett & Co., 1854), 53 and 83. *The American Joe Miller*, 127–28, 67–68, 149. In this last joke book, Jonathan also acts the tightwad, e.g., 119: "Landlord," said Jonathan, the other day, stepping up to the bar in a public house, "jest give us a cents-worth of New England, and put it into two tumblers. Here, Jim, take hold; away with the expense, I say, when a fellow is on a bust."

17. *Elton's Comic All-My-Nack 1848* (New York: Elton, Publisher, 1848), 3 (unnumbered).

18. *The American Comic All-I-Make 1839* (New York: Elton Publisher, 1839), 19 (unnumbered).

19. *The Old American Almanac 1843* (Boston: Thomas Groom & Co., 1843) 4.

20. *Crockett's Yaller Flower Almanac*, 12.

21. *Crockett's Yaller Flower Almanac*, 33; much the same humor occurs in "Jonathan and the Jib" in a jest book, *The Book of 1000 Comical Stories* (New York: Dick & Fitzgerald, 1859), 12.

22. *Elton's Comic All-My-Nack for 1839* (New York: Elton, 1839), 29 (unnumbered).

23. Timothy Hood, Esq., *Hood's Komick Almanack, 1834* (Troy, N.Y.: J. Hosford), 19. Yankee tricks perpetrated by Jonathan also feature in *Mrs. Parington's Carpet-Bag of Fun*, 93–94 and 96.

24. *Crockett's Yaller Flower Almanac*, 13.

25. *The National Comic Almanac, for the Year 1837* (Boston: The President of the American Eating Club, 1837), 17 (unnumbered).

26. *Crockett's Yaller Flower Almanac*, 9.

27. Billy Broadgrin [pseud.], *The Merry Fellow's Pocket Companion* (Boston: Tom Hazard, 1799), 13–14.

28. *Yankee Notions*, 1 (1852): 48.

29. *Yankee Notions*, 1 (1852): 165. A Sunday "Blondie" comic strip, for example, used the same idea within the last few years.

30. *Yankee Notions*, 2 (1853): 201; with an almost identical illustration, a similar anecdote appeared in *Mrs. Partington's Carpet-Bag*, 293–94, with a character called Hezekiah substituting for Jonathan.

31. *Yankee Notions*, 2 (1853): 68.

32. *Yankee Notions*, 3 (1854): 156–57.

33. J. K. Paulding, "Jonathan's Visit to the Celestial Empire," *The New York Mirror*, 18 June 1831; also reprinted in David Sloane, *The Literary Humor of the Urban Northeast* (Baton Rouge: Louisiana State University, 1983), 50–62.

34. Paulding, "Jonathan's Visit," 395.

35. Paulding, "Jonathan's Visit," 394.

36. *Yankee Notions*, 3 (1854): 34.

37. *Yankee Notions*, 3 (1854): 285.

Chapter 8. Literary Development

1. Francis Anbury's *Travels Through the Interior Parts of America*, 2 vols. (London: William Lane, 1791), 2: 37–40, for example, a series of letters written to enlighten the English about the bizarre customs of the American natives, outlines an experience in which a farmer named Jonathan suggests that the startled writer "bundle" with his daughter Jemina.

2. Paulding's four-page "Brother Jonathan" from *New York Mirror*, 10 September 1825; reprinted in Kendall B. Taft, *Minor Knickerbockers* (New York: American Book Company, 1947), and Paulding's *Diverting History of John Bull and Brother Jonathan* both use Jonathan's story in this manner.

3. Bruce I. Granger and Martha Harzog, "Textual Commentary," in *Letters of Jonathan Oldstyle, Gent.* (Boston: Twayne Publishers, 1977), 51–52.

4. "Uncle Jonathan's Reflections," in *The Spirit of the Public Journals* (Baltimore: Geo. Dobbin & Murphy, 1806), 20–24.

5. A retired editor, "Brother Jonathan's Wife: A Lecture" (Philadelphia: Alfred Pierce, 1842), 13.

6. A retired editor, "Brother Jonathan's Wife," 5.

7. James K. Paulding, *John Bull and Brother Jonathan* in *The Bulls and the Jonathans*, edited by William I. Paulding (New York: Charles Scribner and Company, 1867), 9–10.

8. Paulding, *John Bull and Brother Jonathan*, 66.

9. Paulding, *John Bull and Brother Jonathan*, 71.

10. Taft, *Minor Knickerbockers*, 379.

11. Paulding, "Brother Jonathan," in Taft, *Minor Knickerbockers*, 41.

12. Ibid., 31.

13. Ibid., 32.

14. Ibid., 33.

15. Ibid., 36.

16. Ibid., 38.

17. Ibid., 31.

18. Lawrence, *Music for Patriots*, 215, notes that she found this song in *The Book of the Navy*.

19. Lowell, "Jonathan to John," 238–39.

20. Lowell, "Jonathan to John," 238.

21. Since Hosea, of all the Old Testament prophets, is probably the most forgiving, Lowell's choice of name for his persona contains an apt irony.

22. Lowell, "Jonathan to John," 238.

23. Lowell, "Jonathan to John," 238. Two points are relevant to Lowell's peroration. First, the overtones of this stanza are redolent of the biblical warning of Gamaliel (Acts 5:35–39) that God's work cannot be thwarted except temporarily. The stanza has the breath of manifest destiny about it. Second, Lowell himself— though this entire poem is an argument—wrote in one of his letters to J. H. Heath, "I cannot reason on the subject [slavery]. A man who is in the right can never reason. He can only affirm." *Letters*, 1: 93. Both of these internalized assumptions undergird Lowell's poem and aid him to a sophistication and unity lacking in other Jonathan verse.

24. Sloane, *Literary Humor*, 182–201, quotes excerpts. Jonathan appears as a grandsire on 198. Few would want to read all 341 pages of the original.

25. As Edgar Allan Poe said of Neal in "Twice-Told Tales, by Nathaniel Hawthorne. A Review," *Graham's Magazine* (May 1842); reprinted in E.A.P. *Essays and*

Reviews. New York: The Library of America, 1984. "Some of the pieces of Mr. John Neal abound in vigor and originality; but, in general, his compositions of this class are excessively diffuse, extravagant, and indicative of an imperfect sentiment of Art" (573).

26. *New England Quarterly*, 32 (1959): 458.

27. Dennis D. Gartner, "A Critical Edition and Study of James Kirke Paulding's 'The Diverting History of John Bull and Brother Jonathan'" Ph.D. diss. University of Wisconsin, Madison, 1972, 190.

28. See George C. Hastings, "John Bull and His American Descendants," *American Literature*, 1 (1929): 40–68.

29. John Neal, *American Writers*, edited by Fred Lewis Pattee (Durham, North Carolina: Duke University Press, 1937), 200–01. This last phrase paraphrases what Neal advocated for American fiction.

30. In his dissertation, "John Neal: American Romantic," University of Utah, Salt Lake City, 1974, 13, Gerald Robert Grove, Sr., also notes Neal's foreshadowing the "philosophical style" of Melville, particularly in that Neal frequently inserts passages of social criticism or metaphysical speculation into his narrative.

31. [John Neal], *Brother Jonathan* 3 vols. (Edinburgh, William Blackwood, 1825), 1: 14–15.

32. Ibid., 1: 187–88.

33. Ibid., 2: 45–46.

34. Ibid., 3: 452.

35. Ibid., 1: 12–13.

36. Ibid., 1: 122–23.

37. Ibid., 1: 150.

38. Ibid., 1: 153–55.

39. [Frances Trollope], *The Life and Adventures of Jonathan Jefferson Whitlaw* (London: Richard Bentley, 1836).

40. R. N., Pseud.? [Hugo Playfair] *The Playfair Papers*, 3 vols. (London: Saunders and Otley, 1841), 2: 80.

41. *The Playfair Papers*, 2: 132.

42. A Kentuckian, *Jonathan Sharp* (London: Henry Colburn, Publisher, 1845), is still another three-volume British fiction about American adventures and ethics illustrated by a main character who wins and loses a fortune without much attention to ethical distinctions.

43. Jonathan Slick, [Ann Sophia Stephens], *High Life in New York* (New York: Bunce & Brother, Publishers, 1854), 13.

Chapter 9. Conclusion

1. Quoting a 1788 London text, Oscar Sonnech in *Report on "The Star Spangled Banner," "Hail Columbia," "America," "Yankee Doodle"* (Washington, D.C.: Library of Congress, 1909; reprinted. New York: Dover Publications, Inc., 1972), 84, suggested a possible common origin for "Yankee" and "Jonathan" in the early eighteenth century. The terms by then (1713) had come to mean "weak" and "simple." Albert Matthews in "Brother Jonathan Once More," *Publications of the Colonial Society of Massachusetts, Transactions*, 32 (1935): 374, shows that a satire printed in London in 1643 might indicate that the sobriquet was in colloquial English use at that early period. Not even Matthews, however, despite his exhaustive study, can trace the name to a definitive source. Curiously enough, according to H. L. Mencken, *The American Language*, 4th ed. (New York: Alfred A. Knopf,

1936; reprinted. 1947), 302, during the genteel days of the nineteenth century, "Jonathan" came to be another name for "bull."

2. In addition to this study's illustrations, David Grimsted's *Melodrama Unveiled* (Chicago: The University of Chicago Press, 1968), 186–87, has an interesting development of the role that became Jonathan's.

3. Alfred Kazin, "Introduction," *The 42nd Parallel* (New York: New American Library, 1969), xvi.

4. Russel Nye, *The Unembarrassed Muse* (New York: The Dial Press, 1970), 150.

5. Will Wright, *Six Guns and Society* (Berkeley: University of California, 1975), 2.

6. TeSelle, *Speaking in Parables*, 39.

7. TeSelle, *Speaking in Parables*, 49.

8. Peter M. Briggs, "English Satire and Connecticut Wit," *American Quarterly* 37 (1985): 25. David E. E. Sloane, *Literary Humor*, associates Mark Twain (and thus Huck Finn) with the humor of the Northeast (and thus, it seems to me, with Jonathan). Twain, according to Sloane, was bound to the humor of the Northeast "in his consistent fund of political and moral language, his use of urban and vulgar language blending up to the colloquial and informal in much of his own writing in person, and his explicit defense of the rights of man in the context of the American vision and its ramifications for the world community" (22–23).

9. Briggs, "English Satire," 27.

10. One might substitute "Civil" for "Second World" and "Cold" in the following quotation from Arthur Power Dudden's "The Record of Political Humor," *American Quarterly,* 37 (1985): 61, because a similar situation obtained in the 1860s. "The herd-like patriotic unities demanded by the Second World War and the Cold War aftermath effectively suppressed the traditional toleration for jesting at the nation's leaders."

Part of Jonathan's increasing limitation also involved his close identification as a sectional figure. And as Jay B. Hubbell points out in *The South in American Literature* (Duke University Press, 1954), 183, while before 1831 and the establishment of Garrison's *Liberator*, Southerners might readily accept Northern writers as expressing national sentiments, during the next several decades feelings polarized and Southerners came to believe, as Larzer Ziff expresses the point, that "the literary products of the Northeast were a sectional literature masquerading as a national literature." *Literary Democracy* (The Viking Press, 1981; reprinted. New York: Penguin Books, 1981), 181.

11. See Neil Schmitz's discussion of the interdependence between humorous colloquialism and the refusal to be civilized (homogenized) in *Of Huck and Alice: Humorous Writing in American Literature* (Minneapolis: University of Minnesota Press, 1983), 33, and Briggs, "English Satire," 14, on the way humor of necessity becomes formalized in literature.

12. See Lawrence E. Mintz, "Standup Comedy as Social and Cultural Mediation," *American Quarterly*, 37 (1985): 74, on the comedian's (and his comic persona's) essential role as critic.

13. Hayden White, "Structuralism and Popular Culture," *Journal of Popular Culture*, 7 (1974): 766.

14. Ibid.

15. Frederic Jameson, "Ideology, Narrative Analysis and Popular Culture," *Theory and Society*, 4 (Winter 1977): 551.

16. Hannah Arendt, "Society and Culture" in *Culture for the Millions?* edited by Norman Jacobs (D. Van Nostrand Company, Inc., 1961; reprinted Boston: Beacon Press, 1964), 50.

Bibliography

Primary Sources

DRAMATIC WORKS (FOR ANNOTATIONS, SEE APPENDIX B)

Atkinson, Joseph. *Match for a Widow, or the Frolics of Fancy*. Dublin: P. Byrne, 1788.

Barber, James. *Jonathan; or the Man of Two Masters*. London: Dicks' Standard Plays (No. 983), n.d.

Beach, L[azarus]. *Jonathan Postfree, or the Honest Yankee*. New York: David Longworth, 1807.

Colman, George the Younger. *New Hay at the Old Market*. London: T. Cadell & W. Davies, 1795.

Colman, George the Younger. *Who Wants a Guinea?* in *The Modern Theatre; a Collection of Successful Modern Plays*. Selected by Mrs. [Elizabeth Simpson] Inchblad, vol. 3. London: Longman, Rees, Orme, and Brown, 1811.

Cumberland, Richard. *The Brothers* in *The British Theatre; a Collection of Plays*. Edited by Mrs. Inchblad. Vol. 18. Longman, Hurst, Rees, and Orme, 1808.

Dibdin, Thomas. *Banks of the Hudson, or the Congress Trooper: A Transatlantic Romance*. London: John Cumberland, n.d.

Dunlap, William. *A Trip to Niagara: or Travellers in America*. New York: E. B. Clayton, 1830.

Goldsmith, Oliver. *She Stoops to Conquer or The Mistakes of a Night* in *Three English Comedies*. New York: Dell Publishing Co., Inc., 1966.

Gondinet, Edmond. *Jonathan* in *Theatre Complet*. Vol. 2. Paris: Galmann-Levy, Editeurs, 1906.

[Hackett, James]. *Jonathan in England*. New York: Samuel French (No. 320), n.d.

Humphreys, General [David]. *Yankey in England*. No publishing date appears on the microprint of Yale University's copy. This edition is assumed to have been published between 1807 and 1816, probably during 1815.

Lindsley, A. B. *Love and Friendship, or Yankee Notions*. New York: D. Longworth, 1809.

Mathews, Charles. "All Well at Natchitoches," Part 3 in *The London Mathews; Containing an Account of the Celebrated Comedian's Trip to America*. London: Hodgson and Co., n.d.

Mathews, Charles. "A Trip to America" in *Mathews in America; or the Theatrical Wanderer; a Cargo of New Characters, Original Songs and Concluding Piece of the Wild Goose Chase, or the Inn at Baltimore*. Vol. 4. London: Hodgson & Co., n.d.

Minshull, John. *Rural Felicity, A Comic Opera with the Humour of Patrick, and Marriage of Shelty*. New York: Privately published, 1801.

Moncrieff, William. *Tarnation Strange; or More Jonathans; An Anglo-American Farce*. London: J. Limbird, 1842.

Paulding, J. K. *The Bucktails; or Americans in England* in *American Comedies* by J. K. Paulding and William Irving Paulding. Philadelphia: Carey and Hart, 1847.

Peake, R[ichard] B[rindsley]. *Americans Abroad; or Notes and Notions*. London: John Dicks (No. 589), n.d.

Reed, Ferdinanda Wesselhoeft. *Jonathan's Night Shirt*. Boston: The Woman's Journal, 1916.

Robinson, J. *The Yorker's Stratagem; or Banana's Wedding*. New York: T. & J. Swords, 1792.

Shaw, Bernard. *The Apple Cart; A Political Extravaganza*. 1930. Reprint. Baltimore: Penguin Books, 1956.

Sheridan, Richard Brinsley. *The Rivals* in *Three English Comedies*. New York: Dell Publishing Co., Inc., 1966.

Somerset, C. A. *The Bloomer Costume! or Brother Jonathan in England!* British Museum manuscript ADD 43037, vol. 83, Pt. 2 (Licensed 6 October 1851).

Steele, Sir Richard. *The Conscious Lovers*. London: J. Tonson, 1730.

Stevens, George Lionel. *The Patriot; or Union and Freedom*. Boston: Marsh, Capin & Lyon, 1834.

[Tyler, Royall.] *The Contrast*. Philadelphia: Pritchard & Hall, 1790. Reprint. New York: The Dunlap Society, 1887.

Woodworth, Samuel. *The Forest Rose; or American Farmers*. Boston: William V. Spencer, 1855.

JEST BOOKS AND ALMANACS

The American Comic All-I-Make. 1839. New York: Elton Publisher, 1839.

The American Joe Miller: or the Jester's Own Book. Philadelphia: Daniels & Getz, 1853.

[Avery, Samuel P.] Sam Slick, Jr. [pseud.] *Laughing Gas: An Encyclopedia of Wit, Wisdom and Wind*. New York: Garrett & Co., 1854.

Avery, S. P. *Mrs. Partington's Carpet-Bag of Fun*. New York: Garrett & Co., 1854.

The Book of 1000 Comical Stories; an Endless Repast of Fun. New York: Dick & Fitzgerald, 1859.

Broadgrin, Billy. [pseud.] *The Merry Fellow's Pocket Companion: Containing a Large Nunchon of Witty Anecdotes, Bon Mots, and Curious Stories*. Boston: Tom Hazard, 1799.

Brother Jonathan's Almanac, for the Year of Our Lord 1848. Philadelphia: G. G. Sower, 1848.

Brother Jonathan's Almanac, for the Year of Our Lord, 1851. Philadelphia. G. G. Sower, 1851.

Brother Jonathan's Almanac, for 1863. Philadelphia: Sower & Barnes.

Chaplet of Comus; or Feast of Sentiment and Festival of Wit. Boston: Monroe and Francis, 1811.

Collection of Funny, Moral, and Entertaining Stories and Bon Mots. New Haven: D. Bowen, [1787].

The Comic Token for 1835. A Companion to the Comic Almanac. Boston: Charles Ellms, 1835.

Crockett's Yaller Flower Almanac for '36. New York: Elton, 1836.

Elton's Comic All-My-Nack for 1839. New York: Elton, 1838.

Elton's Comic All-My-Nack. 1848. New York: Elton, Publisher, 1848.

Elton's Comic Almynack 1851. New York: Elton, 1851.

Elton's Funny Almanac. 1846. New York: Elton, 1846.

Finn's Comic Almanac, or United States Calendar for 1835. Boston: Marsh, Capeu & Lyon, 1835.

Finn, Henry J., ed. *American Comic Annual.* Boston: Richardson, Lord & Holbrook, 1831.

Fishers Comic Almanac 1841. New York: Turner & Fisher, 1841.

Fishers Comic Almanac 1844 for the Middle Southern and Western States. New Orleans: H. A. Turner, 1844.

Fishers Comic Almanac 1850. Philadelphia: Fisher & Brothers, 1850.

Fishers Comic Almanac 1851. Philadelphia: Fisher & Brother, 1851.

Hood, Timothy. *Hood's Komick Almanack, 1834.* Troy, N.Y.: J. Hosford, 1834.

Jonathan Jaw Stretcher's Yankee All-My-Nack, 1852. Philadelphia: Fisher & Brother. Also Boston: G. W. Cotrell & Co, 1852.

Jonathan Jolly, [pseud.] *The Care Killer; a Collection of Pleasing Tales, Choice Stories, Smart Repartees, and Good Things.* New York: G. Sinclair, 1809.

The Merry Fellow's Companion; Being the Second Part of the American Jest Book. Philadelphia: M. Carey, and W. Spotswood, 1789.

The National Comic Almanac, for the Year 1836. Boston: The President of the American Eating Club, 1836.

The National Comic Almanac, for the Year 1837. Boston: The President of the American Eating Club, 1837.

The New Entertaining Jest-Book, and Chearful [sic] Witty Companion. Philadelphia: W. Woodhouse, 1790.

The Old American Almanac 1843. Boston: Thomas Groom & Co, 1843.

Old Fogy's Comic Almanac for 1858. New York: Philip J. Cozens, Publisher, 1858.

Ripsnorter Comic Almanac 1848. New York: Elton, 1848.

Smith, Seth. *Brother Jonathan's Almanac, for the Year of Our Lord 1847.* Philadelphia: C. G. Sower, 1847.

Turner's Comick Almanack, 1840. New York: Turner & Fisher, 1840.

Turners Comic Almanac, 1850. New York: Fisher & Brothers, 1850.

Uncle Ben's New Jersey Almanac, for 1844. Princeton, N.J.: R. E. Honor, 1844.

(These constitute between one-fourth and one-third of the almanacs and jest books examined, but these are the only ones with references to Jonathan. Many of the other one hundred or so almanacs examined have Yankee anecdotes that do not refer to the main character as Jonathan.)

PERIODICALS AND BROADSIDES

Brother Jonathan. N. D. Willis & H. Hastings Weld, eds. 2, no. 5, 1 August 1840.
A 82.7 × 64 cm. sheet folded twice, published by Wilson and Company, New
York.

Brother Jonathan. 1 January to 23 April 1842. An illustrated literary weekly also
published by Wilson & Company, New York.

[Coffin, Robert Stevenson]. The Boston Bard [pseud.] "Jonathan's Account of the
Pilgrim People or the Natural Free Masons." Boston: G. Graupner, 1826.
Broadside 8 × 11½ inches.

Diogenes, His Lantern. New York. 1852–1853.

[Fessenden, Thomas Green]. "Jonathan's Courtship." [New Haven? 1795?] Broadside.

Harper's Weekly. New York 1857–1867.

Momus. New York. 1860.

Neal, John. *American Writers: a Series of Papers Contributed to Blackwood's
Magazine (1824–1825)*. Durham, North Carolina: Duke Univerisity Press, 1937.

The National Journal. 1823–1824.

The New York Mirror, A Repository of Polite Literature and the Arts. 18 June
1831.

The Port Folio 2 1802. Published by William Fry in Philadelphia.

Punch. London. 1841–1865.

*The Spirit of the Public Journals; or Beauties of The American Newspapers, for
1805*. Baltimore: Geo. Dobbin & Murphy, 1806.

Vanity Fair. New York. 1860–1863.

Yankee Doodle. 1846–1847.

Yankee Notions or Whittling's of Jonathan's Jack-Knife. New York. 1852–1865.

BOOKS AND SHORT WORKS

Batcheler, Horace P. *Jonathan at Home; or A Stray Shot at the Yankees*. London:
W. H. Collingridge, City Press, 1864.

[Blouet, Paul] Max O'Rell, [pseud.] and Jack Allyn. *Jonathan and His Continent;
Rambles Through American Society*. Translated by Madame Paul Blouet. New
York: Cassell Publishing Company, 1889.

"Brother Jonathan's Epistle to His Relations." Boston: White and Potter, Printers,
1852.

"Brother Jonathan's Wife: A Lecture." Philadelphia: Alfred Pierce, 1842.

[Cohen, Alfred J.] Alan Dale, [pseud.] *Jonathan's Home*. Boston: Doyle & Whittle, 1885.

[Haliburton, Thomas Chandler.] Sam Slick, Jr., [pseud.] *The Courtship and
Adventures of Jonathan Homebred; or the Scrapes and Escapes of a Live Yankee*.
New York: Dick & Fitzgerald, Publishers, 1860.

Irving, Washington. *Letters of Jonathan Oldstyle, Gent./Salmagundi; or the Whim-
whams and Opinions of Launcelot Langstaff, Esq. and Others*. Edited by Bruce
I. Granger and Martha Hartzog. Boston: Twayne Publishers, 1977.

Jackson, George Stuyvesant. *Early Songs of Uncle Sam*. Boston: Bruce Humphreys, Inc., 1933.

Jinks, Jonathan, [pseud.] *Ulysses the Great or Funny Scenes at the White House*. Philadelphia: Attic Publishing Co., 1875.

Jonathan, [pseud.] *Brieven uit en over de Vereenigde Staten Van Noord-Amerika*. Schoonhoven: S. E. Van Nooten, 1853.

A Kentuckian, [pseud.] *Jonathan Sharp; or the Adventures of a Kentuckian*. 3 vols. London: Henry Colburn, Publisher, 1845.

Lowell, John Russell. *The Complete Poetical Works*. Boston: Houghton Mifflin Company, 1896.

Moore, Frank. *Songs and Ballads of the American Revolution*. 1855. Reprint. Port Washington, N.Y.: Kennikat Press, 1964.

[Neal, John]. *Brother Jonathan: or the New Englanders*. 3 vols. Edinburgh: William Blackwood, 1825.

Paulding, James K. *The Bulls and the Jonathans; Comprising John Bull and Brother Jonathan and John Bull in America*. Edited by William S. Paulding. New York: Charles Scribner and Company, 1867.

[Pierce, Zerelda.] Brother Jonathan, D. D. [pseud.] *The Church Republic: A Romance of Methodism*. New York: Wilbur B. Ketchum, 1892.

[Playfair, Hugo] R. N., [pseud.?] *The Playfair Papers, or Brother Jonathan, the Smartest Nation in All Creation*. 3 vols. London: Saunders and Otley, 1841.

[Sargent, Winthrop.] *The Loyalist Poetry of the Revolution*. Philadelphia: [Collins, Printer], 1857.

[Stephens, Ann Sophia Winterbotham]. *Jonathan Slick of Weatherfield, Conn.*, [pseud.] New York: Bunce & Brother, Publishers, 1854.

Taft, Kendall B. *Minor Knickerbockers: Representative Selections*. New York: American Book Company, 1947.

Tator, Henry H. *Brother Jonathan's Cottage; or A Friend to the Fallen*. New York: Francis Hart, 1854.

[Trollope, Frances]. *The Life and Adventures of Jonathan Jefferson Whitlaw, or Scenes on the Mississippi*. 3 vols. London: Richard Bentley, 1836.

Uncle True Songster. Philadelphia: Fisher & Brother, n.d.

Secondary Sources

Aderman, Ralph M. "James Kirke Paulding as a Social Critic." *Papers on English Language and Literature*, 1 (1965): 217–29.

Aderman, Ralph M. "James Kirke Paulding's Contributions to American Magazines." *Studies in Bibliography*, 17(1964): 141–51.

Adler, Jerry et al. "The Finer Art of Politics," *Newsweek*, 13 October 1980.

American Antiquarian Society. *A Dictionary Catalog of American Books Pertaining to the 17th Through 19th Centuries: Library of the AAS*. Vol. 3. Westport, Connecticut: Greenwood Publishing Corporation, 1971.

American Caricatures Pertaining to the Civil War, Reproduced from the original lithographs published from 1856 to 1872. New York: Brentano's 1918.

The American Language: An Inquiry into the Development of English in the United States, 4th ed. Edited by H. L. Mencken. New York: Alfred A. Knopf, 1936.

Reprint. 1947.

American Printmaking Before 1876: Fact, Fiction, and Fantasy. Papers presented at a symposium held at the Library of Congress, 12–13 June 1972. Washington, D.C.: Library of Congress, 1975.

[Anburey, Thomas]. *Travels Through the Interior Parts of America; in a Series of Letters*. 2 vols. London: William Lane, 1791.

Applyby, Joyce. *Capitalism and a New Social Order: The Republican Vision of the 1790s*. New York: New York University Press, 1984.

Applyby, Joyce. "Republicanism and Ideology." *American Quarterly*, 37 (1985): 461–73.

Aristotle. *The Nichomachean Ethics*. Translated by D. P. Chase. 1847. Reprint. London: The Walter Scott Publishing Co., Ltd., n.d.

Arpad, Joseph John. "David Crockett: An Original." M.A. thesis, University of Iowa, Iowa City, 1965.

Atkinson, Fred Washington. *American Drama in Atkinson Collection*. Part I, 1796–1830. Unpublished MS. at University of Chicago. 1 March 1918.

Auburn, Mark S. *Sheridan's Comedies: Their Contents and Achievements*. Lincoln: University of Nebraska Press, 1977.

Balch, Marston. "Jonathan the First.' *Modern Language Notes*, 46 (1931): 281–88.

Baragwaneth, A. K., commentator. *Currier & Ives Favorites*. New York: Crown Publishers, Inc., 1979.

Baumgardner, Georgia B. *American Broadsides: Sixty Facsimiles dated 1680 to 1800 reproduced from Originals in the American Antiquarian Society*. Barre, Massachusetts: Imprint Society, 1971.

Becker, Stephen. *Comic Art in America: A Social History of the Funnies, The Political Cartoons, Magazine Humor, Sporting Cartoons and Animated Cartoons*. New York: Simon and Schuster, 1959.

Bergson, Henri. *Laughter: An Essay on the Meaning of the Comic*. Translated by Clondesley Brerton and Richard Rothwell. 1911. Reprint. New York: The Macmillan Company, 1924.

Bernard, John. *Retrospections of America, 1797–1811*. 1887. Reprint. New York: Benjamin Blom, 1969.

Bier, Jesse. *The Rise and Fall of American Humor*. New York: Holt, Rinehart and Winston, 1968.

Bishop, Joseph Bucklin. *Our Political Drama: Conventions, Campaigns, Candidates*. New York: Scott-Thaw Co., 1904.

Blair, Walter. *Native American Humor: 1800–1900*. New York: American Book Company, 1937.

Blair, Walter. "Americanized Gothic Braggarts." *Critical Inquiry*, 4 (Winter 1977): 331–49.

Blair, Walter and Hamlin Hill. *America's Humor: From Poor Richard to Doonesbury*. Oxford: Oxford University Press, 1978.

Blair, Walter and Raven I. McDavid, Jr. *The Mirth of a Nation: America's Great Dialect Humor*. Minneapolis: University of Minnesota Press, 1983.

Board of Music Trade of the United States of America. *Complete Catalogue of Sheet Music and Musical Works, 1870*. 1871. Reprint. New York: Da Capo,

1973.

Boorstin, Daniel. *The Americans: The National Experience*. New York: Vintage Books, 1965.

Borkat, Roberta F. S. "'Lord Chesterfield Meets Yankee Doodle': Royall Tyler's *The Contrast*." *The Midwest Quarterly* 17 (July 1976): 436–39.

Bratton, J. S. *The Victorian Popular Ballad*. Totowa, New Jersey: Rowman and Littlefield, 1975.

Bridgman, Richard. *The Colloquial Style in America*. New York: Oxford University Press, 1966.

Briggs, Peter M. "English Satire and Connecticut Wit." *American Quarterly* 37 (1985): 13–29.

Briggs, Susan and Asa, collectors and editors. *Cap and Bell: Punch's Chronicle of English History in the Making, 1841–61*. London: Macdonald, 1972.

Brigham, Clarence. "An Account of American Almanacs and Their Value for Historical Study." *Proceedings of the American Antiquarian Society*. New Series, 25 (1925): 195–209.

Brigham, Clarence S. "David Claypoole Johnston, the American Cruikshank." *Proceedings of the American Antiquarian Society*, 50 (1940): 98–110.

Brigham, Clarence S. *Journals and Journeyman: A Contribution to the History of Early American Newspapers*. Philadelphia: University of Pennsylvania Press, 1950. Reprint. Westport, Connecticut: Greenwood Press, Publishers, 1971.

Brodwin, Stanley, "Strategies of Humor: The Case of Benjamin Franklin." *Prospects*, 4 (1979): 121–67.

Browne, Ray et al., eds. *Frontiers of American Culture*. Indiana: Purdue University Studies, 1968.

Butterfield, Roger. *The American Past: A History of the United States from Concord to Hiroshima, 1775–1945*. New York: Simon and Schuster, 1947.

Caricatures Pertaining to the Civil War; Reproduced from a Private Collection of Originals Designed for Currier & Ives, New York, and Published by Them in Sheets from 1856 to 1892. New York: Wright & Swasey, 1892.

Cawelti, John G. *Adventure, Mystery, and Romance: Formula Stories as Art and Popular Culture*. Chicago: The University of Chicago Press, 1976.

Chesnut, Mary Boykin. *A Diary from Dixie*. Edited by Ben Ames Williams. Boston: Houghton Mifflin Company 1949. Reprint. Cambridge, Massachusetts: Harvard University Press, 1980.

[Clemens, Samuel]. Mark Twain. *How to Tell a Story and Other Essays*. New York: Harper & Brothers Publishers, 1897.

Coad, Oral Summer. "The Plays of Samuel Woodworth." *Sewanee Review* 27 (1919): 163–75.

Coffin, Tristram Potter and Hennig Cohen, eds. *The Parade of Heroes: Legendary Figures in American Lore*. Garden City, N.Y.: Anchor Press, Doubleday, 1978.

Cohen, Hennig and William B. Dillingham, eds. *Humor of the Old Southwest*. Boston: Houghton Mifflin Company, 1964.

Collison, Robert. *The Story of Street Literature: Forerunner of the Popular Press*. Santa Barbara, California: ABC–Clio Press, 1973.

Comstock, Helen. *American Lithographs of the Nineteenth Century*. New York: M. Barrows and Company, Inc., Publishers, 1950.

Conningham, Frederick A. *Currier & Ives Prints: An Illustrated Check List*. 1949. Updated by Colin Simkin. Reprint. New York: Crown Publishers, Inc., 1970.

Cooper, Lane. *An Aristotelian Theory of Comedy: With an Adaptation of the Poetics and a Translation of the "Tractatus Coislinianus."* New York: Harcourt, Brace and Company, 1922.

Crouse, Russel. *Mr. Currier and Mr. Ives: A Note on Their Lives and Times*. Garden City, New York: Garden City Publishing Company, Inc., 1936.

Curvin, Jonathan. "Realism in Early American Art and Theatre." *The Quarterly Journal of Speech* 30 (1944): 450–55.

Curvin, Jonathan W. "The Stage Yankee." *Studies in Speech and Drama, in Honor of Alexander M. Drummond*. 139–51. Ithaca: Cornell University Press, 1944.

[Damon, Samuel Foster.] *Yankee Doodle*. Providence, Rhode Island: Bibliographical Society of America, 1959.

Dannet, Sylvia G. L. *A Treasury of Civil War Humor*. New York: Thomas Yoseloff, 1963.

Davis, Charles E. and Martha B. Hudson. "Humor of the Old Southwest: A Checklist of Criticism." *Mississipi Quarterly* 27 (1974): 179–99.

Dickson, H. E. "A Note on Charles Mathews' Use of American Humor." *American Literature* 12 (1940): 78–83.

Dickson, Harold E. *Arts of the Young Republic: The Age of William Dunlap*. Chapel Hill: The University of North Carolina Press, 1968.

A Dictionary of Americanisms: on Historical Principles. Edited by Mitford M. Mathews. 2 vols. Chicago: The University of Chicago Press, 1951.

A Dictionary of Slang and Unconventional English: Colloquialisms and Catchphrases, Solecisms and Catachreses, Nicknames, Vulgarisms, and Such Americanisms as have been naturalized. Edited by Eric Partridge. 7th ed. New York: The Macmillan Company, 1970.

Dorman, James H., Jr. *Theater in the Ante Bellum South, 1815–1861*. Chapel Hill: The University of North Carolina Press, 1967.

Dorson, Richard M. *American Folklore*. Chicago: The University of Chicago Press, 1959.

Dorson, Richard M. *Jonathan Draws the Long Bow*. New York: Russell & Russell, 1970.

Dorson, Richard M. "The Yankee on the Stage—A Folk Hero of American Drama." *New England Quarterly* 13 (1940): 467–93.

Dos Passos, John. *The 42nd Parallel: First in the Trilogy "U.S.A."* New York: Houghton, Mifflin, 1930. Reprint. New York: New American Library, 1969.

Downer, Alan S. "Early American Professional Acting." *Theatre Survey* 12 (1971): 79–96.

Drake, Milton, comp. *Almanacs of the United States*, 2 vols. New York: The Scarecrow Press, Inc., 1962.

Dudden, Arthur Power. "The Record of Political Humor." *American Quarterly* 37 (1985): 50–70.

Eastman, Max. *Enjoyment of Laughter*. New York: Simon and Schuster, 1936.

Elliot, Emory. *Revolutionary Writers: Literature and Authority in the New Republic, 1725–1810*. New York: Oxford University Press, 1982.

Emerson, Everett, ed. *American Literature, 1764–1789: The Revolutionary Years*.

Madison: The University of Wisconsin Press, 1977.

Emerson, Ralph Waldo. *The Works of RWE: Comprising His Essays, Lectures, Poems, and Orations*. 12 vols. London: George Bell and Sons, 1882.

Endo, Shusaku. *Silence*. Translated by William Johnston. Tokyo: Sophia University Press, 1969. Reprint. New York: Taplinger Publishing Company, 1980.

Enkvist, Nils Erik. *Caricatures of Americans on the English Stage Prior to 1870*. Helsingfors: Societas Scientiarum Fennica, 1951. Reprint. Port Washington, New York: Kennikat Press, Inc., 1968.

Feibleman, James. *In Praise of Comedy: A Study in Its Theory and Practice*. New York: Russell & Russell, 1962.

Feidelson, Charles, Jr. *Symbolism and American Literature*. Chicago: The University of Chicago Press, 1953.

Fleming, E. McClung. "The American Image as Indian Princess, 1765–1783." *Winterthur Portfolio* 2 (1965): 65–84.

Fleming, E. McClung. "From Indian Princess to Greek Goddess: The American Image, 1783–1815." *Winterthur Portfolio* 3 (1967): 37–66.

Ford, William Chauncy. *Broadsides, Ballads, etc.: Printed in Massachusetts, 1639–1800*. Massachusetts Historical Society Collections, Vol. 75. Boston: The Massachusetts Historical Society, 1922.

Fox, Celina. "Patriotism Through Prints." Review of *The Great Book of Currier and Ives* by Walton Rawls. *Times Literary Supplement*, 27 November 1981.

Freud, Sigmund. *Jokes and Their Relation to the Unconscious*. Translated and edited by James Strachey. New York: W. W. Norton & Company, Inc., 1963.

Frye, Northrup. *Anatomy of Criticism: Four Essays*. Princeton, New Jersey: Princeton University Press, 1957.

Gallagher, Kent G. *The Foreigner in Early American Drama: A Study in Attitudes*. The Hague: Mouton & Co., 1966.

Gartner, Dennis D. "A Critical Edition and Study of James Kirke Paulding's 'The Diverting History of John Bull and Brother Jonathan.'" Ph.D. diss., University of Wisconsin, Madison, Wisconsin, 1972.

Garwood, Irving. *American Periodicals from 1850 to 1860*. Macomb, Illinois: Commercial Art Press, 1931.

George, Mary Dorothy. *Catalogue of Political and Personal Satires: Preserved in the Department of Prints and Drawings in the British Museum*. Vol. 5, 1771–1783. London: Printed by Order of the Trustees, 1935.

George, Mary Dorothy. *Catalogue of Political and Personal Satires, Preserved in The Department of Prints and Drawings in the British Museum*. Vol. 9, 1811–1819. London: Printed by Order of the Trustees, 1949.

George, M. Dorothy. *English Political Caricature to 1792: A Study of Opinion and Propaganda*, 2 vols. Oxford: At the Clarendon Press, 1959.

Girgus, Sam G., ed. *The American Self: Myth, Ideology, and Popular Culture*. Albuquerque: University of New Mexico Press, 1981.

Granger, Bruce Ingham. *Political Satire in the American Revolution, 1763–1783*. Ithaca, New York: Cornell University Press, 1960.

Grimsted, David. *Melodrama Unveiled: American Theatre and Culture, 1800–1850*. Chicago: The University of Chicago Press, 1968.

Griswold, Rufus W. *The Poets and Poetry and America*. 2nd ed. Philadelphia:

Carey and Hart, 1842.

Groce, George C. and David H. Wallace. *The New York Historical Society's Dictionary of Artists in America, 1564–1860.* New Haven: Yale University Press, 1957.

Grotjahn, Martin. *Beyond Laughter.* New York: McGraw-Hill Book Company, Inc., 1957.

Grove, Gerald Robert. "John Neal: American Romantic." Ph.D. diss., University of Utah, Salt Lake City, Utah, 1974.

Hall, Harold E. "James Kirke Paulding: A Pioneer in American Fiction" Ph.D. diss., University of Pennsylvania, Philadelphia, Pennsylvania, 1953.

Hart, James D. *The Popular Book: A History of American Literary Taste.* Oxford University Press, 1950. Reprint. Berkeley: University of California Press, 1963.

Hastings, George E. "John Bull and His American Descendants." *American Literature* 1 (1929): 40–68.

Havens, Daniel F. *The Columbian Muse of Comedy: The Development of a Native Tradition in Early American Social Comedy, 1787–1845.* Carbondale: Southern Illinois University Press, 1973.

Herold, Amos L. *James Kirke Paulding: Versatile American.* New York: Columbia University Press, 1926.

Hess, Stephen and Milton Kaplan. *The Ungentlemanly Art: A History of American Political Cartoons.* New York: The Macmillan Company, 1968.

Hill, Yankee [George H.] *Scenes from the Life of an Actor: Compiled from the Journals, Letters, and Memoranda of the Late.* New York: Garrett & Co., 1853.

Hirshson, Stanley P. *Farewell to the Bloody Shirt: Northern Republicans & the Southern Negro, 1877–1893.* Indiana University Press, 1962.

Hodge, Francis. "Charles Mathews Reports on America," *Quarterly Journal of Speech* 36 (1950): 492–99.

Hodge, Francis. *Yankee Theatre: The Image of America on the Stage, 1825–1850.* Austin: University of Texas Press, 1964.

Holliday, Carl. *The Wit and Humor of Colonial Days.* 1912. Reprint. New York: Frederick Ungar Publishing Co., 1960.

Horn, Maurice and Richard E. Marschall, eds. *The World Encyclopedia of Cartoons.* New York: Gale Research Company, 1980.

Hubbell, Jay B. *The South in American Literature: 1607–1900.* Durham, N. C.: Duke University Press, 1954.

The Image of America in Cartoon Caricature. Fort Worth, Texas: Amon Carter Museum of Western Art, 1975.

Inge, M. Thomas, ed. *The Frontier Humorists: Critical Views.* Hamden, Connecticut: Archon Books, 1975.

Israel, Calvin, ed. *Discoveries & Considerations: Essays on Early American Literature & Aesthetics, presented to Harold Jantz.* Albany, New York: State University of New York Press, 1976.

Jacobs, Norman, ed. *Culture for the Millions? Mass Media in Modern Society.* D. Van Nostrand Company, Inc., 1961. Reprint. Boston: Beacon Press, 1964.

Jameson, Frederic. "Ideology, Narrative Analysis and Popular Culture." *Theory and Society* 4 (Winter 1977): 543–59.

Jameson, Frederic. *The Political Unconscious: Narrative as a Socially Symbolic*

Act. Ithaca, New York: Cornell University Press, 1981.

[Kelly, Jonathan] F[alconbridge]. *Dan Marble; a Biographical Sketch of That Famous and Diverting Humorist with Reminiscences, Comicalities, Anecdotes, etc., etc*. New York: DeWitt & Davenport, 1851.

Kernodle, Portia. "Yankee Types on the London Stage, 1824–1880." *Speech Monographs* 14 (1947): 139–47.

Ketchum, Alton. *Uncle Sam: The Man and the Legend*. New York: Hill & Wang, 1959.

Knight, Sarah Kemble. *The Journal of Madam Knight*. New York: Peter Smith, 1920. Reprint. 1935.

Kutolowski, Kathleen Smith. "Freemasonry and Community in the Early Republic: The Case for AntiMasonic Anxieties." *American Quarterly* 34 (1982): 543–61.

Lammon, Lorraine Welling. "American Caricature in the English Tradition: The Personal and Political Satires of William Charles." *Winterthur Portfolio* 2 (1976): 1–52.

Lang, Hans-Joachim. "Critical Essays and Stories by John Neal." *Jahrbuch fur Amerikastudien* 7 (1962): 204–96.

Langer, Susanne. *Feeling and Form: A Theory of Art*. New York: Charles Scribner's Sons, 1953.

Lauber, John. "*The Contrast*: A Study in the Concept of Innocence." *English Language Notes* 1 (September 1963): 33–37.

Lawrence, Vera Brodsky. *Music for Patriots, Politicians, and Presidents: Harmonies and Discords of the First Hundred Years*. New York: Macmillan Publishing Co., Inc., 1975.

Lease, Benjamin. *That Wild Fellow: John Neal and the American Literary Revolution*. Chicago: The University of Chicago Press, 1972.

Lemay, J. A. Leo. "The American Origins of 'Yankee Doodle.'" *William and Mary Quarterly* 33 (1976): 435–64.

Lemay, J. A. Leo. *The Frontiersman from Lout to Hero: Notes on the Significance of the Comparative Method and the Stage Theory in Early American Literature and Culture*. Worcester, Massachusetts: American Antiquarian Society, 1979.

Levy, Lester S. *Grace Notes in American History: Popular Sheet Music from 1820 to 1900*. Norman: University of Oklahoma Press, 1967.

Levy, Lester S. *Picture the Songs: Lithographs from the Sheet Music of Nineteenth Century America*. Baltimore: The Johns Hopkins University Press, 1976.

Library of Congress. *Catalog of Broadsides in the Rare Book Division*. Vol. 4. Boston: G. K. Hall & Co., 1972.

Lipset, Seymour Martin. *The First New Nation: The United States in Historical and Comparative Perspective*. New York: Basic Books, 1963.

Lorant, Stephen. *The Presidency: A Pictorial History of Presidential Elections from Washington to Truman*. New York: The Macmillan Company, 1951.

Lossing, Benson J. *Pictorial History of the Civil War in the United States of America*, 3 vols. in 1. Hartford: Thomas Belknap, Publisher, 1877.

Lowe, John. "Theories of Ethnic Humor: How to Enter, Laughing." *American Quarterly* 38 (1986): 439–60.

Lynn, Kenneth S. *The Comic Tradition in America*. London: Victor Gollancz Ltd., 1958.

Mac Gregor, Alan Leander. "Tammany: The Indian as Rhetorical Surrogate." *American Quarterly* 35 (1983): 391–407.

Made in America, Printmaking 1760–1860: An Exhibition of Original Prints from the Collections of The Library Company of Philadelphia and The Historical Society of Pennsylvania. Philadelphia: Philadelphia Library Company, 1973.

Marcus, Alan I. "National History Through Local: Social Evils and the Origin of Municipal Services in Cincinnati." *American Studies* 22 (1981): 23–39.

Martin, Harold C. "The Colloquial Tradition in the Novel: John Neal." *New England Quarterly* 32 (1959): 455–75.

Mason, Laurie, comp. *Print Reference Source: A Select Bibliography, 18th–20th Centuries.* Millwood, N.Y.: Kraus-Thomson Organization Limited, 1975.

Mathews, Mrs. [Anne]. *Memoirs of Charles Mathews, Comedian.* 2nd ed. 4 vols. London: Richard Bentley, 1839.

[Mathews, Brander]. "The American on the Stage." *Scribner's Monthly* 18 (1879): 321–33.

[Mathews, Charles]. *Mathews in America! A New Dramatic at Home: Written for an intended to be delivered by Mr. Mathews Abroad; containing a New Budget of Songs, Tales and Anecdotes.* 3rd ed. London: Duncombe, Book and Music Seller, n.d.

[Mathews, Charles]. James Smith. *Sketches of Mr. Mathews' Celebrated Trip to America, Comprising a Full Account of His Admirable Lecture on Peculiarities, Characters, and Manners.* London: J. Limbrid, n.d.

Matthews, Albert. "Brother Jonathan." *Publications of the Colonial Society of Massachusetts, Transactions* 8 (1901): 94–126.

Matthews, Albert. "Brother Jonathan Once More." *The Colonial Society of Massachusetts, Transactions* 32 (1935): 374–86.

Matthews, Albert. "Uncle Sam" *Proceedings of the American Antiquarian Society* New Series, 1 (1909): 21–65.

Matthiessen, F. O. *American Renaissance: Art and Expression in the Age of Emerson and Whitman.* London: Oxford University Press, 1941. Reprint. 1974.

Maurice, Arthur Bartlett and Frederick Tabor Cooper. *The History of the Nineteenth Century in Caricature.* 1904. Reprint. New York: Cooper Square Publishers, 1970.

McCloskey, John C. "Campaign of Periodicals after the War of 1812 for National American Literature." *Publications of Modern Language Association,* 50 (1935): 262–73.

McFadden, George. *Discovering the Comic.* Princeton, New Jersey: Princeton University Press, 1982.

McNamara, Brooks, ed. *American Popular Entertainments: Jokes, Monologues, Bits and Sketches.* New York City: Performing Arts Journal Publications, 1983.

Meine, Franklin J. *American Humor: An Exhibition of Books and Prints from the Collection of Franklin J. Meine.* 11 January to 21 March 1939. Chicago: The Newberry Library, 1939.

Mendel, Werner M. D., ed. *A Celebration of Laughter.* Los Angeles: Mara Books Incorporated, 1970.

Meserve, Walter J. *American Drama to 1900: A Guide to Information Sources.* Vol. 28. American Literature, English Literature, and World Literature in English from Information Guide Series. Detroit, Michigan: Gale Research Company, 1980.

Meserve, Walter J. *An Emerging Entertainment: The Drama of the American People to 1828*. Bloomington: Indiana University Press, 1977.

Mintz, Lawrence E. "Standup Comedy as Social and Cultural Mediation." *American Quarterly* 37 (1985): 71–80.

Moody, Richard. *America Takes the Stage: Romanticism in American Drama and Theatre, 1750–1900*. Bloomington: Indiana University Press, 1955. Reprint. New York: Kraus Reprint Co., 1969.

Moore, Frank, ed. *The Rebellion Record: A Diary of American Events, with Documents, Narratives, Illustrative Incidents, Poetry, Etc*. 4 vols. New York: G. P. Putnam, 1862.

Morgan, Winifred Alice. "An American Icon: Brother Jonathan in the Popular Media Between the Revolutionary and the Civil Wars." Ph.D. Diss., The University of Iowa, Iowa City 1982.

Morison, Samuel Eliot. *The Oxford History of the American People, 1789–1877*. Oxford University Press, 1965. Reprint. New York: New American Library, 1972.

Morse, John D., ed. *Prints in and of America to 1850*. Charlottesville: The University Press of Virginia, 1970.

Moses, Montrose J. *The American Dramatist*. Boston: Little Brown & Co., 1925. Reprint. New York: Benjamin Blom, 1964.

Moses, Montrose J. and John Mason Brown, eds. *The American Theatre as Seen by Its Critics: 1752–1934*. New York: W. W. Norton & Company, 1935.

Mott, Frank Luther. *A History of American Magazines, 1741–1850*. New York: D. Appleton and Company, 1930.

Mott, Frank Luther. *A History of American Magazines, 1850–1865*. Cambridge, Massachusetts: Harvard University Press, 1938.

Murrell, William. *A History of American Graphic Humor*, Vol. 1. 1747–1865. New York: Whitney Museum of American Art, 1933.

[Neal, John]. "Matthews [*sic*] in America." *Blackwood's Magazine* 15 (1824): 424–28.

[Neal, John]. X. Y. Z. [pseud.] "Speculations of a Traveller Concerning the People of the United States; with Parallels." *Blackwood's Magazine* 16 (1824): 91–97.

Neal, John. *Wandering Recollections of a Somewhat Busy Life: An Autobiography*. Boston: Roberts Brothers, 1869.

Nethercot, Arthur H. "The Dramatic Background of Royall Tyler's *The Contrast*." *American Literature* 12 (1941): 435–46.

Nevins, Alan and Frank Weitenkampf. *A Century of Political Cartoons: Caricature in the United States from 1800 to 1900*. New York: Charles Scribner's Sons, 1944.

Nichols, Charles L. "Notes on the Almanacs of Massachusetts." *Proceedings of the American Antiquarian Society*, New Series, 22 (1912): 15–134.

Nicoll, Allardyce. *A History of Early Nineteenth Century Drama, 1800–1850*. 2 vols. New York: The Macmillan Company, 1930.

Northall, W. K., ed. *Life and Recollections of Yankee Hill*. New York: W. F. Burgess, 1850.

Nye, Russel. *The Unembarrassed Muse: The Popular Arts in America*. New York: The Dial Press, 1970.

O'Connor, Flannery. *The Habit of Being: Letters*. Edited by Sally Fitzgerald. New York: Farrar, Straus, Giroux, 1979.

O'Donnell, Thomas F. "Introduction." *The Dutchman's Fireside* by James Kirke Paulding. 1831. Reprint. New Haven, Conn.: College & University Press, Publishers, 1966.

Odell, George C. D. *Annals of the New York Stage*. Vols. 1–6. New York: Columbia University Press, 1928–1931.

Olson, Elder. *The Theory of Comedy*. Bloomington: Indiana University Press, 1968.

O'Neal, David L. *Early American Almanacs: The Phelps Collection, 1679–1900*. Peterborough, New Hampshire: Antiquarian Booksellers, 1978.

Owens, Louis D. "James K. Paulding and the Foundations of American Realism." *Bulletin of the New York Public Library* 79 (1975–76): 40–50.

The Oxford English Dictionary. Edited by A. H. Murray et al. 12 vols. Oxford: At the Clarendon Press, 1833. Reprint. 1933.

Paulding, William I. *Literary Life of James K. Paulding*. New York: Charles Scribner and Company, 1867.

Persons, Stow. *The Decline of American Gentility*. New York: Columbia University Press, 1973.

Peters, Harry T. *America on Stone, The Other Printmakers to the American People: A Chronicle of American Lithography other than that of Currier and Ives, from Its Beginning, Shortly Before 1820, to the Years when the Commercial Single Stone Hand-Colored Lithograph Disappeared from the American Scene*. New York: Doubleday, Doran and Company, 1931.

Peters, Harry T. *Currier & Ives: Printmakers to the American People*. Garden City, New York: Doubleday, Doran & Co., Inc., 1942.

Pratt, John Lowell, ed. *Currier & Ives: Chroniclers of America*. New York: Promontory Press, 1974.

Quimby, Maureen O'Brien. "The Political Art of James Akin." *Winterthur Portfolio* 7 (1971): 59–112.

Quinn, Arthur Hobson. *A History of the American Drama: From the Beginning to the Civil War*. New York: Harper & Brothers, 1923.

Quinn, James J., Jr. "The Jonathan Character in the American Drama." Ph.D. Diss., Columbia University, New York, 1955.

Rawls, Walton. *The Great Book of Currier & Ives' America*. New York: Abbeville Press, Publishers, 1979.

Reilly, Deborah. *Eminent Irreverie: The Work of George Cruikshank, Illustrator*. An Exhibit of Book and Periodical Illustrations from the University of Wisconsin-Madison Libraries. The University of Wisconsin-Madison Libraries, 1984.

Remini, Robert V., ed. *The Age of Jackson*. University of South Carolina Press. Reprint. New York: Harper & Row, Publishers, 1972.

Richards, Irving T. "John Neal: A Bibliography." *Jahrbuch fur Amerikastudien* 7 (1962): 296–319.

Rickels, Milton and Patricia. *Seba Smith*. Boston: Twayne Publishers, 1977.

Robertson, James Holman. "James Kirke Paulding, A Study in Literary Nationalism." Ph.D. Diss., University of Michigan, Ann Arbor, 1949.

Rourke, Constance. *American Humor: A Study of the National Character.* New York: Harcourt Brace Jovanovich, Inc., 1931. Reprint. 1939.

Rourke, Constance. *The Roots of American Culture and Other Essays.* Edited by Van Wyck Brooks. New York: Harcourt, Brace and Company, 1942.

Rubin, Joan Shelley. "'Information, Please!' Culture and Expertise in the Interwar Period." *American Quarterly* 35 (1983): 499–517.

Sachs, Viola. *The Myth of America: Essays in the Structures of Literary Imagination.* The Hague: Mouton, 1973.

Sagendorph, Rob. *America and Her Almanacs: Wit, Wisdom & Weather 1639–1970.* Dublin, New Hampshire: Yankee, Inc., 1970.

Saxton, Alexander. "George Wilkes: The Transformation of a Radical Ideology." *American Quarterly* 33 (1981): 437–58.

Saxton, Alexander. "Problems of Class and Race in the Origins of the Mass Circulation Press." *American Quarterly* 36 (1984): 211–34.

Schaeffer, Neil. *The Art of Laughter.* New York: Columbia University Press, 1981.

Schlesinger, Arthur M. Jr. *The Age of Jackson.* Boston: Little, Brown and Company, 1946.

Schmitz, Neil. *Of Huck and Alice: Humorous Writing in American Literature.* Minneapolis: University of Minnesota Press, 1983.

Sears, Donald A. *John Neal.* Boston: Twayne Publishers, 1978.

Seydow, John J. "The Sound of Passing Music: John Neal's Battle for American Literary Independence," *Costerus* 7 (1973): 153–82.

Shackelford, George T. M. *Nineteenth Century American Prints from the Dartmouth College Collection.* Hanover, New Hampshire: Carpenter Galleries, Dartmouth College, 1977.

Sharp, James Roger. *The Jacksonians Versus the Banks: Politics in the States after the Panic of 1837.* New York: Columbia University Press, 1970.

Shaw, Albert. *Abraham Lincoln: His Path to the Presidency.* New York: The Review of Reviews Corporation, 1929.

Shaw, Albert. *Abraham Lincoln: The Year of His Election.* New York: The Review of Reviews Corporation, 1929.

Siebert, Donald T., Jr. "Royall Tyler's 'Bold Example': *The Contrast* and The English Comedy of Manners." *Early American Literature* 13 (Spring 1978): 3–11.

Silverman, Kenneth. *A Cultural History of the American Revolution: Printing, Music, Literature, and the Theatre in the Colonies and the United States from the Treaty of Paris to the Inauguration of George Washington, 1763–1789.* New York: Thomas Y. Crowell Company, 1976.

Sloane, David E. E. *The Literary Humor of the Urban Northeast, 1830–1890.* Baton Rouge: Louisiana State University Press, 1983.

Sommers, Jerome J. "James H. Hackett: The Profile of a Player." Ph.D. Diss. The University of Iowa, Iowa City, 1966.

Sonneck, Oscar George Theodore. *Report on "The Star-Spangled Banner," "Hail Columbia," "America," "Yankee Doodle."* Washington, D.C.: Library of Congress, 1909. Reprint. New York: Dover Publications, Inc., 1972.

Spielmann, M. H. *The History of "Punch."* New York: The Cassell Publishing Company, 1895.

Stauffer, David McNeely. *American Engravers Upon Copper and Steel. Pt. II. Check-List of the Works of the Earlier Engravers.* New York: The Grolier Club, 1907.

Stowell, Marian Barber. *Early American Almanacs: The Colonial Weekday Bible.* New York: Burt Franklin Publisher, 1977.

Sunday Intelligencer. Chicago. 20 May 1890.

Tandy, Jennette. *Crackerbox Philosophers in American Humor and Satire.* New York: Columbia University Press, 1925.

Tanselle, G. Thomas. *Royall Tyler.* Cambridge, Massachusetts: Harvard University Press, 1967.

Tatham, David. *The Lure of the Striped Pig: The Illustration of Popular Music in America, 1820–1870.* Barre, Massachusetts: Imprint Society, 1973.

Taubman, Howard. *The Making of the American Theatre.* New York: Coward McCann, Inc., 1965.

Tave, Stuart M. *The Amiable Humorist: A Study in the Comic Theory and Criticism of the Eighteenth and Early Nineteenth Centuries.* Chicago: The University of Chicago Press, 1960.

Taylor, Charles Henry. "Some Notes on Early American Lithography." *American Antiquarian Society, Proceedings*, New Series, 32 (1922): 68–80.

Taylor, Joshua C. *The Fine Arts in America.* Chicago: The University of Chicago Press, 1979.

TeSelle, Sallie McFague. *Speaking in Parables: A Study in Metaphor and Theology.* Philadelphia: Fortress Press, 1975.

Thieme, Ulrich. *Allgemeines Lexikon Der Bildenden Kunstler: Von der antike bis zur gegenwart.* Vol. 8. Leipzig: Verlag von E. A. Seeman, 1913.

Thompson, Lawrence S. *Nineteenth and Twentieth Century Drama.* Boston: G. K. Hall & Co., 1975.

Thorp, Willard. *American Humorists.* Minneapolis: University of Minnesota Press, 1964.

Torrance, Robert M. *The Comic Hero.* Cambridge, Massachusetts: Harvard University Press, 1978.

Traver, John Hatswell. "James Kirke Paulding and the English Romance Vogue 1800–1850." M.A. Thesis., University of Iowa, Iowa City, 1950.

Van Deusen, Glyndon G. *The Jacksonian Era, 1828–1848.* New York: Harper & Row, 1959. Reprint. Harper Torchbook, 1963.

Vernon, Grenville, comp. *Yankee Doodle-Doo: A Collection of Songs of the Early American Stage.* New York: Payson & Clark Ltd., 1927.

W———, H———. "Yankeeana," *The London and Westminster Review*, 32 (1839): 136–45.

Walker, Nancy. *The Tradition of Women's Humor in America.* Huntington Beach, California: American Studies Publishing Company, 1984.

Walsh, William S., ed. *Abraham Lincoln and the London Punch: Cartoons, Comments and Poems, Published in the London Charivari, During the American Civil War (1861–1865).* New York: Moffat, Yard and Company, 1909.

Wecter, Dixon. *The Hero in America: A Chronicle of Hero-Worship.* New York: Charles Scribner's Sons, 1941.

Weiss, Harry B. "American Chapbooks 1722–1842." *Bulletin of the New York*

Public Library 47 (1945): 491–98.

Weiss, Harry B. "American Chapbooks 1722–1842; A Preliminary Check List of American Chapbooks." *Bulletin of the New York Public Library* 49 (1945): 587–96.

Weiss, Harry B. *A Book About Chapbooks: The People's Literature of Bygone Times*. Trenton, New Jersey, 1942. Reprint. Hatboro, Pennsylvania: Folklore Associates, Inc., 1969.

Weiss, Harry B. "A Brief History of American Jest Books." *Bulletin of the New York Public Library* 47 (1943): 273–89.

Weiss, Harry B. "Chapman Whitcomb, Early American Publisher and Peddlar of Chapbooks." *The Book Collector's Packet* 3 (April 1939): 1–3.

Weiss, Harry B. "Early American Chapbooks." *American Collector* 13 (1944): 10–11.

Weitenkampf, Frank. *Political Caricature in the United States in Separately Published Cartoons*. New York: The New York Public Library, 1953.

Wemyss, Francis Courtney. *Theatrical Biography: or The Life of an Actor and Manager*. Glasgow: R. Griffin & Co., 1848.

Wendrick, Jon S. "For Education and Entertainment—Almanacs in the Early American Republic, 1783–1815." Ph.D. Diss., Claremont Graduate School, 1974.

Wernick, Robert. "Getting a Glimpse of History form a Grandstand Seat." *Smithsonian* 16 (August 1985): 68–86.

White, Hayden. "Structuralism and Popular Culture." *Journal of Popular Culture* 7 (1974): 759–85.

Wright, Will. *Six Guns and Society: A Structural Study of the Western*. Berkeley: University of California Press, 1975.

Zall, P. M. "The Old Age of American Jestbooks." *Early American Literature* 15 (Spring 1980): 3–13.

Zenderland, Leila, ed. *Recycling the Past: Popular Uses of American History*. University of Pennsylvania Press, 1978.

Ziff, Larzer. *Literary Democracy: The Declaration of Cultural Independence in America*. The Viking Press, 1981. Reprint. New York: Penguin Books, 1981.

Index